Managing Employee Performance

Psychology at Work
Series editor: Clive Fletcher

This series interprets and examines people's work behaviour from the perspective of occupational psychology. Each title focuses on a central issue in management, emphasizing the role of the individual's workplace experience.

Books in the series include:

Creating the Healthy Organization
Well-being, Diversity and Ethics at Work
Sue Newell

Impression Management
Building and Enhancing Reputations at Work
*Paul Rosenfeld, Robert A. Giacalone
and Catherine A. Riordan*

Managing Employee Performance
Design and Implementation in Organizations
Richard Williams

Managing Innovation and Change
A Critical Guide for Organizations
Nigel King and Neil Anderson

Managing Teams
A Strategy for Success
Nicky Hayes

Recruitment and Selection
A Framework for Success
Dominic Cooper and Ivan Robertson

Psychology
at Work

Managing Employee Performance

Design and Implementation in Organizations

Richard S. Williams

THOMSON

™

LEARNING   Australia • Canada • Mexico • Singapore • Spain • United Kingdom • United States

Managing Employee Performance: Design and Implementation in Organizations

Copyright © Richard S. Williams 2002

The Thomson Learning logo is a registered trademark used herein under licence.

For more information, contact Thomson Learning, Berkshire House,
168–173 High Holborn, London, WC1V 7AA or visit us on the World Wide Web at:
http://www.thomsonlearning.co.uk

British Library Cataloguing-in-Publication Data
A catalogue record for this book is available from the British Library

ISBN 1-86152-780-2

First published 1998 by International Thomson Business Press, under the title Performance Management: Perspectives on Employee Performance

This edition 2002 by Thomson Learning

Typeset by LaserScript, Mitcham, Surrey
Printed by TJ International, Padstow, Cornwall
Cover design by Metamorphosis
Text design by Malcolm Harvey Young

Contents

Figures

Tables

Boxes

Series editor's preface

Understanding the psychology of individuals and teams is of prime importance in work settings as rapid and far-reaching changes continue to occur. Organizational structures are shifting radically to the point where individual managers and professionals have far greater autonomy, responsibility and accountability. Organizations are seeking to reduce central control and to "empower" individual employees. These employees combine in teams that are frequently cross-functional and project based rather than hierarchical in their construction. The traditional notion of careers has changed; increasingly, an individual's career is less likely to be within a single organization, which has implications for how organizations command loyalty and commitment. The full impact of information technology has now been felt, with all the consequences this has for the nature of work and the reactions of those doing it.

The capacity of people to cope with the scale and speed of change has become a major issue and the literature on work stress only increases. The belief in the importance of individuals' cognitive abilities and personality make-up in determining what they achieve and how they contribute to teamwork has been demonstrated in the explosive growth in organizations' use of psychometric tests and related procedures. Perhaps more than ever before, analysing and understanding the experience of work from a psychological perspective is necessary to achieve the twin goals of effective performance and quality of life. Unfortunately, it is the latter of these that all too often seems to be overlooked in the concern to create competitive, performance driven, or customer focused cultures within companies.

It is no coincidence that the rise in the study of business ethics and increasing concern over issues or fairness paralleled many of the organizational changes of the late twentieth century. Ultimately, an imbalance between the aims and needs of the employees and the aims and needs of the organization is self-defeating. One of the widely recognized needs for the twenty-first century is for a greater emphasis on innovation rather than on simply reacting to pressures. However, psychological research and theory indicate that innovation is much more likely to take place where individuals feel secure enough to take the risks involved, and where organizational reward systems encourage experimentation and exploration which they have signally failed to do in the last century. Seeking to help organizations realize the potential of their workforce in a mutually enhancing way is the business challenge psychology has to meet.

The central theme of the *Psychology at Work* series is to interpret and explain people's work behaviour in the context of a continually evolving pattern of change, and to do so from the perspective of occupational and organizational psychology. Each of the books draws together academic research and practitioner experience, relying on empirical studies, practical examples, and case studies to communicate their ideas. The reader, whether a student, manager or psychologist, will find that they provide a succinct summary of accumulated knowledge and a guide to how to apply it in business. The themes of some of the books cover traditional areas of occupation psychology, while others focus on topics that cut across such boundaries, tackling subjects that are of growing interest and prominence. They are directly relevant for practitioners, consultants and students of HR and occupational psychology but much of what they deal with is of great value to managers, and students of management, more generally. This broad appeal is demonstrated by the fact that an earlier version of the series, the *Essential Business Psychology* series, was highly commended by the Management Consultancies Association book award. The *Psychology at Work* series shares the aims, and some of the titles, as the original series but the individual books have been substantially updated and the range of titles is expanded. Although the books share a common aim and series heading, they have not been forced into a rigid stylistic format. In keeping with the times, the authors have had a good deal of autonomy in deciding how to organize and present their work. I think all of them have done an excellent job; I hope you will find that too.

Clive Fletcher

1 What is performance management?

The idea of performance management is far from new – it has long been recognized that performance needs to be managed. This is true whether we are concerned with performance at the organizational level, the individual level, or any level in between. And over the years we have seen many practices, techniques, tools, systems and philosophies which have as their aim the management of performance. Indeed, the term performance management itself may be seen as yet another philosophy or system, and as such it came to particular prominence in the late 1980s/early 1990s. But its precise nature remains indistinct: as I shall go on to show, there are a number of perspectives on performance management.

So, performance management is no single thing. That said, one main interpretation has come to dominate in practice – one which focuses on the individual and which, for the most part, is essentially an evolutionary extension of traditional appraisal practice. But this has many deficiencies, not least of which is that it clings on to outmoded values about employees, their motivation and performance. By contrast, the models that are advocated in the textbooks on this subject – both the practitioner-oriented literature and that of a more academic kind – are broader in their scope. And they promulgate rather different values, such as participation, a philosophy of improvement and concern for employee well-being.

If we accept these values then we might expect to see a different approach not just to performance management itself but also to the way in which systems are designed and developed. So, for example, an involving approach to design and implementation might mean that systems will better meet the needs and interests of those most directly affected by performance management. It is said that performance management should be owned and driven by the line – if this is so then we might expect to see line managers being brought into the development process as a way of helping to bring about their acceptance of the system. A participative approach is one way of showing that employees are valued and trusted.

Going hand in hand with participation is the need for diagnosis and analysis. This theme is clear in much of the writing on performance management that we have seen over the past decade or so. Emphasis is also placed on the need to maintain, monitor and manage performance management systems. Though evaluation is often seen as something that is tacked on afterwards, it is a necessary part of the plan–do–check–act cycle.

We would expect an improvement philosophy to show itself in a developmental approach to performance management rather than the excessive emphasis on control and external reward that characterizes so much of contemporary practice. The latter are important but they need to be balanced by more of a concern for the employee – their well-being, fairness of treatment. And for the sceptics who see such thinking as unduly altruistic, there is increasing evidence to indicate that organizational benefits are to be obtained.

For the most part, however, it is not concern for the employee that has driven the introduction of performance management. Indeed, as might be expected, no single force was responsible; rather, there were a number of interrelated influencing factors. They are as germane today as they were a few years ago. So, by way of background, let me first briefly examine these influences. I'll then go on to look at the nature of performance management.

Factors influencing the introduction of performance management

Market conditions

The increasingly competitive environment of the 1980s, which continued throughout the recessionary early 1990s and remains a dominant factor today, has been identified by many commentators (e.g. Connock 1991; Storey and Sisson 1993) as a major influence leading to increased concern for performance improvement. Some (e.g. Lawler 1995) go so far as to say that the nature of competition is the 'most significant difference' about the business environment of the 1990s:

> Many businesses have become global, and as a result, success requires much higher levels of performance in three areas: the quality of goods and services produced, the cost at which they are produced, and the speed with which the producers innovate and get new products and services to the market.
>
> *(Lawler 1995: 52)*

In some sectors new market conditions have been created, particularly in the public sector; for example amongst schools, hospitals and other units within the health service, executive agencies within central government, and within local authorities through compulsory competitive tendering and 'Best Value'. All this has led to a much sharper focus in the public sector on performance and performance management.

The competitiveness theme is widespread in recent literature on organizational and employee performance, as the extracts in Table 1.1 show. However, important though it is, competitiveness is only one element in the drive to increase productivity and performance. In the same way that there are several forces pressing on organizations, so too there is a range of responses available to organizations. The sources quoted in Box 1.1 represent just a few of the perspectives from which the 'problem' of performance and productivity management has been approached. For example, Flood and Olian (1996) and Fay (1995) take a human resource management perspective, Peppard and Preece (1995) and Bredrup (1995a) emphasize the business process, and Bounds *et al.* (1994) are concerned with total quality management (TQM). These represent three overall approaches for managing performance which continue to be important today.

Today's concern for competitiveness may be seen as a continuation or development of the long-standing search for greater productivity. There have been many 'productivity improvement programmes' (e.g., Lawlor 1985; Prokopenko 1987) but some authorities (e.g., Heap 1992) have seen the traditional UK approach to improving productivity as being overly concerned with cost-cutting. Productivity has risen in the short term, but at what long-term expense? Increasingly, then, we have seen

| Box 1.1 | **Competitiveness and organizational performance** |

'The world of business has become a struggle to gain competitive advantage in a much larger and more demanding marketplace. Markets now stretch across international boundaries, trade barriers have crumbled and distribution channels have become more efficient. State intervention in many markets has diminished and organizations now confront an unequalled number of competitors. Consumer preferences have been ratcheted up, with increasingly demanding calls for higher quality products and services, delivered faster, and at a lower price.'

(Flood and Olian 1996: 5)

'Managers of today are under increasing pressure to improve the competitive position of their organization, either to steal a march on their competitors or to simply keep up with the ever accelerating pace of competition. ... At a macro level, it is easy to discern the changes taking place in the environment and the consequential demands and challenges which such developments place on organizations. Globalization of markets, commodization of products and services, and intense competition all challenge the way that organizations traditionally compete. New information and communication technologies are changing the very nature of business itself.'

(Peppard and Preece 1995: 157)

'A clear trend ... is that competition will increase due to more globalization and more demanding customers. As customers are exposed to better products and services their expectations for better quality, service and value will increase. Higher expectations have to be met by improved performance to obtain customer satisfaction.'

(Bredrup 1995a: 61)

'The changes that/are affecting organizations and work design include the increasing intensity and scope of international competition, a drive by American organizations to cut costs (in part to meet foreign competition relying on lower labour costs), a continued move toward automation of production processes, a reliance on more sophisticated information processing technologies, and greater use of communication technology in place of face-to-face interactions.' ▶

(Fay 1995: 23)

> 'Over time, managers have faced a growing intensity of global competition and pervasive change. ... Relentless advances in technology open and close markets as products rapidly move through ever-shorter life cycles. ... Better communications and logistical innovations have increased accessibility to even the remotest corners of the earth. As technological and economic development continues, the number of global competitors will continue to increase. Customers now expect more because competitors offer more.'
>
> *(Bounds* et al. *1994: 5)*

arguments for a broadening of the productivity concept, with greater emphasis being placed on the 'top-line' or performance element (e.g., Heap 1992; Andersen 1995).

Management theories and movements: excellence and quality

Also influential have been changes in thinking about the nature of the management of organizations and about performance. Two particular examples of this are the 'search for excellence' movement and the concern for quality. The latter has been especially influential because it has reshaped the way in which we think about performance and because of the changes to manufacturing and service delivery processes that have resulted.

Though the research carried out by Peters and Waterman (1982) has come to be questioned (e.g., Hitt and Ireland 1987), there is no doubt that their eight principles of excellence (Table 1.1) have been influential. For example, the ideas of getting close to the customer and finding out what the customer wants so as to identify and meet changing consumer demand and expectations/requirements are now widely accepted (Lawler 1995). They have been reinforced in the public sector, for example, by many of the changes pushed through by central Government. Similarly, 'sticking to the knitting' is an idea that we see reflected in the notion of the 'core competence' of an organization (Prahalad and Hamel 1990). And the case for productivity or competitiveness through people has been argued by many (e.g., Pfeffer 1994).

Table 1.1	**Characteristics of 'excellent' companies**

- A bias for action
- Close to the customer
- Autonomy and entrepreneurship
- Productivity through people
- Hands-on, value-driven
- Stick to knitting
- Simple form, lean staff
- Simultaneous loose–tight properties

Source: Peters and Waterman 1982

Technological developments

From one point of view technology is part of performance management, one of the tools, that is, for managing performance. Product and process technology have been identified by Pfeffer (1994), for example, as one of the traditional bases of competitive success. And, indeed, technology, especially information technology, has been in many cases a solution to a performance problem which has led to that business gaining competitive advantage: American Airlines and their SABRE system is a particular case in point (McKenney 1995). Others in the industry then were left to catch up, often doing so with a comparable technological solution of their own.

Over the years we have seen many technological developments which have led organizations to make changes to their systems for managing performance, that is, their manufacturing process or the service delivery process. Examples include automation, computer-aided design (CAD), computer-aided manufacturing (CAM), just in time (JIT), and lean production, and business process re-engineering (BPR) typically will involve the application of information technology (IT). All of these have their implications for the people expected to operate them.

Organizational restructuring and change

Like technology, organizational restructuring may be seen as part of performance management. Much restructuring seems to have been as a response to the prevailing economic conditions and we have seen many different manifestations: '"de-layering", "downsizing", "flexibility", "team-working", "service level agreements", "high performance work systems", "strategic business units", "core and periphery", "teleworking", "franchising"' (Storey and Sisson 1993: 80) are many of the terms which illustrate the different forms of restructuring that we have come to see. In addition there have been changes of ownership and mergers. All these developments have been seen in both the private and public sectors.

Though the sorts of structural changes listed above may cut costs (and so boost productivity) they do not necessarily do anything to increase performance, at whatever level and however defined. Potentially, they offer an opportunity for doing so: for example, Fletcher and Williams point out that 'Delayering might be seen as facilitating performance management, in that it places more power to determine organizational performance in the hands of individual managers' (Institute of Personnel Management 1992: 82). Extending this still further we have ideas like 'empowerment' and 'control through involvement' (Lawler 1995) which seek, amongst other things, to push authority lower down the hierarchy (where there still is a hierarchy, that is!). But such structural changes might be seen very differently by employees who remain in the organization, as in the negative consequences of 'downsizing' (Cascio 1993; Feldman 1995).

One consequence claimed for such restructuring as delayering and decentralization has been an alteration in the **role of the line manager** – the quote from Fletcher and Williams above gives one example. But there may have been other changes as well, such as having more extensive personnel management and employee development responsibilities for larger numbers of staff. In other words, the **management** role comes to be emphasized more than the technical aspects of managers' jobs.

Government policies

Certain of these have had a particular impact on the public sector, as in the creation of new markets mentioned above. Other legislative changes – local management of schools (LMS), care in the community, and many others – have already affected service provision and will continue to do so. This is true also of other legislative changes which have affected organizations more generally, namely those bearing on employment and industrial relations.

Industrial relations changes

As Fletcher and Williams comment:

> The 1980s saw a number of legislative changes, which together with other factors (including high unemployment) made inroads into traditional collective bargaining. One result of this has been to facilitate the movement towards dispensing rewards on a more individual, rather than collective, basis, and to allocate more of those rewards on the basis of merit.
>
> *(Institute of Personnel Management 1992: 84)*

Here again, the employment-related legislation now in force seems set to remain. Performance management as typically practised is wholly consistent with this individualization of the employment relationship – goal-setting, appraisal, and performance-related pay all operate, for the most part, on an individual basis.

The inadequacies of performance appraisal

A final influencing factor is the claim that performance appraisal is deficient as a tool for managing employee performance. This argument is particularly evident in the North American literature on performance management (e.g., Schneier *et al.* 1986; Heisler *et al.* 1988), although there are examples of it elsewhere (e.g., South Africa – Spangenberg 1994). Table 1.2 summarizes the problems which continue to be potential pitfalls for performance management.

At one level, then, performance management may be seen as a reaction against performance appraisal. Indeed, much more generally, performance management policies and practices appear very much to be a **response** to the sorts of pressures and influences summarized above. And organizations have responded in many different ways: thus, it is clear that there is no single approach to performance management. Evidence from surveys of practice support this view, as do the writings of academics and practitioners.

Table 1.2	**Sources of performance appraisal problems**

1 CONTEXT

   1.1 Organizational characteristics
- Emphasis on the past clashes with managerial preference for current information
- No commitment to appraisal
- Conducting of appraisals not reinforced, e.g. no rewards for conscientious appraisals
- Performance appraisals not declared an important managerial function
- Redundant in democratic participative climate

   1.2 Position characteristics
- Inability to observe performance

2 SYSTEM CHARACTERISTICS

   2.1 Implementation
- No user participation in system development
- Failure to develop performance measures from job analysis
- Rating systems administered subjectively
- Results used to discriminate on the basis of race, sex, etc.

   2.2 Performance appraisal policies
- No standard policy regarding rater's tasks/roles in appraisal
- No standard policy regarding frequency of appraisals

3 PERFORMANCE APPRAISAL ELEMENTS

   3.1 Rater and rating process
Observation
- Lack of knowledge of ratee's job
- Possession of erroneous or incomplete information
- Differing expectations because of level in hierarchy and role

Judgement
- Bias and errors in human judgement
- Stereotypes and prejudices

   3.2 Performance appraisal instrument
Performance measures (criteria)
- Ambiguity of performance measures: incompleteness
- Lack of specificity and behaviour-based language
- Irrelevant performance criteria
- Criteria not communicated explicitly to ratees

Performance appraisal system
- Inability of system to reflect dynamic nature of jobs and organizational context
- Credibility loss from outdated systems

4 PERFORMANCE APPRAISAL OUTCOMES
Evaluation
- Failure to recognize excellent performance
- Promotional decision errors
- Staffing jobs with inadequate skills mix

Guidance and development
- Failure to recognize potential
- Failure to build skills through training

Motivation
- Grievances because of subjectivity and bias

Source: Spangenberg 1994: 3

Perspectives on performance management

One of the things that writers on performance management agree about is that performance management is difficult to define – this is true, of course, of many other initiatives, such as total quality management (TQM) and business process re-engineering (BPR). None the less, it seems possible to discern three main perspectives or types of model:

- performance management as a system for managing organizational performance;
- performance management as a system for managing employee performance;
- performance management as a system for integrating the management of organizational and employee performance.

What are the main features of these perspectives? I'll set these out first before going on to identify some underlying themes.

Performance management as a system for managing organizational performance

A good illustration of this view is found in Rogers (1990), who writes about corporate, authority-wide systems of performance management in local government:

The characteristics of such systems are that they are corporate systems which include the following processes as part of an annual integrated cycle of management:

- setting corporate policy and resource aims and guidelines
- specifying, within the framework provided by (1) above, a detailed set of plans, budgets, objectives, targets and standards of performance
- regularly and systematically reviewing the performance of all services.

(Rogers 1990: 29)

Another illustration of this conception is presented by Bredrup (1995), who sees performance management as comprising three main processes – planning, improving and reviewing. Of course, these three processes could be taken as applying to the management of performance at whatever level of analysis one chooses – organization-wide, business unit, department, team, individual, etc. (Mabey and Salaman 1995). But Bredrup's schematic representation (see Figure 1.1) of his model shows rather more clearly the organizational perspective.

Figure 1.1 **Performance management: planning, improvement and review**

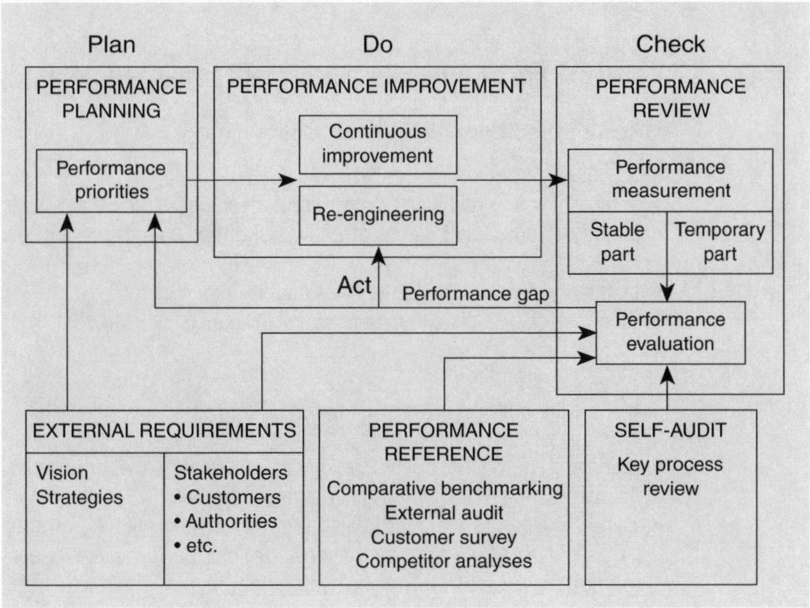

Source: Bredrup 1995a

Thus, in this model **performance planning** is concerned with such activities as formulating the organization's vision and strategy and defining what is meant by performance. **Performance improvement** takes a process perspective, that is, including such activities as business process re-engineering, continuous process improvement, benchmarking, and total quality management. **Performance review** embraces performance measurement and evaluation.

One of the reasons why this model is of particular interest is because it incorporates many of the management ideas, philosophies, practices, etc. that have emerged in the 1980s and 1990s. This is true also of other, recent portrayals of performance management: an illustration of this comes from one of the Institute of Personnel and Development's (IPD) books on performance management, as shown in Table 1.3.

Performance management of the kind depicted so far hardly is new and perhaps is more familiar to us as strategic/business planning, operations management and the like. In other words, the focus of this model is on the determination of the organization's strategy and the implementation of that strategy through the organization's structure, technology, business systems and procedures, etc. Employees are **not**

Table 1.3	**Components of effective performance management**

Effective performance management means:

- articulating your company's vision
- establishing key results, objectives and measures at key business unit level
- identifying business process objectives and the key indicators of performance for those processes
- identifying and installing effective departmental measures
- monitoring and controlling four key performance measures
  1   quality
  2   delivery
  3   cycle time
  4   waste
- managing the continuous improvement of performance in those key areas – 'benchmarking' your performance against the best
- being prepared to aim for 'breakthrough' improvements in performance when this is required by a significant shortfall in your performance measured against the performance of your major competitors

Source: Lawson 1995: 12–13

the primary focus, although they will be affected by changes in technology, structure, operating systems, etc.

Performance management as a system for managing employee performance

There are several variants of this model, with performance management commonly being represented as a cycle. Here are a few examples. Ainsworth and Smith (1993) have a three-step cycle, as in Figure 1.2. Guinn (1987) also proposes a three-step process: planning, managing and appraising, as shown in the upper half of Table 1.4. Torrington and Hall (1995) likewise have three: planning, supporting and reviewing performance. Common in much of this writing is the idea that manager and managed should have a shared view of what is expected of the employee; involvement and participation of a direct kind are typically advocated as the means by which this shared view may be arrived at. Supporting performance is seen as a responsibility of the line manager who also has a particular part to play in reviewing performance. Here again we have an activity that often is presented as being shared between

| Figure 1.2 | **Performance management: planning, assessment and feedback** |

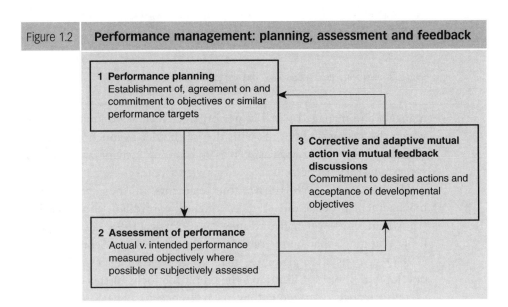

Source: Ainsworth and Smith 1993

Table 1.4	**Elements in the performance management system**

(a)

Planning	Managing	Appraising
Establish performance targets	Monitor behaviour and objectives	Formal meeting of employee and manager
Identify job behaviours	Reinforce desired behaviours and objective attainment	Written record
Identify basis for measuring performance	Redirect inappropriate behaviours	Focus on future and employee's development
Provide direction, initial energizing of behaviour	Provide control	Provide for replanning and new objective establishment

(b)

Direct	Energize	Control	Reward
Key result areas	Set goals	Monitor	Evaluate
Performance indicators	Establish behavioural expectations	Provide feedback	Reinforce
Required behaviours		Redirect	
		Develop	

Source: (a) Guinn 1987, cited in Heisler *et al*. 1988: 151 (b) Heisler *et al*. 1988: 156

manager and managed – that is, performance review is a joint activity in which the responsibility rests with the job holder as much as with the manager. Moreover, review is seen as an ongoing activity rather than as something that happens just once or twice a year.

Heisler *et al.* (1988) have four elements in their performance management process: directing, energizing, controlling and rewarding (shown in the lower half of Table 1.4). Hartle (1995) also proposes four: planning, managing, reviewing and rewarding. Schneier *et al.* (1987) give us five: planning, managing, reviewing, rewarding and developing. Table 1.4 illustrates the employee focus of this conception of performance management by its reference to behaviours and the motivational language that is used, e.g. providing direction, energizing.

Performance management as a system for integrating the management of organizational and employee performance

This model may be regarded as a combination of the first two, although this perhaps is rather too simple a view as there are variations on the basic theme. This variation reflects the two main models identified above, that is, the extent to which there is an emphasis on organizational as compared to employee performance.

In the second category of model described above the stress is firmly on employee performance; that said, several of the particular models within that category recognize that the management of employee performance takes place within a framework of organizational goals. But there is a sense in which this framework is taken as given. For example, in presenting their employee-focused view of performance management Ainsworth and Smith make certain assumptions:

> This assumes that the important corporate issues of 'mission' and the setting of corporate goals have been addressed and resolved. It assumes that objectives for the sub-sections of the organization (the departments, divisions or business units) have been set within the key results areas, and that the senior management group has identified just where the competitive advantage and value added dimensions of the business lie. It further assumes that all of this has been communicated to and understood by those involved.
>
> *(Ainsworth and Smith 1993: 5–6)*

In other models which present performance management as an integrative system the organizational framework is made even more explicit. The performance management cycles presented by McAfee and Champagne (1993) and Storey and Sisson (1993) – shown in Figure 1.3 – represent illustrations. Rather more elaborate versions of this sub-type are to be found, as illustrated in Table 1.5. Though they are intended to enhance organizational performance, what characterizes all these models is their emphasis on employee-focused interventions:

> Performance management supports a company's or organization's overall business goals by linking the work of each individual employee or manager to the overall mission of the work unit.
>
> *(Costello 1994: 3)*

Figure 1.3 **Performance management cycles**

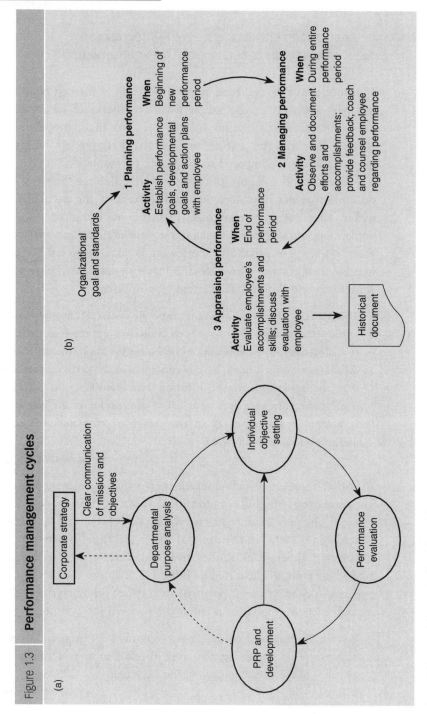

Source: (a) Storey and Sisson 1993; (b) McAfee and Champagne 1993

Table 1.5 Integrative models of performance management

A 'textbook' performance management system	The main building blocks of performance management	Requirements of the performance management process	Improving the performance of the organization and the contribution of staff
The organization has a shared vision of its objectives, or a mission statement, which it communicates to all its employees.	The development of the organization's mission statement and objectives.	A clear statement of the organization's mission – i.e. what the organization needs to do to compete and survive in its current business environment.	In order to maximize performance, focus the efforts of the organization on explicit, challenging and realistic aims and objectives.
The organization sets individual performance management targets which are related both to operating-unit and wider organizational objectives.	Associated with this, the development of the business plan (business being interpreted in the broadest sense of the word).	A mechanism to enable the performance of individuals within the organization to be aligned with that mission statement and a way of adjusting performance requirements to meet new challenges which may arise.	Target and improve the understanding, commitment and contribution of individual staff in the delivery of those objectives.
It conducts a regular, formal review of progress towards these targets.	Enhancing communications within the organization, so that employees are not only aware of the objectives and the business plan but can contribute to their formulation.	A set of human resource management policies which support the organization's strategic aims and which give individuals an incentive to work towards their own personal objectives. This involves creating an environment where high performance is actively encouraged and human resource policies are in tune with corporate goals.	Support the delegation of responsibility to front-line staff by using management through objectives.

A 'textbook' performance management system	The main building blocks of performance management	Requirements of the performance management process	Improving the performance of the organization and the contribution of staff
It uses the review process to identify training, development and reward outcomes.	Clarifying individual responsibilities and accountabilities (which means, amongst other things, having job descriptions, clear role definitions, and so on, and being willing to be held accountable).	A clear statement of the organization's future goals – their vision and the direction in which they intend to move.	Provide quantitative and qualitative standards for judging individual and organizational performance.
It evaluates the effectiveness of the whole process and its contribution to overall organizational performance to allow changes and improvements to be made.	Defining and measuring individual performance (with the emphasis on being measured against one's own objectives rather than being compared with others). Implementing appropriate reward strategies. Developing staff to further improve performance, and their career progression, in the future.	A process which enables the critical capability factors within the organization to be developed as part of the performance management process. This is particularly relevant with regard to the development of people – their competence, skills and knowledge need to be a critical part of the development of capability.	Provide feedback to the organization and to individual staff about their actual performance. Identify and implement training and other actions necessary to improve individual performance.

Source: Bevan and Thompson 1991; Fletcher 1993, 1994; Lockett 1992; Audit Commission 1995a

The central aim of performance management is to develop the potential of staff, improve their performance and, through linking an employee's individual objectives to business strategies, improve the company's performance.

(Incomes Data Services 1992: 1)

[Performance management] is about directing and supporting employees to work as effectively and efficiently as possible *in line with the needs of the organization.*

(Walters 1995: x)

Rather different are those models which, while claiming to be integrative, place more emphasis on managing organizational performance. For example, Rogers puts forward an elaboration of his corporate model which adds the management of employee performance:

corporate systems . . . include the following processes as part of an annual integrated cycle of management:

- setting corporate policy and resource aims and guidelines
- specifying, within the framework provided by (1) above, a detailed set of plans, budgets, objectives, targets and standards of performance
- regularly and systematically reviewing the performance of all services.

. . . systems which integrate the procedures for managing organizational performance with those for managing the performance of individuals . . . have the following additional characteristics:

- Procedures and systems for planning, monitoring and appraising the performance of individuals which are integrated with those for managing organizational performance.

Some, though not all . . . have a fifth characteristic:
- Systems, such as performance related pay, for rewarding individual achievements.

(Rogers 1990: 29–30)

What's being said in all of this, of course, is that there is a need to manage performance at several levels: this is made explicit in a number of models. Thus, Rummler and Brache (1995) specify three interdependent levels of performance: organization, process and job/performer. Spangenberg (1994), drawing on Mohrman (1990) and Rummler and

Brache, presents one of the most comprehensive of the integrated models and identifies three levels of performance: organization, process/function and team/individual. And at each level he envisages a five-step annual performance cycle, as illustrated in Table 1.6.

Performance management: some underlying themes

A number of interrelated themes run through these several perspectives on performance management. I will introduce these themes here before returning to them in later chapters.

The first is indicated by the way in which the different models have been categorized, that is, the level at which performance management operates (Mabey and Salaman 1995). At the one extreme we have models which are concerned with managing organizational performance; at the other extreme are those which define performance management as being the management of employee performance. Some of the latter explicitly recognize the organizational context within which employee performance must be located. Some commentators (e.g., Storey and Sisson 1993) have argued that in these models the management of employee performance comes to be given heightened, strategic importance. The more comprehensive of the models present performance management as being concerned with the management of performance at all levels – organizational, individual and everything in between. Related to this is the theme of **integration** and **linking**; many of the models present performance management as an **holistic** process.

Implied by many models is a view of the **nature of organizations** – essentially a 'rationalistic, directive view of the organization' (Mabey and Salaman, 1995: 186). An element of this theme is the need for an organization to have a vision and strategy and a statement of goals and objectives. Related to this theme is one to do with the **nature of performance** – in other words, what is performance? For ease of illustration let me confine myself to the two extremes – organizational performance and individual performance. At the organizational level a goal-oriented perspective seems to be dominant. But other conceptions of organizations and organizational performance are to be found, for example ones which emphasize process and adaptation/learning.

These same points apply to individual performance, which is primarily seen in terms of outputs/results. But the idea that

Table 1.6	**Spangenberg's integrated model of performance**

Organization	Process/function	Team/individual
1 PERFORMANCE PLANNING		
• Vision • Mission • Strategy • Organizational goals set and communicated	• Goals for key processes linked to organizational and customer needs	• Team mission, goals, values and performance strategies defined • Individual goals, responsibilities, and work-planning aligned with process/function goals
2 DESIGN		
• Organization design ensures structure supports strategy	• Process design facilitates efficient goal achievement	• Teams are formed to achieve process/function goals • Job design ensures process requirements reflected in jobs; jobs logically constructed in ergonomically sound environment
3 MANAGING PERFORMANCE (AND IMPROVEMENT)		
• Continual organization development and change efforts • Functional goals (in support of organizational goals) managed, reviewed and adapted quarterly • Sufficient resources allocated • Interfaces between functions managed	• Appropriate sub-goals set; process performance managed and regularly reviewed • Sufficient resources allocated • Interfaces between process steps managed	• Active team-building efforts, feedback, co-ordination and adjustment • Developing individual understanding and skills; providing feedback • Sufficient resources allocated
4 REVIEWING PERFORMANCE		
• Annual review, input into strategic planning	• Annual review	• Annual review
5 REWARDING PERFORMANCE		
• Financial performance of organization	• Function rewards commensurate with value of organizational performance and function contribution	• Rewards commensurate with value of organization performance, and: for team – function and team contribution; for individual – function/team performance and individual contribution

Source: Spangenberg 1994: 30–1

performance can be equated with behaviour is also evident. Defining individual performance – both conceptually and operationally – must surely be one of the key issues in performance management. There is also the related question of what **causes** performance.

What is performance management for, especially in relation to the management of individual performance? In broad terms the overall purpose is to contribute to the achievement of organizational performance. But performance management systems typically have many elements to them and what remains a controversial issue is the balance between development and reward purposes. Also, what's in it for the worker? Where do job satisfaction, employee well-being and the like fit within performance management systems? As I will go on to show, employee interests are not especially evident in performance management practice.

One theme that is especially clear is the **importance of communication**. One aspect of this might be termed **organizational communication**, and in many of the models this is seen as essentially downward, although some do recognize the value of upward communication. The second aspect is the day-to-day **interpersonal communication** that takes place between manager and managed. Indeed, and this is another theme, the line manager takes on particular importance in the employee-focused models of performance management both as an agent of communication and as **owner** of the performance management process. And in many of the models there is a recognition of mutuality – for example, manager and managed should **jointly** set employee goals. Hence, in much of the advocacy one sees a particular set of values, those stressing **participation** and **involvement**.

Models vary in the extent to which they are **prescriptive** of what organizations should do and how they should do it (Mabey and Salaman 1995). The tendency in most of the models referred to earlier is towards prescription, at least to the extent of prescribing **what** should be done. Some go further and prescribe **how**. However, the models generally are unsatisfactory as descriptions of practice since the reality of what happens falls short in many respects of what the textbooks and popular literature advocate.

Another theme is that there is variation in the **nature** and **scope** of the policies/practices that are implied or specified. This relates to the earlier theme concerning the level at which performance management operates. Models emphasizing the management of organizational performance tend to give more prominence to the business process, and performance management interventions will often be of a structural or technological kind. There are, of course, implications for employees but these typically will be consequential rather than policies being directed specifically at them. But where the concern is with employee performance the sorts of interventions are those which are generally taken as falling within the ambit of personnel management or human resource management (HRM). And the scope may be broad or narrow, that is, all of HRM or just a sub-set (Storey and Sisson 1993). The former would, for example, include recruitment and selection as performance management activities on the grounds, say, that these offer the first opportunity to convey expectations of what performance will be required from the employee. The narrowest conception embraces results-oriented appraisal and, probably, appraisal-related pay – control would seem to be the main underlying intent here.

The importance of organizational culture features in many models. Two points of view may be distinguished – that performance management must fit the organization's culture and that performance management is an instrument of culture change. The latter perspective in essence involves the imposition of top management's values on the rest of the organization – a **unitarist** view which ignores the plurality of interests that we would expect to find in an organization.

What consensus is there about the components of performance management?

The weight of opinion amongst British writers seems to view performance management as an essentially employee-centred set of interventions. It aims to harness the contribution of individual employee performance to organizational performance. Thus, at the heart of performance management we find a cycle of activity which includes policies and procedures for some or all of the following aspects of individual performance:

- directing/planning;
- managing/supporting;
- reviewing/appraising;
- developing/rewarding.

The consensus position recognizes also that these activities take place within a given organizational context, two facets of which are afforded particular emphasis:

- the organization's mission, objectives, and business plan;
- communication about that mission etc.

All this seems very reasonable, sensible and rational. We decide where the organization is heading and what it is trying to do, we communicate that to all our employees, and we have systems for planning the work of individuals so that their efforts can be appropriately directed. This is easier said than done, of course; and when we look at the survey evidence about performance management practice it seems that it isn't happening.

Performance management in practice: survey evidence

During the 1990s, several surveys of performance management practice were carried out by a variety of organizations. A large-scale postal study was carried out in 1991 by the then Institute of Manpower Studies (IMS; now Institute for Employment Studies) for the Institute of Personnel Management (IPM) as it was at the time (now Chartered Institute of Personnel and Development – CIPD). This was extended by a smaller, more qualitative investigation by Fletcher and Williams (Institute of Personnel Management 1992) into 26 organizations, nine of which provided attitude survey data about employee experience of performance management. Also of interest is a later survey carried out by the Institute of Personnel and Development (reported in Armstrong and Baron 1998) and two surveys done by the Industrial Society (1994, 1998). The following account will draw mostly on these surveys. However, in addition, there are various case study reports and other accounts of practice, e.g. by Incomes Data Services (1992), Rogers (1990), Local Government Management Board (1993), and the Audit Commission (1995a, b, c), the last including some survey evidence about employees' attitudes towards performance management.

Who was surveyed?

The IMS sent its questionnaire to 1,863 private- and public-sector organizations of varying sizes and industrial sector. (Fuller details are given in the research report; Institute of Personnel Management 1992.) The usable response rate was 46 per cent. The survey was carried out between March and June 1991. The later IPD survey was of 2,750 UK personnel practitioners from a range of types and sizes of organizations. The response rate was 20.4 per cent. The Industrial Society carried out one survey in April 1994, sending a questionnaire to 4,351 personnel and human resource managers who were drawn randomly from the Society's database. The response rate was 23.6 per cent. Their second survey mailed 5,500 human resource specialists, again from the Society's database; the response rate was a low 9 per cent.

Unfortunately, not enough details about the nature of the later IPD survey nor of the two Industrial Society surveys are reported to allow the exact make-up of the several surveys to be compared. Similarly, the content of the surveys was not exactly the same. Consequently, we are not comparing like with like and the surveys are probably best regarded as a series of snapshots taken at different points in time.

What did the surveys ask about?

The IMS survey was clearly organized around a particular conception of performance management – harnessing the contribution of employee performance in the pursuit of organizational performance. By contrast, the first Industrial Society survey took a narrower view – essentially a survey of appraisal and appraisal-related pay practice rather than performance management more broadly defined. The second survey, however, was broader in scope. The later IPD survey gathered information about the features of performance management.

What did the surveys find?

To sketch an overall picture only the main findings will be summarized here, with others being given in later chapters.

How many organizations have policies and practices aimed at managing employee performance?

According to the IMS survey, 'Just under 20 per cent of respondents had a 'formal performance management programme', 66 per cent had other types of policies to manage employee performance and 14 per cent had no policies at all' (Institute of Personnel Management 1992: 17). The IPD survey revealed that by 1998 the proportion of organizations claiming to have formal processes had increased to just over two-thirds.

Which employees?

The surveys are broadly agreed in reporting that performance management applies more to managerial levels than to manual staff. The IMS surveys are the more informative about this: Figure 1.4 shows the findings from the earlier survey, with those from 1998 painting much the same picture. The IPD survey indicates much the same view

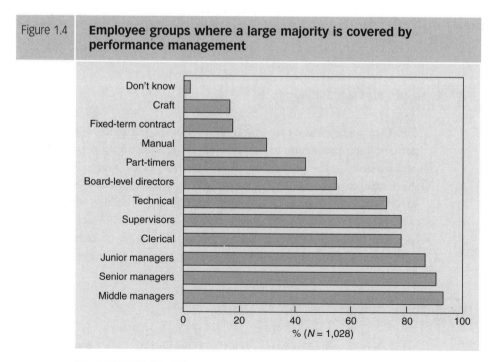

Figure 1.4 **Employee groups where a large majority is covered by performance management**

% (N = 1,028)

Source: Industrial Society 1994

overall, albeit with a slightly higher proportion of respondents (just over half) reporting performance management applying to manual staff.

Aims of performance management

The IMS survey identified improving organizational effectiveness, motivating employees, and improving training and development as the three main reasons for introducing performance management. In similar vein, the Industrial Society discovered the identification of individual training needs to be a main purpose of schemes. Other purposes included setting objectives/targets and providing feedback on performance; changing the organizational culture and linking pay to productivity were also important reasons amongst organizations with formal performance management systems.

Do organizations have mission statements and do they communicate them to employees?

From the IMS survey we learn that there is a difference between organizations which have formal performance management policies and those which don't: this is clearly illustrated in Figure 1.5. Having a mission statement is one thing; but telling all employees what it is seems to be something else! It would appear that mission statements are not universally communicated, even by organizations which claim

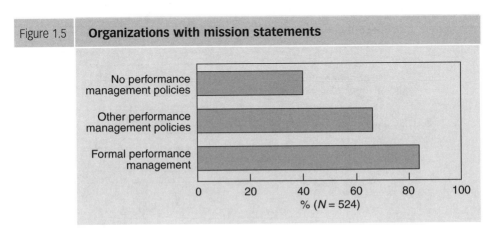

Figure 1.5 **Organizations with mission statements**

Source: Institute of Personnel Management 1992

27

to have performance management policies. Figure 1.6 shows that communication is even less likely in organizations without performance management policies.

Communicating requirements and performance review

Amongst organizations having performance management systems performance requirements, and their measurement criteria, are commonly expressed in objective, output-based terms; this is particularly the case for managers.

Generally speaking, line management is the most commonly used channel of communication, followed by the appraisal process. For both, the incidence of use is less for those organizations which do not have performance management policies.

How is performance reviewed, and by whom? Amongst organizations having formal performance management or some other policies a 'joint discussion between employee and line manager' was by far the most common approach to performance review. For those organizations with no performance management policies the most common approach was 'no review'! According to the IMS survey self-, peer and upward appraisal all seem to be rare, although review findings are commonly seen by a third party in organizations which have performance management policies. The Industrial Society surveys report surprisingly high figures for the incidence of self-appraisal – 71 per cent in 1994,

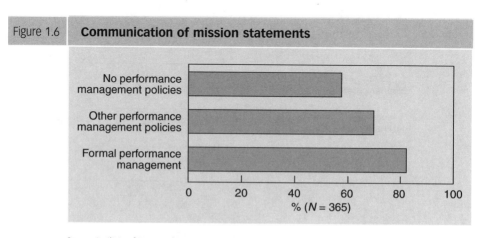

Figure 1.6   **Communication of mission statements**

Source: Institute of Personnel Management 1992

and a somewhat lower 58 per cent in 1998. The IPD survey reports 45 per cent of responding organizations as using self-appraisal, 20 per cent using upward feedback, 11 per cent using 360° feedback (the Industrial Society report 14 per cent in their second survey), and nine per cent using peer appraisal.

Performance and pay

How directly is pay linked to performance? This varies according to level of employee and the presence of formal performance management. For senior managers, over half the organizations with formal systems maintain a direct link between the achievement of performance requirements and pay. This is significantly higher than in organizations with other sorts of policies (39 per cent) and those with no policies at all (20 per cent). For other white-collar employees there is a similar overall pattern, but with fewer organizations reporting a direct link. And for manual employees there is still less of a tendency to link pay directly to performance.

The type of pay system linking pay and performance varies. For manual employees bonus schemes are the most common but for white-collar staff appraisal-related pay is the most frequently used, with the incidence of use rising with the level of employee. In addition, appraisal-related pay is more likely to be used by formal performance management organizations than by other organizations. A link with pay continues to be a feature of performance management: the IPD survey reports 43 per cent of organizations as having performance-related pay (PRP).

A concluding comment: does performance management exist?

From their findings the IMS researchers concluded that 'There was no consistent definition of performance management among those professing to operate it' (Institute of Personnel Management 1992: 5). That said, the sophistication of their survey allowed them to identify a number of characteristics which distinguished formal performance management organizations from those having other policies for managing employee performance. These characteristics are shown in Table 1.7. Though organizations professing to have formal

Table 1.7	**Distinguishing characteristics of formal performance management organizations**

Performance management organizations were more likely to:

- have mission statements which are communicated to all employees;
- regularly communicate information on business plans and progress towards achieving these plans;
- implement policies such as total quality management (TQM) and performance related pay (PRP);
- focus on senior managers' performance rather than other manual and white-collar employees;
- express performance targets in terms of measurable outputs, accountabilities and training/learning targets;
- use formal appraisal processes and CEO presentations as ways of communicating performance requirements;
- set performance requirements on a regular basis;
- link performance requirements to pay, particularly for senior managers.

Source: Institute of Personnel Management 1992: 5

performance management policies *tended* to engage in practices and activities of the kind advocated in the textbooks, the IMS researchers were able to identify only 3 per cent of organizations (out of the 856 respondents) which closely matched their textbook model.

From the survey evidence presented in this chapter it is clear that formal employee performance management of the holistic, comprehensive, integrative kind that is advocated in much of the literature is rare. The dominant approach to managing employee performance still rests on objective-setting and annual appraisal. In some instances this will be supplemented by PRP, although it is significant that the IPD survey found two-thirds of organizations claiming to use personal development plans. To this extent, then, the reality of contemporary performance management practice is probably best seen as 'a logical progression in the history of the development of appraisal systems' (Lundy and Cowling 1996: 307).

So, much of today's practice is merely an extension of what has gone before. That systems evolve is understandable, but perhaps we also need to see signs of revolution. There is evidence of some changes in thinking – for example a broader perspective on the nature of performance. At the organizational level, I look at this in Chapters 2 and 3, which focus on the organizational context for performance management. I then shift attention to the individual level and examine employee performance and its determinants, in Chapters 4, 5 and 6. The key role of the line manager in reviewing, supporting and rewarding performance is developed in Chapters 7 and 8. Finally, in Chapters 9 and 10, I turn to design, development and management. Throughout these chapters I emphasize themes of diagnosis, analysis and participation and the need to recognize and balance the goals of the several groups who have an interest in performance management.

2 The organizational context I: Vision, mission and strategy

In this and the following chapter I will examine the organizational context within which employee-centred performance management exists. As shown in the previous chapter, there is widespread agreement in the performance management literature that organizations should have a vision, mission and strategy. I will consider what these terms mean and the implications for performance management.

In Chapter 3 I will go on to consider the nature of organizational performance, as it is clear that a central purpose of performance management, even as an employee-focused intervention, is to contribute to the delivery of performance at the organizational level.

Vision, mission and strategy

Advocacy of the need for vision, mission and strategy is by no means confined to the performance management literature. As we would expect it is particularly prevalent in texts on strategic management (e.g. Luffman *et al.* 1996), but it is also found widely elsewhere in writings on various aspects of management and organization, for example Bounds *et al.* (1994) on quality management, Torrington and Hall (1995) on personnel management, and Wild (1995) on operations management.

What do we mean by the terms *vision, mission* and *strategy*? Box 2.1 gives some definitions. As can be seen, the terms are partly overlapping and by no means clearly distinguished – these variations reflect company practice, as Campbell and Yeung (1991a) discovered in their research among forty-two organizations. So, though not all writers distinguish between vision and mission Campbell and Yeung (1991b) suggest that the former term denotes some desired future state, whereas the latter is more concerned with the present and may be a more enduring statement about an organization's intent. The term strategy may be interpreted in two senses – *content* or *process* – as implied in Brown's definition in Box 2.1. In some models, strategy content is seen as part of mission; for example, Campbell and Yeung see a strong mission as having the following four linked elements working together in a mutually reinforcing way:

- **purpose**: why the organization exists;
- **strategy**: the competitive position and distinctive competence;
- **values**: what the company believes in;
- **behaviour standards**: the policies and behaviour patterns that underpin the distinctive competence and the value system.

Box 2.1	**Definitions of vision, mission and strategy**

Vision

'A vision indicates what the company is aiming at in the future. It serves as the long-term road map for the company.'

(Bredrup 1995d: 92)

'A *vision* statement outlines what purposes managers want the organization to serve over the long term and what the organization should become.'

(Bounds et al. 1994: 218)

'Vision is the term used to describe a picture of a relatively remote future in which business has developed under the best possible conditions and in accordance with the hopes and dreams of the owner or chief executive. A vision provides a benchmark for what one hopes to achieve in business, and can be a guide to the level of ambition of strategic planning.'

(Karlöf 1993: 150–1)

Mission

'A mission defines the scope of the business activities the company pursues. ... A mission answers the question: "What business should the company be in?"'

(Bredrup 1995d: 94–5)

'The *mission* should describe the organization's current purpose in terms of what the organization will do over the near term. This statement should set the organization apart from those serving the same customer need.'

(Bounds et al. 1994: 218)

'Mission is an organization's character, identity and reason for existence. It can be divided into four inter-relating parts: purpose, strategy, behaviour standards and values. Purpose addresses why an organization is in being: for whose benefit is all this effort being put in? Strategy considers the nature of the business, the desired positioning vs other companies and the source of competititve advantage. Behaviour standards are the norms and rules of "the way we do things around here". Values are the beliefs and moral principles that lie behind the behaviour standards, beliefs that have normally been formulated within the organization by a founding dynasty or a dominant management team.'

(Campbell and Yeung 1991b: 145)

Strategy

'The MEANS by which organizations meet, or seek to meet, OBJECTIVES. There can be a strategy for each product or service, and an overall strategy for the organization.'

(Thompson 1990: x)

'According to some, strategy refers to a plan for interacting with the competitive environment in order to achieve organizational goals. Such plans are generally characterized as formal, explicit, devised by senior executives, long-termist, and have a significant effect on how the organization behaves in its environment. ... An alternative view of strategy suggests that it can be less structured, and more informal and implicit in its formulation. The idea here is that strategy is something intrinsic to the process of leading and managing. Rather than being a set plan, strategy is a set of principles or heuristics for managing that are encoded in a system of management and which allow for considerable flexibility and adaptability in dealing with the exigencies of a changing environment.'

(Brown 1995: 167)

Collectively the terms vision, mission and strategy are a series of statements about the direction in which an organization wishes to head in the future and the means by which it wishes to get there. We can see these features in the examples shown in Boxes 2.2 and 2.3.

These examples also illustrate certain other features of such statements over which there is some measure of agreement:
- the **values** which guide the organization;
- the **distinctive features** that characterize the organization;
- the interests of all **stakeholders**.

Box 2.2	**Example of a mission statement**

The Co-operative Bank

We, The Co-operative Bank Group, will continue to develop a successful and innovative financial institution by providing our customers with high quality financial and related services whilst promoting the underlying principles of co-operation which are:

- **Quality and Excellence**
  To offer all our customers consistent high quality and good value services and strive for excellence in all that we do.
- **Participation**
  To introduce and promote the concept of full participation by welcoming the views and concerns of our customers and by encouraging our staff to take an active role within the local community.
- **Freedom of Association**
  To be non-partisan in all social, political, racial and religious matters.
- **Education and Training**
  To act as a caring and responsible employer encouraging the development and training of all our staff and encouraging commitment and pride in each other and the Group.
- **Co-operation**
  To develop a close affinity with organizations which promote fellowship between workers, customers, members and employers.

▶

- **Quality of Life**
  To be a responsible member of society by promoting an environment where the needs of local communities can be met now and in the future.
- **Retentions**
  To manage the business effectively and efficiently, attracting investment and maintaining sufficient surplus funds within the business to ensure the continued development of the Group.
- **Integrity**
  To act at all times with honesty and integrity and within legislative and regulatory requirements.

(Source: Strength in Numbers, *a Co-operative Bank promotional document, p. 7)*

| Box 2.3 | **Example of a strategy statement** |

Universities Superannuation Scheme (USS) Ltd
Corporate Aim
To carry out the duties of trusteeship and the administration of USS for the benefit of members, pensioners and participating institutions in an efficient and cost-effective manner in accordance with quality management principles.

Strategic Objective One: Trusteeship – *To exercise the powers and duties conferred by the USS trust deed and rules in a lawful and fair manner.*

- We undertake to act within the powers provided by the trust deed and rules, with UK and EC legislation and in accordance with all relevant regulations, guidelines and codes of practice.
- We will exercise discretion fairly and consistently in the interests of the scheme membership as a whole.
- We will ensure that the directors and staff of USS Ltd are fully trained and are aware of their duties and obligations. We will control investment managers and the officers to whom they delegate responsibility and receive full and regular reports from them. ▶

- We will make sure that there are resources to meet the benefits promised, taking appropriate professional advice where necessary.
- We will maintain communication with members. We will keep members' guide up-to-date and provide this to all members. Reports of actuarial valuations and annual reports and accounts will be available for members to view.
- We will seek to maintain and develop good working relationships with participating employers, with the aim of constant improvement.

Strategic Objective Two: Administration – *To strive constantly for higher standards of scheme administration and service at an acceptable cost.*

- We will demonstrate a high level of operational efficiency, committing ourselves to quality management principles and always aiming to increase cost-effectiveness.
- We will take into account the best practices in other organizations and the availability of new equipment and technology. We will develop and improve our own procedures and maintain comprehensive up-to-date procedure notes and work instructions.

Strategic Objective Three: Investment – *To maximize the long-term investment return on assets consistent with the liabilities of the scheme.*

- We will set demanding but realistic targets for all managers and monitor investment performance.

Strategic Objective Four: Company Management – *To strive constantly for improved management of the trustee company at an acceptable cost and in accordance with the company's Memorandum and Articles of Association and quality management principles.*

- We will develop and maintain employment policies and practices consistent with being a fair and considerate employer.
- We will adopt quality management principles, and in that light will take account of best practice elsewhere and our own experience to improve our systems and procedures.

(Objectives 2, 3 and 4 have been abbreviated.)

(Source: abstracted from Corporate Aims and Objectives, *a USS Ltd Company leaflet)*

Values

What do we mean by values? Ravlin defines values as 'a set of core beliefs held by individuals concerning how they should or ought to behave over broad ranges of situations' (1995: 598). We all have values which develop through the process of socialization that we experience across the life-span. But in the present context values are being regarded as a property of the organization, in that all the employees are expected to subscribe to a particular set of values which have been articulated by the organization's leadership. Bringing about a congruence of individual values with organizational values is what Campbell and Yeung (1991a) refer to as creating a **sense of mission** – that is, employees' personal commitment to the organization's mission.

However, there exists the possibility of disagreement or even conflict should the values of individuals be at odds with those set out in the mission statement. Also, day-to-day business pressures may conflict with the espoused values. For example, Stiles *et al.* (1997) studied the performance management activities of a distribution company, a telecommunications company and a bank, all three of which had introduced values statements. But managers at the sharp end saw short-term demands to satisfy budgetary and financial targets as continuing to drive their activity, not the 'worthier' corporate values.

In the organizational context the term values is commonly associated with the term **organization (or organizational) culture**. This remains an elusive concept, with Brown listing fifteen definitions, his own preference being as follows:

> Organizational culture refers to the pattern of beliefs, values and learned ways of coping with experience that have developed during the course of an organization's history, and which tend to be manifested in its material arrangements and in the behaviours of its members.
>
> *(Brown 1995: 8)*

Within this definition is the idea that there are **levels of culture**, as exemplified by Schein (1992) and Kotter and Heskett (1992), and illustrated in Figure 2.1. In these conceptions actual behaviours and organizational practices and procedures are the outward manifestations of more deep-seated values (the root of organizational culture) and learned norms and rules (the behaviour standards that guide what people do).

| Figure 2.1 | Levels of organizational culture |

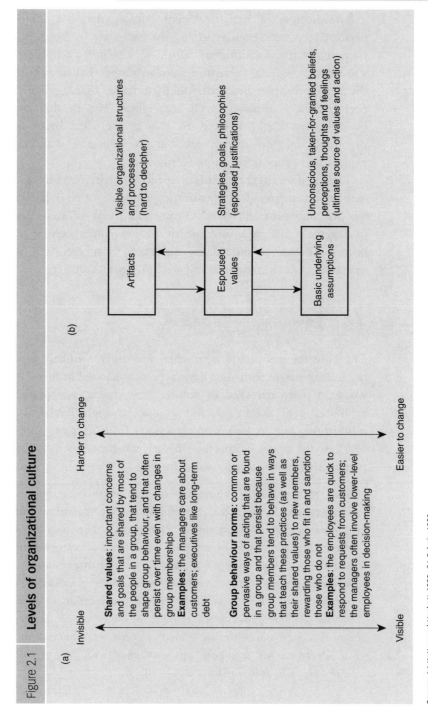

Source: (a) Kotter and Heskett 1992; (b) Schein 1992

The notion of organizational culture may be important for performance management in at least two ways, depending on which elements of the definition of culture we choose to emphasize. First, if we stress the values/behaviour standards aspects then culture provides the moral principles and behavioural guidelines that regulate employees' performance – quality, excellence, ethics, etc. in the case of The Co-operative Bank. Related to this is the view that culture and organizational performance are causally related. I shall come on to explore this proposition in just a moment.

Second, if we stress the artifact aspects, then performance management may be seen as part of an organization's culture – that is, part of 'the way we do things around here'. From this point of view performance management may be an instrument for maintaining culture (reinforcing norms of behaviour and values) or possibly for modifying it (inculcating new values). I will return to this second theme later.

Culture and organizational performance

The core themes in the argument that organizational culture affects organizational performance have been summarized in Box 2.4. In other words, a particular kind of culture – a 'strong' corporate culture – facilitates goal alignment and engenders high levels of employee motivation, and 'is better able to learn from its past' (Brown 1995: 185). At the centre of this argument is what is termed the **integration perspective** on organizational culture:

> Integration studies of culture implicitly assume that a 'strong' culture is characterized by consistency, organization-wide consensus, and clarity. According to Integration studies, consistency occurs because people at the higher levels of an organization articulate a set of espoused values, sometimes in the form of a philosophy of management or mission statement; these values are then reinforced by a variety of cultural manifestations which presumably generate organization-wide value consensus. In Integration studies, there is clarity concerning what the organizational values are and should be, what behaviours are preferable. ... Organizational members apparently know what they are to do and they agree why it is worthwhile to do it.
>
> *(Martin 1995: 377)*

| Box 2.4 | **Organizational culture and organizational performance** |

[The] argument of the corporate-culture school is:

- That organizations have cultures.
- That they become more effective when they develop the right 'strong' cultures (which need careful definition).
- That these cultures create consensus and unity and motivate staff.
- That cultures have an effect on corporate performance.
- That when necessary, cultures can be – and should be – changed.
- That it is the responsibility of senior managers to change them.

The corporate-culture approach presumes that organizational cultures can be assessed, managed, constructed and manipulated in the pursuit of enhanced organizational effectiveness. Employees' norms, beliefs and values can (and when necessary should) be changed so that they can contribute the appropriate behaviour, commit themselves to the organization, support management and strategy. This prevalent view holds that the norms and values shared by members of the organization create consensus, induce unity and when appropriate generate appropriate behaviour. Cultures integrate the organization (Meek 1988).

(Source: Mabey and Salaman 1995: 283)

Martin notes that this perspective 'has gained wide acceptance, in part because such a harmonious and clear environment is attractive, particularly to managers who would like to think that they could create a vision and enact a culture that would inspire such consensus' (1995: 378). The appeal of this view of culture as a means of 'social control' (O'Reilly 1989) is thus readily apparent. But what is wrong with this integration perspective?

The fundamental criticism is that it is based on the assumption that an organization has a single culture. Drawing on Meek (1988), Mabey and Salaman state that 'managerialist approaches to corporate culture tend to ignore systemic conflicts within the organization, ignore structures of power and interest, ignore structures of hierarchy and inequality, and ignore difference and differentiation of groups and of cultures' (1995: 291). Many of these issues were evident in the three companies studied by Stiles *et al.* (1997) – in all three, objective-setting was intended to support the corporate strategy and values. However, objectives were set top-down without negotiation, so that they ended up being seen as imposed. Added to this, restructuring (downsizing) had diminished career opportunities leaving managers doubtful that achieving their objectives was going to be in their interests – advancement opportunities were reduced and good performance did not guarantee job security.

A more realistic alternative is the 'differentiation' perspective in which organizations are viewed as 'composed of overlapping, nested subcultures that coexist in relationships of intergroup harmony, conflict, or indifference' (Martin 1995: 378). In other words, we have here a view of organizational culture which is anything but consensual, unifying, unitarist and managerialist.

A second difficulty is the assumption that a strong culture is in some sense(s) a 'good thing'. This assumption has been challenged by several commentators (e.g., Legge 1995; Mabey and Salaman 1995), and Brown (1998) gives us five reasons why the assumption might not hold true, as shown in Box 2.5.

A third area of difficulty is that the evidence we have of a positive association between culture and performance is far from compelling. Of particular importance in this regard is the work of Kotter and Heskett, who claim that 'Corporate culture can have a significant impact on a firm's long-term economic performance' (1992: 11). What is the basis for their claim?

Dysfunctional cultures

Kotter and Heskett carried out two studies. The essence of the first was to associate a 'culture strength' index with a number of measures of economic performance for a 'large and diverse sample of companies' in the US. The culture strength index was derived from a questionnaire sent to the top six officers in the selected companies; economic performance was assessed using a range of measures (e.g. return on investment (RoI), increase in share price) over a twelve-year period. They concluded that 'There is a positive correlation between corporate culture and long-term economic performance but ... not a very strong one' (Kotter and Heskett 1992: 20–1). Kotter and Heskett went on to add: 'The statement "Strong cultures create excellent performance"

Box 2.5	**Reasons to doubt the 'strong culture equals high performance' equation**

1 A strong culture may facilitate goal alignment, but the goals set by a culture may not always be positive in two senses: they may not be ethical, and they might not encourage good economic performance. In the first case we can imagine an organization such as a political or religious sect that brainwashes its members into pursuing violent ends, or an economic organization that pursues environmentally catastrophic objectives. An example of the second case would be an organization with a culture which dictated that care for employees was of greater value than profitability or market share, with the result that economic objectives were made subservient to human resource objectives.

2 It cannot be assumed that all strong cultures are associated with high levels of employee motivation. The point is that strong cultures may encourage many different attitudes towards the organization and to work other than the purely positive. As regards motivation, therefore, strong cultures can work both ways.

3 It is probably true that an organization which appreciates its past and which encodes information about past decisions in stories and anecdotes is advantaged compared with similarly placed organizations which do not. However, it is also true that organizations can become too wrapped up in the past and fail to focus on the present and future. It is also possible for organizations to reapply lessons learned in the past to current situations when the old rules no longer apply, perhaps because of technological innovation or increased competition. In other words, there is a thin dividing line between being able to learn from the past and being a prisoner of the past.

4 There are in fact quite a few well-known examples of organizations with both strong cultures and strong economic performances. Yet even these companies do not necessarily lend credence to the strong culture argument. The reason for this is the problem of determining causality. After all, it may be that good economic performance is the cause of a strong culture rather than a strong culture being responsible for high performance. Organizational success often consolidates ▶

> cultural beliefs and values. It therefore seems more than reasonable to suggest that economic success can strengthen a culture.
>
> 5 The strong culture argument fails to take account of the fact that few organizations have a single, unitary culture. Most scholarly commentators suggest that not only do organizations tend to have multiple subcultures, but that there are often highly complex operational and power relationships between them. Certainly some or even all of these subcultures may be strong in the sense of being cohesive, but this may mean that they function to undermine the initiatives of other subcultures rather than to support them.
>
> *(Source: abstracted from Brown 1998: 230)*

appears to be just plain wrong' (1992: 21). In so concluding they recognized the possibility that strong cultures may be **dysfunctional** for an organization.

This idea is also evident in some British work, that by Bate (1984). Bate's interest was in the impact of culture on organizational problem-solving. Based on interviews and discussions in three companies, he identified six characteristics or aspects of culture (which he called 'cultural orientations'), as shown in Box 2.6. Though these orientations are of interest in themselves, their apparently adverse consequences for organizational problem-solving are of more significance for the present discussion.

So, if we assume that there is such a thing as 'strong' culture we apparently have evidence which indicates that it isn't necessarily the good thing that so much of the literature contends. Kotter and Heskett (1992) were not, however, deterred by their initial finding and proceeded to a further study. They concentrated on twenty-two organizations and the core of their data-gathering was to seek opinions from financial analysts on the nature of those organization's cultures. These opinions were supplemented with findings from employees and managers in seventeen of the twenty-two companies.

Adaptive cultures

In this further research Kotter and Heskett claim to have found support for their hypothesis that 'a culture is good only if it "fits" its context,

Box 2.6	**Cultural orientations**

Unemotionality: 'Avoid showing or sharing feelings or emotions'
Depersonalization of issues: 'Never point the finger at anyone in particular'
Subordination: 'Never challenge those in authority and always wait for them to take the initiative in resolving your problems'
Conservatism: 'Better the devil you know'
Isolationism: 'Do your own thing and avoid treading on other people's toes'
Antipathy: 'On most things people will be opponents rather than allies'

The data show that the six cultural associations discussed appear to be linked with the following range of problematic predispositions: a low commitment to and involvement in the change process; a disowning of problems and an abdication of responsibility for the search for solutions; a lack of openness in confronting and dealing jointly with issues; avoidance of data-gathering on the causes of problems; overcaution and a lack of decisiveness and creativity in problem-solving; erection of barriers to change; and a taking of adversary positions on all issues regardless of whether any potential measure of agreement between the parties exists.

(Source: Bate 1984: 64)

whether one means by context the objective conditions of its industry, that segment of its industry specified by a firm's strategy, or the business strategy itself' (1992: 28). Furthermore, they contend that 'only cultures that can help organizations anticipate and adapt to environmental change will be associated with superior performance over long periods of time' (1992: 44). As to the nature of adaptive cultures, Table 2.1 sets out the core values and common behaviour identified by Kotter and Heskett.

More recent research in the UK (Ogbonna and Harris 2000) shows some consistency with the Kotter and Heskett findings. Ogbonna and Harris found that cultures that are externally oriented (e.g., risk taking, readiness to meet new challenges) tend to be more strongly associated with organizational performance (operationalized using a range of

Table 2.1	**Adaptive v. unadaptive corporate cultures**	
	Adaptive corporate cultures	Unadaptive corporate cultures
Core values	Most managers care deeply about customers, stockholders and employees. They also strongly value people and processes that can create useful change (e.g. leadership up and down the management hierarchy).	Most managers care mainly about themselves, their immediate work group or some product (or technology) associated with that work group. They value the orderly and risk-reducing management process much more highly than leadership initiatives.
Common behaviour	Managers pay close attention to all their constituencies, especially customers, and initiate change when necessary to serve their legitimate interests, even if that entails taking some risks.	Managers tend to behave somewhat insularly, politically and bureaucratically. As a result, they do not change their strategies quickly to adjust to or take advantage of changes in their business environments.

Source: Kotter and Heskett 1992: 51

measures) than do those cultures which are predominantly internally focused (indeed a bureaucratic culture may have a negative effect).

Brown describes the findings of Kotter and Heskett as 'truly stunning' (1995: 189), but rightly points to the methodological difficulties with the research. For example, a rather narrow view is taken of organizational performance – namely, economic performance; yet, as we shall see later the multi-faceted nature of performance is given greater emphasis today. Similar points may be made about the Ogbonna and Harris work, e.g. cross-sectional, correlational. Any underlying premise that certain cultures *cause* high performance is likely to be far too simplistic – as Brown implies (Box 2.5), causality may work the other way. Though we can't dismiss the possible importance of organizational culture for performance we are some way from understanding what the relationship is. Earlier ideas about 'strong' (that is, widely shared) cultures now seem somewhat ill-conceived. To the extent that there is a relationship it now seems likely that certain cultures are more supportive of high performance than are others.

The organization's distinctive features

The literature on strategic management typically advocates the analysis of strengths, weaknesses, opportunities, and threats (**SWOT analysis**) as a key element in the process of developing a strategy. Many tools exist for this, some being more concerned with the organization's environment (opportunities and threats), whilst others are internally directed and in essence are concerned with the question 'What is the organization good at?'

In much of the 1990s writing on strategy and competitiveness emphasis has been placed on the importance of an organization's strengths as a source of advantage. Of particular interest is the concept of **core competence** (Prahalad and Hamel 1990). Hubbard (1995) points out that this term is not clearly defined and identifies other, similar terms, namely **distinctive competence** (Selznick 1957) and **capabilities**, but what they together signify is a concern for the internal features of organizations; this lies at the heart of **resource theory** (or **resource-based theory**):

> At its simplest level, the resource view is based around a number of linked or sequential questions: what is the firm good at? Does this derive from a unique set of resources and/or a particular set of capabilities? Can the firm utilize its resources more effectively than its competitors? Can these strengths be easily copied by others? (In which case there is little competitive advantage to be obtained.) Is the firm able to keep its resources from depreciating rapidly? Is it able to reproduce and develop resource strengths and capabilities for future benefit?
>
> *(Purcell 1995: 81–2)*

Resources and capabilities may be tangible or intangible and certainly include the people (their skills, abilities, etc.) of an organization. Indeed, some have argued that traditional sources of competitive success such as technology have become less important, whereas employees and the way they work remain a 'crucial, differentiating factor' (Pfeffer 1994: 14). This echoes the view put by Storey and Sisson about the management of employee performance, namely that it 'is elevated to a higher plane: it comes to be regarded as an issue of strategic importance' (1993: 132).

Stakeholders

Stakeholders are those who have some interest or stake in an organization's success. As Figure 2.2 illustrates, an organization is likely to have several stakeholders and these will vary in nature and importance from organization to organization and over time according to such factors as the values that top management places on particular stakeholders, the organization's environment, its activities and so forth. The examples in Boxes 2.2 and 2.3 give illustrations of the various stakeholders which these two organizations apparently regard as especially important.

A stakeholder to whom considerable importance has been attached in recent years is the customer. The excellence literature particularly influenced this, as did the emphasis on quality. Bounds *et al.*, for example, present a strategic management model 'driven by customer needs' (1994: 211). Their argument is that 'managers and employees put customers first on the list of stakeholders, because the value perceived by customers is the ultimate source of all opportunities to create new wealth' (1994: 224).

Important though the customer is, there is today the view that an effective/successful organization seeks to meet the interests not of just

| Figure 2.2 | **The stakeholder model** |

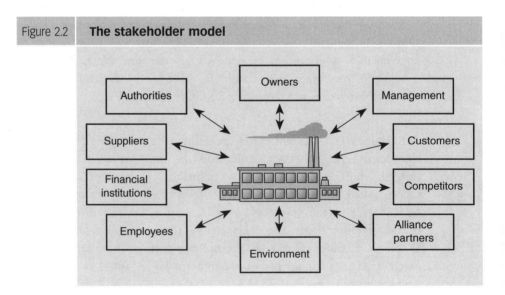

Source: Bredrup 1995b

one stakeholder deemed to have superior importance but rather of several stakeholders. Illustrative of this view is the work of Kotter and Heskett (1992) mentioned earlier: they see customers, shareholders and employees as key stakeholders. Likewise, Schein writes of the need to maintain 'good relationships with the major stakeholders of the organization' and to keep their needs 'in some kind of balance' (1992: 53). He includes: '(1) the investors and stockholders, (2) the suppliers of the materials needed to produce, (3) the managers and employees, (4) the community and government, and last but not least, (5) the customers willing to pay for the good or service' (1992: 53).

The analysis of stakeholder needs and interests is of particular importance for performance management as different stakeholders have different views of the nature of performance and of standards of performance that are expected. Numerous approaches to stakeholder analysis may be found in the literature – e.g. Beer *et al.* (1995) offer a model of organizational effectiveness which is focused on meeting stakeholder needs; and Bredrup and Bredrup (1995) apply stakeholder analysis to the determination of organizational performance requirements, a theme that I will come back to in the next chapter.

A concluding comment

Helpful though stakeholder analysis may be, it is not without its difficulties. Though it may reveal commonalities of interest it is likely also to reveal conflicts – over the direction in which the organization should be going, the means of getting there, etc. And very often these conflicts will reveal ethical dilemmas (Newell 1995). Some balance among the several interests therefore needs to be achieved – that is, stakeholder analysis itself isn't enough, we need stakeholder **synthesis** as well (Winstanley and Stuart-Smith 1996). In other words, an organization needs to incorporate stakeholder requirements within mission and strategy, and this particular aspect of organizational decision-making is only partly rational – it is as much a political process.

If the mission/strategy statement is to provide direction and serve as a basis for action, to promote particular values and act as a guide to behaviour and such like it seems only reasonable that those who will be affected by it should have some say in shaping its content. Some research (Brabet and Klemm 1994) indicates that an involving approach

Box 2.7	**Implications for practice**

It doesn't matter overmuch whether the terms vision, mission and strategy (or similar) are used, but do formulate some statement of the direction in which the organization is heading and how it is to get there.

Incorporate in this statement the organization's values, distinctive features (what it is good at), and the needs of stakeholders. Values lie at the heart of organizational culture – this is not easily changed. Do not assume that the organization has a 'strong' (widely shared) culture or that such can be created easily, especially if this means imposing a particular set of values.

In seeking to manage culture consider adopting a participative and involving approach and place emphasis on adaptability and customer-focus. Remember though that the latter, though important, are only one stakeholder group: analyse the needs of all stakeholders and seek to maintain some balance in satisfying those needs and interests.

can be effective in developing a shared strategy and in gaining employee commitment; in other words, this may help to produce not just the mission statement but also the **sense of mission**. In the next chapter I will give some examples of how a participative approach has been used in defining organizational performance.

3 The organizational context II: Performance

The importance of vision, mission and strategy as the framework for performance management is strongly emphasized in much of the practitioner-oriented literature (as we saw in Table 1.5, page 17). Taken together they set out what the organization is to become in the long term and how that desired position is to be arrived at. They state the purpose(s) of the organization and what it is to achieve – at least in general terms, then, they offer some statement of the organizational performance that is wanted. Also, a framework for guiding the performance of individual employees is provided – by stating the overall goal(s) and by specifying the values and standards that govern behaviour.

This, then, brings me on to consider the nature of organizational performance, and related terms like **productivity** and **effectiveness**. None of these terms is straightforward to define, whether conceptually or operationally. Indeed, Mansfield described this whole area as a 'nightmare of ambiguity and contradictions' (1986: 21). In considering how performance is defined in operational terms, we necessarily have to pay some attention to performance measures and their place in performance management.

In years past a book like this probably would have had the word productivity in the title somewhere. More recently, there has been a shift in emphasis – as we saw in Chapter 1, there is today a much broader concern for competitiveness. This is not to say that interest in productivity has disappeared altogether – far from it – so let me look first at this and how it fits within contemporary conceptions of organizational performance.

Productivity

Reiterating Guzzo's claim that 'productivity may mean different things to different people'(1988: 63), Pritchard has recently noted the wide range of meanings attaching to the term productivity:

> The term has been used to refer to individuals, groups, organizational units, entire organizations, industries, and nations. It has been used as a synonym for output, efficiency, motivation, individual performance, organizational effectiveness, production, profitability, cost/effectiveness, competitiveness, and work quality.
>
> *(Pritchard 1995: 448)*

That said, Campbell and Campbell earlier suggested that 'there is a clear consensus that it is useful to reserve the term productivity for efficiency indices' (1988: 83). If we accept this view then we find that there is some agreement over a common core: 'This common core is the ratio of outputs to inputs, a ratio that reflects the efficiency with which resources are transformed into outputs' (Guzzo 1988: 63). Expressed in these terms, productivity clearly is a systems concept: inputs are subject to some conversion process(es) which lead to the production of outputs.

So, in seeking to measure productivity we are basically concerned with the question of how well (how efficiently) available inputs are converted into outputs. The answer to this question may be expressed in terms of a whole host of indicators; Table 3.1 gives some examples.

Inputs and outputs

Table 3.1 also illustrates some of the many ways in which inputs and outputs may be operationalized, and a few more examples are provided in Table 3.2.

Inputs

In a general sense, by **inputs** we mean all the resources, employees, raw materials, energy, buildings, equipment, etc. that are required to manufacture a product or deliver a service. Reducing inputs – essentially, cutting costs – for the same (or greater) levels of output is

Table 3.1	**Examples of productivity indices**

- GNP/Population, i.e. labour productivity at the national level
- Yield of crop per acre of land cultivated
- Output per worker employed, e.g. number of units produced/number of hours worked; £ value of units produced/number of employees
- Number of calls per salesperson per day
- Average revenue per call
- Number of revenue passenger miles generated/available passenger miles (i.e. passenger load factor for an airline)
- Train miles per member of staff
- Number of criminal offences cleared up per police officer
- Average number of patients treated per general surgery bed per year
- Sales per square foot
- Return on investment
- Return on sales

Table 3.2	**Examples of input and output indices**

Inputs
- Number of employees
- Hours worked
- Staff costs
- Area of sales space available
- Units/cost of energy used
- Amount/cost of raw materials used

Outputs
- Number of passengers carried
- Number of surgical operations carried out
- Number of units sold
- £ value of units sold
- Number of users of a local authority leisure centre
- Quantity/value of goods carried by a delivery company
- Number of benefits paid through the Social Security system

commonly adopted as a means of increasing productivity (Heap 1992). Structural change such as downsizing would be an example of this. However, though short-term productivity may improve, long-term gains are not to be guaranteed: output may not go up, and could even go down – thereby reducing the productivity gains. For example, we know that downsizing can adversely affect the morale of staff, not just while the cuts are taking place but also for some time afterwards – the survivors remain affected. One example of this comes from the study by Stiles *et al.* (1997) mentioned in Chapter 2. They investigated performance management systems in three companies, all of which had experienced undesirable consequences following job losses – Box 3.1 summarizes some of the main findings.

Box 3.1	**Improving productivity? Negative effects of downsizing on performance management**

[There] was evidence that downsizing and delayering had a significant effect on employees attempting to reach their objectives. Restructuring had impacted severely on job security and career ladders, and motivation to reach targets was affected by employees' perceptions that:

(i)   there was little benefit, in terms of advancement, of achieving one's objectives (though fear of losing one's job was obviously a strong counterbalance),

(ii) fulfilling one's objectives entailed ... that the objectives or targets would be raised substantially the following year, and

(iii) achieving good performance did not necessarily entail that an employee's job was safe.

(Source: Stiles et al. *1997: 61)*

Output as quantity

Output is typically taken to mean what an organization produces or the service it delivers. Though outputs are part of productivity, the two terms clearly cannot be regarded as one and the same. By contrast, the terms output and production may be taken as synonyms. Output has traditionally been measured in quantitative terms as the examples in Tables 3.1 and 3.2 show. But such global measures will often be disaggregated into different types. For example, an airline may wish to break down the number of passengers carried according to class of travel – first, business and economy – further subdividing according to the type of ticket sold. An insurance company is likely to be interested in the numbers sold of each of the different types of policy that it provides. Police forces will be interested in the clear-up rates for different crimes.

One particular kind of output is referred to as a **throughput** – 'a special sort of output that is intended for internal consumption' (Brinkerhoff and Dressler 1990: 30). As already noted, productivity is a systems concept. When we apply the systems idea to an organization we discover that any organization as a system is likely to comprise a number of subsystems. The output from one subsystem will be an input to another subsystem (or subsystems) – the latter being an internal customer of the former, in other words. Managing the performance of the organization as a whole is, of course, as much about the management of throughputs as it is about the management of the product or service that eventually gets delivered to the external customer.

Though producing more output without an increase in inputs is one general strategy for improving productivity, greater output in itself doesn't necessarily mean a rise in productivity. If inputs have increased correspondingly or, worse, at a greater rate, then productivity will at best have remained stable and may even have deteriorated.

Output as quality

As well as the quantitative aspect of output there also is a **quality** dimension. In recent years quality has become a central feature of organizational performance in both the private and public sector (Cameron 1995; Kirkpatrick and Lucio 1995; Wilkinson and Willmott 1995a). Wilkinson and Willmott, for example, note that 'quality initiatives are reportedly occurring in three-quarters of companies in the United States and the United Kingdom' (1995b: 1).

Though the management of quality is apparently widespread, the nature of the concept remains open to several interpretations. Reeves and Bednar (1994) identify four main types of definition, each of which has its own strengths and weaknesses: these are summarized in Table 3.3. In the view of Reeves and Bednar it is the last of the four which is the most prevalent today. As the table shows, many of the definitions include the **customer**, typically interpreted in both the **external** and the **internal** sense. Indeed, the development of a customer perspective has come about hand in hand with the rise in the importance of quality. The table shows how definitions of quality have broadened over time: application of the term has extended from manufacturing to service, from being concerned narrowly with

Table 3.3	Strengths and weaknesses of quality definitions	
Definition	**Strengths**	**Weaknesses**
Excellence	Strong marketing and human resource benefits Universally recognizable – mark of uncompromising standards and high achievement	Provides little practical guidance to practitioners Measurement difficulties Attributes of excellence may change dramatically and rapidly Sufficient number of customers must be willing to pay for excellence
Value	Concept of value incorporates multiple attributes Focuses attention on a firm's internal efficiency and external effectiveness Allows for comparisons across disparate objects and experiences	Difficulty extracting individual components of value judgement Questionable inclusiveness Quality and value are different constructs
Conformance to specifications	Facilitates precise measurement Leads to increased efficiency Necessary for global strategy Should force disaggregation of consumer needs Most parsimonious and appropriate definition for some customers	Consumers do not know or care about internal specifications Inappropriate for services Potentially reduces organizational adaptability Specifications may quickly become obsolete in rapidly changing markets Internally focused
Meeting and/or exceeding expectations	Evaluates from customer's perspective Applicable across industries Responsive to market changes All-encompassing definition	Most complex definition Difficult to measure Customers may not know expectations Idiosyncratic reactions Pre-purchase attitudes affect subsequent judgements Short-term and long-term evaluations may differ Confusion between customer service and customer satisfaction

Source: Reeves and Bednar 1994: 437

attributes of the product (or service) – the **what** of quality – to include the **how** of quality, and from internally (company) defined attributes to a customer perspective.

Transformation processes

Viewing productivity as a systems concept tells us that inputs are converted into outputs via some transformation process or processes. Similarly, an organization, as a system, comprises many subsystems and it is these which are concerned, directly or indirectly, with the transformation processes that convert inputs to outputs. Numerous writers have proposed categorizations of generic organizational subsystems: for example, Katz and Kahn (1978) and Mullins (1996) each identify five subsystems, as shown in Box 3.2. Though the two schemes depict different ways of viewing an organization, their

Box 3.2	**Organizational subsystems**

Production or technical subsystem: The production system is concerned with the throughput, the energic or informational transformation whose cycles of activity comprise the major functions of the system.

Supportive subsystems: Supportive subsystems carry on the environmental transactions of procuring the input or disposing of the output or aiding in these processes. Some transactions are a direct extension of the production activities of the organization, importing the material to be worked on or exporting the finished product. Others are indirectly related to the production cycle but supportive of it, maintaining a favourable environment for the operation of the system.

Maintenance subsystems: Maintenance activities are not directed at the material being worked on but at the equipment for getting the work done. ... Whereas the supportive systems of procurement and disposal are concerned with insuring production inputs, that is, materials and resources for the work of the organization, the maintenance system is concerned with inputs for preserving the system either through appropriate selection of personnel or adequate rewarding of the personnel selected.

Adaptive subsystems: Nothing in the production, supportive and maintenance subsystems would suffice to ensure organizational ▶

survival in a changing environment. Except for the functions of procurement and disposal, these subsystems face inward; ... In most formal organizations there arise, therefore, structures that are specifically concerned with sensing relevant changes in the outside world and translating the meaning of those changes for the organization. There may be structures that devote their energies wholly to the anticipation of such changes. All these comprise the adaptive subsystem of the organization and bear such names as product research, market research, long-range planning, research and development, and the like.

Managerial subsystems: These systems comprise the organized activities for controlling, co-ordinating, and directing the many subsystems of the structure.

(Source: Katz and Kahn 1978: 52, 52–3, 54–5, 55)

Task – the goals and objectives of the organization. The nature of inputs and outputs, and the work activities to be carried out in the transformation or conversion process.

Technology – the manner in which the tasks of the organization are carried out and the nature of work performance. The materials, systems and procedures, and equipment used in the transformation or conversion process.

Structure – patterns of organization, lines of authority, formal relationships and channels of communication among members. The division of work and co-ordination of tasks by which the series of activities are carried out.

People – the nature of the members undertaking the series of activities: such as their attitudes, skills and attributes; needs and expectations; interpersonal relations and patterns of behaviour; group functioning and behaviour; informal organization and styles of leadership.

Management – co-ordination of task, technology, structure and people, and policies and procedures for the execution of work. Corporate strategy, direction of the activities of the organization as a whole and its interactions with the external environment.

(Source: Mullins 1996: 85)

relevance here is that they highlight the several aspects of organizations which are related to organizational productivity and performance and which need to be managed.

Much of the effort to improve organizational productivity has focused on the organization's transformation processes, very often with the aim of reducing costs (Heap 1992). Modern-day approaches, and their associated tools and techniques, include total quality management (TQM), new wave manufacturing, and business process re-engineering (BPR). The boundaries of these approaches are by no means hard and fast, with many of the tools and techniques falling into more than one of them. For example, just-in-time is sometimes presented as a key element in quality management (e.g., Dale 1994) and sometimes as a new wave manufacturing strategy (e.g., Harrison 1994). Similarly, benchmarking is presented as an important measurement tool in its own right (Andersen 1995) as well as in the context of both TQM (Dale and Boaden 1994) and BPR (Peppard and Rowland 1995).

From productivity to performance

One of the factors that has contributed to the multiplicity of productivity definitions that we have is that different disciplines have brought their particular perspectives to bear on the concept, as Table 3.4 shows. As is clear from the table, the notion of efficiency remains central to conceptualizations of productivity, but it is equally clear that the term has come to have broader interpretations, perhaps so broad that the term lost some of its meaning. This in part stems from the changed view of what we mean by output – the importance of the quality dimension is afforded greater emphasis *and* we need to consider what the customer wants. In other words, productivity is more than efficient production; it is also about producing a quality product or providing a quality service that is wanted, considerations that a narrow definition of productivity ignore. This has led some (e.g., Lawlor 1985; Pritchard 1992) to argue that the concept of productivity needs to combine ideas of efficiency and **effectiveness**. That is, the conception of productivity comes to be so broad that it is like the managerial perspective shown in Table 3.4.

Arguably, however, broadening the term in this way is unhelpful – if it includes so much it loses its meaning and usefulness. Others, therefore, have sought to present this widening of the productivity

Table 3.4	**Different disciplines' perspectives on productivity**

The Economist
The economist sees productivity as the ratio of outputs over their associated inputs. . . . Put another way, productivity is the efficiency of the transformation of inputs into outputs.

The Accountant
Approaches to productivity based on an accounting perspective attempt to describe and improve the financial performance of the organization. This is done through the construction of a series of financial ratios, such as dollars of sales divided by the cost of labour or dollars of profit divided by the capital employment to produce it. Most of these measures have an output/input format and are thus a type of efficiency measure, but they are focused primarily on financial efficiency. Typically, multiple measures are constructed to get an overall picture of organizational functioning.

The Industrial Engineer
The industrial engineer views productivity as the efficiency of throughput as measured by output to input ratios. It is based on the model of a machine, where productivity is the ratio of useful work (the output) divided by the energy used to produce the work (input). . . . Measurement is typically focused on the operational units within the organization rather than the total organization and usually attempts to assess the functioning of a 'man-machine' system.

The Psychologist
[This] focuses primarily on the aspects of productivity that the individual can control, that is, behaviour. The assumption is that by changing individuals' behaviour, productivity will be changed.

The Manager
The broadest but least precisely indentifiable perspective is that of the manager. In this perspective, productivity includes all aspects of the organization seen as important to effective organizational functioning. It includes efficiency and effectiveness, but also includes quality of output, work disruptions, absenteeism, turnover, and customer satisfaction. No one specific definition of what productivity is nor how it should be measured are specified. Anything that should make the organization function better ipso facto deals with productivity.

Source: Pritchard 1992: 448–9

concept in terms of a paradigm shift. One such is Andersen, who writes of a new productivity paradigm:

> The key to the new productivity paradigm is to accept that productivity, in the sense of efficiency, is only one of several important dimensions of the organization that must be measured and improved. We need to move on to include in the equation both effectiveness as well as some of the softer

and more intangible dimensions. The new productivity paradigm is actually the performance paradigm, where we actually measure the entire performance, including productivity, of the organization.

(Anderson 1995: 12)

Bredrup regards effectiveness and efficiency as two of three dimensions of organizational performance, the integration of which 'will ultimately decide the competitiveness of a company.' (1995a: 85):

- effectiveness – to what extent are customer needs met;
- efficiency – how economically are the resources of the company utilized;
- changeability – to what extent is the company prepared for future changes.

Organizational performance: a multidimensional concept

Though popular today, this view that organizational performance should be broadly defined is not exactly new. If we look back at academic (and other) writings on organizational performance and effectiveness we find that they reflect the now widely accepted idea that performance is multi-faceted. This is well illustrated by the list of thirty criterion measures identified by Campbell (1977) and shown in Table 3.5. So performance is measured in terms of output (inappropriately referred to as productivity in the table) and outcome, profit, internal processes and procedures, organizational structures, employee attitudes, organizational responsiveness to the environment, and so on. The picture is a confusing one: can organizational performance be all of these things?

The paradox of organizational performance and effectiveness

The paradoxical and confusing nature of organizational performance has been noted by numerous writers:

We want our organizations to be adaptable and flexible, but we also want them to be stable and controlled. We want growth, resource acquisition,

Table 3.5	**Criteria of organizational effectiveness**

1 *Overall effectiveness.* The general evaluation that takes into account as many criteria facets as possible. It is usually measured by combining archival performance records or by obtaining overall ratings or judgements from persons thought to be knowledgeable about the organization.

2 *Productivity.* Usually defined as the quantity or volume of the major product or service that the organization provides. It can be measured at three levels: individual, group and total organization via either archival records or ratings, or both.

3 *Efficiency.* A ratio that reflects a comparison of some aspect of unit performance to the costs incurred for that performance.

4 *Profit.* The amount of revenue from sales left after all costs and obligations are met. Per cent return on investments and per cent return on total sales are sometimes used as alternative definitions.

5 *Quality.* The quality of the primary service or product provided by the organization may take many operational forms, which are largely determined by the kind of product or service provided by the organization.

6 *Accidents.* The frequency of on-the-job accidents resulting in lost time.

7 *Growth.* Represented by an increase in such variables as total manpower, plant capacity, assets, sales, profits, market share and number of innovations. It implies a comparison of an organization's present state with its own past state.

8 *Absenteeism.* The usual definition stipulates unexcused absences, but even within this constraint there are a number of alternative definitions (for example, total time absence versus frequency of occurrence).

9 *Turnover.* Some measure of the relative number of voluntary terminations, which is almost always assessed via archival records.

10 *Job satisfaction.* Has been conceptualized in many ways but the modal view might define it as the individual's satisfaction with the amount of various job outcomes he or she is receiving.

11 *Motivation.* In general, the strength of the predisposition of an individual to engage in goal-directed action or activity on the job. It is not a feeling of relative satisfaction with various job outcomes but is more akin to a readiness or willingness to work at accomplishing the job's goals. As an organizational index, it must be summed across people.

12 *Morale.* It is often difficult to define or understand how organizational theortists and researchers are using this concept. The modal definition seems to view morale as a group phenomenon involving extra effort, goal communality, commitment and feelings of belonging. Groups have some degree of morale, whereas individuals have some degree of motivation (and satisfaction).

13 *Control.* The degree of, and distribution of, management control that exists within an organization for influencing and directing the behaviour of organization members.

14 *Conflict/cohesion.* Defined at the cohesion end by an organization in which the members like one another, work well together, communicate fully and openly, and co-ordinate their work efforts. At the other end lies the organization with verbal and physical clashes, poor co-ordination, and ineffective communication.

15 *Flexibility/adaptation*. (Adaptation/Innovation). Refers to the ability of an organization to change its standard operating procedures in response to environmental changes.

16 *Planning and goal-setting*. The degree to which an organization systematically plans its future steps and engages in explicit goal-setting behaviour.

17 *Goal consensus*. Distinct from actual commitment to the organization's goals, consensus refers to the degree to which all individuals perceive the same goals for the organization.

18 *Internalization of organizational goals*. Refers to the acceptance of the organization's goals. It includes their belief that the organization's goals are right and proper. It is *not* the extent to which goals are clear or agreed upon by the organization members (goal clarity and goal consensus, respectively).

19 *Role and norm congruence*. The degree to which the members of an organization are in agreement on such things as desirable supervisory attitudes, performance expectations, morale, role requirements and so on.

20 *Managerial interpersonal skills*. The level of skill with which managers deal with superiors, subordinates and peers in terms of giving support, facilitating constructive interaction, and generating enthusiasm for meeting goals and achieving excellent performance. It includes such things as consideration, employee centredness and so on.

21 *Managerial task skills*. The overall level of skills with which the organization's managers, commanding officers or group leaders perform work-centred tasks, tasks centred on work to be done, and not the skills employed when interacting with other organizational members.

22 *Information management communication*. Completeness, efficiency and accuracy in analysis and distribution of information critical to organizational effectiveness.

23 *Readiness*. An overall judgement concerning the probability that the organization could successfully perform some specified task if asked to do so.

24 *Utilization of environment*. The extent to which the organization successfully interacts with its environment and acquires scarce and valued resources necessary to its effective operation.

25 *Evaluations by external entities*. Evaluations of the organization, or unit, by the individuals and organizations in its environment with which it interacts. Loyalty to, confidence in and support given the organization by such groups as suppliers, customers, shareholders, enforcement agencies and the general public would fall under this label.

26 *Stability*. The maintenance of structure, function and resources through time and, more particularly, through periods of stress.

27 *Value of human resources*. A composite criterion that refers to the total value worth of the individual members, in an accounting or balance sheet sense, to the organization.

28 *Participation and shared influence*. The degree to which individuals in the organization participate in making the decisions that directly affect them.

29 *Training and development emphasis*. The amount of effort the organization devotes to developing its human resources.

30 *Achievement emphasis*. An analogue to the indivdual need for achievement referring to the degree to which the organization appears to place a high value on achieving major new goals.

Source: Campbell 1977: 36–9

and external support, but we also want tight information management and formal communication. We want an emphasis on the value of human resources, but we also want an emphasis on planning and goal setting.

(Quinn et al. 1996)

Theoreticians (e.g., Cameron 1986, 1995; Meyer and Gupta 1994) have attempted to capture these contradictions in their models. Hall, for example, offers four central principles (1996: 275, 277):

1 Organizations face multiple and conflicting environmental constraints.
2 Organizations have multiple and conflicting goals.
3 Organizations have multiple and conflicting internal and external constituencies.
4 Organizations have multiple and conflicting time frames.

All this isn't simply of theoretical interest; it also is of practical significance for measuring performance and evaluating effectiveness, as Dawson notes:

[Practitioners] need to note that when they are trying to assess the performance of an organization they need to adopt a variety of approaches. Performance is multifaceted and thus a variety of assessment methods are required in order to construct a profile of an organization's performance. Only in this way can its members gauge those things that are being done well and those things that are being done badly.

(Dawson 1996: 50)

Performance measurement

The need for performance measurement

If performance measurement simply means the retrospective collection of historical results it is likely that little useful purpose will be served from the point of view of performance management (Bredrup 1995c; Zairi 1994). Many commentators (e.g., Chakravarthy 1986; Eccles 1991) have noted that commonly used indicators, especially accounting-based ones, paint a picture of the past. But if measurement is to be useful in performance management it has to be forward-looking and concerned with performance improvement.

Table 3.6	**Important purposes for a performance measurement system**

- *Decision support.* Ideally measurement should indicate where to act, perhaps how to act and hopefully monitor the effect of the action. Decisions should be based on knowledge and measurement plays an important role to provide information.
- *Monitor effect of strategic plans.* Implementation of strategic plans has to be monitored to make necessary corrections to ensure achievement of long-term goals. Indicators have to be chosen to monitor consequences and achievements.
- *Performance evaluation.* Evaluation is required for a number of reasons, such as tracking improvement potentials, setting new yardsticks, satisfying requirements from stakeholders, distributing incentives, etc.
- *Diagnosis.* A company needs indicators with a diagnostic purpose. If business achievements are decreasing, the performance measurement systems should be able to give some warnings in advance and provide input to a search for reasons. However, it is difficult to isolate the cause/effect relationship.
- *Management of a continuous improvement process.* A continuous improvement process often provides stepwise 'blue savings' like released capacity, reduced future costs or increased value for the customer. Measurement is important to justify further investments and effort in the process, to manage the process and ensure consistency with strategy and to transform improvements into business achievements.
- *Motivation.* Measuring progress is necessary to justify further effort in the improvement process. Resistance against change is considerable in most organizations and lacking progress is enough ammunition to kill a project or a process.
- *Comparison.* Evaluation of performance and performance planning depends on a reference to identify performance gaps. Comparative benchmarking is possible to identify these gaps.
- *Record development.* Documentation of development could be demanded by stakeholders like customers, authorities, alliance partners, etc. or used actively as a marketing tool. Measurement to monitor and record supplier performance to give input to their improvement processes could result in productivity improvement.

Source: Bredrup 1995c: 172

Bredrup (1995c), for example, suggests eight important reasons that might be served by a measurement system, as shown in Table 3.6.

Multiple performance indicators

The consequence of all of the above is that for any organization we need a range of indicators if we are to measure performance and make judgements about effectiveness. Thus, we would expect to see measures of outcome, output, throughput, internal functioning, etc., including the five main areas suggested by Walters (1995: 172):

- contribution to the achievement of strategic objectives;
- measures of quality;
- measures of quantity and volume;
- measures of efficiency and value for money;
- measures of external and internal customer satisfaction.

The balanced scorecard

One approach which has become popular in recent years which attempts to capture some of the contradictory nature of organizational performance is termed the balanced scorecard (Kaplan and Norton 1992, 1993, 1996). This aims to measure performance in terms of four sets of indicators, each taking a different perspective (Kaplan and Norton 1996: 76):

- **Financial**: to succeed financially, how should we appear to our shareholders?
- **Customer**: to achieve our vision, how should we appear to our customers?
- **Internal business process**: to satisfy our shareholders and customers, what business processes must we excel at?
- **Learning and growth**: to achieve our vision, how will we sustain our ability to change and improve?

One application of the balanced scorecard is shown in Table 3.7; the Europe/Middle East/Africa (EMEA) region of AT&T used it to help determine the objectives required to implement their vision. Though it is practically useful and helpful in terms of recognizing some of the complexity of organizational performance, critics have said that the approach does not go far enough. For example, Atkinson et al. (1997) point to a number of weaknesses, including the failure to pay sufficient attention to employees and suppliers or to the broader community within which the organization operates. Consistent with the stakeholder argument set out in the previous chapter, Atkinson and his colleagues highlight the need to incorporate a much wider range of stakeholders. As an example, they show how the Bank of Montreal has defined different classes of performance measures with reference to different stakeholder groups (Table 3.8).

Table 3.7	**An application of the business scorecard**

Perspective	Strategic objectives to make the vision a reality
Financial To our EMEA shareholders	Pursue economic value-added opportunities Improve gross profit margin Reduce manufacturing and purchase costs
Customer How we differ from customers	Develop customer partnerships based on trust, professionalism and shared values Become preferred supplier Outperform other best suppliers Improve responsiveness and reliability in supply of products and services
Internal processes How we must excel	Increase effectiveness of salesforce Improve delivery performance Improve responsiveness to opportunities in the marketplace Build technological capabilities close to the customer
Growth and innovation How we can continue to improve and create value	Build skills and offer a portfolio for creative solutions Enter CATV, mobile and LD markets Create customer- and project-focused teams Build capability to differentiate on software and service provision

There are other models that explicitly recognize the multidimensional nature of organizational performance. For example, in the 'Excellence Model' of the European Foundation for Quality Management excellence is based on satisfying the needs of all the relevant stakeholder groups. People (that is, employees), Customers and Society Results therefore are features of this model, thereby signalling that it is not just business results that need to be achieved.

A concluding comment

Concern for organizational productivity hasn't disappeared but it has been overtaken by a wider-ranging desire to improve all aspects of the organization's performance and maintain competitiveness. Today, we

Table 3.8	**Primary and secondary measures for stakeholder groups at the Bank of Montreal**		
	Stakeholder group	Primary measures	Secondary measures
	Shareholders	Return on common shareholders' investment	Revenue growth Expense growth Productivity Capital ratios Liquidity ratios Asset quality ratios
	Customers	Customer satisfaction and quality of service	Customer surveys for different market/product requests
	Employees	Employee commitment Employee competence Employee productivity	Different elements of employee opinion survey Different elements of customer service index (re. employee competence) Financial ratios of employee costs to revenues by different classifications
	Community	Public image	Different external surveys

Source: Atkinson *et al.* 1997: 35

see the concept of performance as embracing productivity (efficiency) as well as effectiveness, adaptability and responsiveness. It is clear, then, that organizational performance is far from being a simple concept. When we talk about *the* performance of an organization we are not talking about some unitary thing.

Consequently, performance has come to be measured by using multiple indicators. Some are 'hard', and include financial and non-financial metrics. Others are of a 'softer' kind, concerning quality, employee attitudes and the like. Hence, we see measures both of results and of processes. Moreover, our measures need to accommodate the perspectives of the several stakeholder groups – both internal and external – who have an interest in the effectiveness or success of the organization. For any one facet of performance, different stakeholders may have different, perhaps conflicting, expectations. It may be unrealistic to suppose that all stakeholders' expectations can be satisfied all of the time – perhaps the most that we can hope for is that they can be maintained in some state of balance.

Box 3.3	**Implications for practice**

Accept that the nature of organizational performance is paradoxical:

- multiple and conflicting environmental constraints
- multiple and conflicting goals
- multiple and conflicting internal and external constituencies
- multiple and conflicting time frames.

Use some framework like the balanced scorecard (amended as appropriate to accommodate a wider range of stakeholders) or the EFQM Excellence Model to reflect the complexity of organizational performance.

Within that framework use a range of indicators of organizational functioning, e.g. input, output, efficiency/productivity, throughput, outcomes/consequences, along with qualitative measures and indicators of the softer and less tangible aspects of performance. Use these indicators in a diagnostic, forward-looking, improvement-oriented way.

4 Individual performance I: Outputs and results

As we saw in Chapter 1, the predominant conception of performance management in the UK is that it is an intervention (or set of interventions) targeted at individual employees with the aim of directing and enhancing their performance so as to improve organizational performance. At the heart of performance management we have a cycle of activity which starts with defining/planning employee performance requirements, managing/supporting performance, reviewing it, and providing for development and reward.

In this and the next two chapters I will explore the nature of individual performance and the causes of performance. As well as considering performance as a concept I will review how it is operationalized in practice. There are two main perspectives – outputs and behaviours. I will start with outputs in this chapter and in the next deal with the behavioural view. Then, in Chapter 6, I will go on to consider theories which seek to explain, or at least describe, the causes or determinants of performance.

Expressing performance requirements: what happens in practice?

We know from surveys of appraisal practice (Gill 1977; Long 1986) that a results-orientation has come to be the dominant approach in the UK for expressing performance requirements. An associated trend has been a shift away from trait-oriented appraisal. The move towards results was confirmed by the IMS survey of performance management that I referred to in Chapter 1 (Institute of Personnel Management

1992). The IMS asked about the six means of expressing performance requirements listed in Table 4.1.

The level of the job is a significant factor influencing not just the nature of the method used to express performance requirements but also the incidence of use. Amongst organizations having formal performance management policies **clear and measurable accountabilities, objectives/targets, main job activities and tasks**, and **lists of competences** tended to be used to express performance requirements for senior managers. For other white-collar employees **clear and measurable accountabilities** were used less than **main job activities and tasks** and **written job descriptions**. For manual employees the most frequently used methods were **main job activities and tasks** and **written job descriptions**, but all of the means (listed in Table 4.1) were less frequently used for these categories of staff than for managers. These findings imply a preference for objective rather than subjective standards (such as managerial judgement) so it is hardly surprising that commonly used indicators are 'output-based measures' and 'objectives' (whether or not agreed with the employee). The more recent surveys (Armstrong and Baron 1998; Industrial Society 1998) confirm this preference for objectives-based approaches.

Table 4.1	**Means of expressing performance requirements**
	• Clear and measurable accountabilities: reflecting approaches to setting unambiguous targets linked to measurable outcomes for which the jobholder is explicitly answerable
	• Broad responsibilities and roles: including descriptions of the key elements of jobs expressed as areas of obligation and functional responsibility in general terms
	• Objectives/targets: reflecting the aims of the job and the main outputs expected of a competent performer
	• Main job activities and tasks: describing the important components of jobs in terms of activity areas and duties
	• Written job descriptions: explaining core responsibilities and lines of accountability
	• Lists of competences: statements of performance outcomes, often expressed in behavioural or output terms

Source: Institute of Personnel Management 1992: 5

Performance as output: some definitions

As the evidence from practice shows, a wide range of terms is used to denote performance as output. The language used includes:

- accountabilities;
- key result areas;
- results;
- duties, tasks and activities;
- objectives;
- goals;
- outputs;
- targets;
- critical success factors;
- competences and standards.

Illustrative definitions of various of these terms are shown in Box 4.1 from which it is clear that performance is being conceptualized, in effect, as a property of the job. Also clear is that there is a high degree of conceptual overlap and redundancy among the several terms. Like Locke and Latham (1984), I will take the view that they can be used synonymously but organizations may find some pragmatic value in drawing distinctions amongst them where it suits their purposes. For example, Legal & General (Life and Pensions) distinguish between principal accountabilities and objectives. Cambridgeshire County Council make a similar distinction:

> **Accountabilities**: These describe the principal purposes for which each job exists. They do not change from year to year unless the job changes. There are normally about eight per job, covering all aspects of the job.
> **Goals**: These reflect the immediate priorities of the job. They indicate specific measurable levels of achievement expected within a given period of time. They can be related to standards and used to influence how a job holder meets particular accountabilities.
>
> *(Audit Commission 1995b: 5.62)*

Also, as we saw above, different terminology (and approaches for expressing performance requirements) may be used for different types or levels of job.

Though this output-oriented interpretation of performance is especially evident in the practitioner literature (e.g., Ainsworth and

| Box 4.1 | **Conceptions of performance as output** |

Accountabilities: 'Principal accountabilities define the key result areas of the job. ... The list of principal accountabilities should cover all the key aspects of the job which together contribute to achieving its overall purpose' (Armstrong 1994: 49). The terms '**main tasks**' or '**main duties**' may be used as synonyms.

Key result areas: important areas of activity in which achievement determines or indicates success (Ainsworth and Smith 1993: 7).

Targets: 'Targets are often known by other names such as objectives and goals but really these terms all describe the same thing. Targets explain what should be achieved at the end of an activity – a point to be hit or a desired result. The emphasis in this definition is important because the focus is on output rather than input or effort' (Hale 1993: 64).

Goals: A *goal* is what an employee is trying to accomplish on the job. It is the object or aim of an action. There are many familiar concepts that are similar in meaning to that of goal; e.g., *task*: a piece of work to be accomplished; *performance standard*: a measuring rod for evaluating performance (usually referring to a minimum acceptable amount or quality); *quota*: an assigned amount of work or production; *work norm*: a standard of acceptable conduct as defined by a work group; *objective*: the ultimate aim of an action; *deadline*: a time limit for accomplishing some task; and *budget*: a spending limit for an individual, project department, or organization

'In most instances, the distinctions between these concepts are not of great importance; thus we use the word goal as an umbrella term. No distinction is made, for example, between the terms goal and objective. This is because both of these concepts have the same two elements in common: they imply or specify a *direction* for action to take, and they imply a specified *amount* or quality of work to be accomplished' (Locke and Latham 1984: 5).

Competences and standards: standards state in terms of outcome what is expected of an individual performing a particular occupational role. They do not look at the underlying abilities ▶

> or traits of the individual – they describe the expectations which the individual is required to meet. A standard is expressed in two parts:
>
> - an element of competence;
> - its associated performance criteria.
>
> The element describes something which the individual should be able to do. Performance criteria describe the standards of performance required for the successful achievement of that element (Management Charter Initiative 1990a: 3).

Smith 1993; Armstrong 1994; Lockett 1992), we also find it in academic writings. Drawing on earlier work by Kane (1986), one example comes from Bernardin *et al.*:

> Performance is defined as: The *record of outcomes* produced on a *specified job function* or activity during a *specified time period*. ... Performance on the job as a whole would be equal to the sum (or average) of performance on the critical or essential job functions. The functions have to do with the work which is performed and *not* with the characteristics of the person performing.
>
> *(Bernardin* et al. *1995: 470–1)*

Bernardin and his colleagues argue that a focus on results should be the preferred approach to performance management as it takes a customer perspective and enables individuals' efforts to be linked to organizational goals.

A similar example comes from the work of Pritchard and his colleagues (Pritchard *et al.* 1988, 1989; Pritchard 1990a, 1990b). They developed what they termed a Productivity Measurement and Enhancement System (ProMES). Fundamental to this system is the identification of important job outputs, called *products*: 'Products are activities or objectives that an organizational unit is expected to accomplish' (Pritchard 1990a: 80). Though defined in terms of unit accomplishments, these products are intended to provide a focus for individuals' action. Another feature of ProMES that is of particular interest is the involving way in which the system operates. This is described in Box 4.2.

Pritchard and his colleagues note several benefits for their approach. One is that it helps to make clear to employees what is required – their

| Box 4.2 | **Pritchard's Productivity Measurement and Enhancement System (ProMES)** |

The first step in the development of ProMES is to identify what are called *products*. Products are activities or objectives that an organizational unit is expected to accomplish.

To identify products, a team of supervisors and representative incumbents is formed and led by a facilitator to identify the salient products. This design team would make a listing of these products and discuss and refine it until consensus was reached.

A typical unit would have from three to five products. This list is then reviewed by higher levels of supervision and management for completeness and accuracy. Any disagreements are discussed with the originating group and resolved. At this point, a set of products has been identified and agreed on by multiple levels of the organization.

Once the products have been determined, the next step is to develop *indicators* to these products. An indicator is a measure of how well the organization is generating the product in question. To identify the indicators, the design team is asked to think of things they would use to show how well they are generating their products. There may be one or several indicators for each product.

As with the products, the group works on the indicators until the members are satisfied that the list comprehensively covers all the products and represents valid measures of the products. Great care must be exercised at this point to ensure that good indicators are generated. It is easy to end up with indicators that are incomplete or that tap easily measured aspects of the product rather than what is really important but more difficult to measure. It is also important that the indicator be consistent with the product in the sense that generating a large amount of the indicator does in fact achieve the product. This issue needs much more care than it might at first seem. Once the members of the group have finalized the indicators, the process of approval up the organizational hierarchy is done as it was with the products.

Typically, there will be a total of from eight to fifteen indicators for a given unit. ▶

> Once the products and indicators are identified and approved, the next step is to establish *contingencies*. A contingency is a graphic function representing the relationship between the amount of an indicator and the degree of contribution that amount of the indicator makes to overall productivity. (See Pritchard *et al.* 1989 for a fuller description of how contingencies are developed.)
>
> Once the contingencies are completed and approved by management, the last step is to put the system together. This would be accomplished by first collecting the indicator data for a given period of time. Assume that the time period selected was a month-long period. The data for the different indicators would be collected at the end of the month. Then, based on the contingencies, effectiveness scores would be determined for each indicator. ... Once the effectiveness value for each indicator is determined, they can be summed to get the overall effectiveness of the unit.
>
> This information is then put into a regularly occurring, formal productivity feedback report that is circulated to the members of the unit and their management. They then meet to discuss the report and assess reasons for increases and decreases in their productivity and plan changes that will improve their productivity.
>
> *(Source: summarized from Pritchard 1990a, 1990b)*

unit's objectives, how attainment will be measured and the level of attainment that is expected. Indeed, clarity about expectations is intended to be an outcome of all of the means of expressing performance as goals, results, competences, etc., and some British research (Winterton and Winterton 1996) reports that adoption of the MCI National Standards can lead to this outcome as well as various other performance-related benefits, e.g. increased commitment and motivation.

However, for Pritchard and his colleagues it is not just the statement of the products themselves which is important but also the **involving** process of system development. One further benefit that this brings is acceptance of the measurement system on the part of those to whom it applies. As noted in Chapter 1, the participation theme is widespread in the performance management literature and many benefits are claimed for involving employees. For example, an authoritative review (Rodgers and Hunter 1991) of management by objectives (MbO) suggests considerable benefits for employee participation in setting their goals:

> Participation in decision making promotes understanding throughout the organization. Managers who rely on only their own ideas are more like a one-person orchestra than a conductor of musicians. But with participatory input from lower levels, useful information that is known to subordinates is made known to top management. Awareness of alternative courses of action is increased and knowledge of the consequences of decisions is enhanced. Problems are found with the design of the work process and the methods necessary to attain work objectives. Periodic changes to work methods result: job responsibilities are reallocated, lines of authority are redrawn, and technical systems are restructured. Subordinates are made aware of top management's objectives, and top managers are made aware of problems involved with implementing the objectives they see as important.
>
> *(Rodgers and Hunter 1991: 323)*

These sorts of benefits – the enhancement of communication, improvements in the structure and operation of the work system – are all consistent with the outcomes desired of performance management, and in evaluating the operation of a performance management system we would want to gather information about such processes as organizational communication, the extent to which participation/involvement is provided for and the extent to which it is perceived by job holders as having happened.

Unfortunately, the survey evidence that we have provides us with only a few clues about the extent of employee participation in determining job content and performance requirements. So, we know that there is a higher incidence of agreeing performance objectives with employees in formal performance management organizations than in those with other policies or with no policies. But of all organizations responding to the IMS performance management survey, fewer than half report such participation taking place for the majority of their employees. That said, within performance management organizations the expression of performance requirements by some means or other is the norm. Though it does not extend to all hierarchical levels/types of job it is clear that for the most part the preferred approach is one which emphasizes targets, results, accountabilities, etc. – in other words, an overall philosophy that might loosely be labelled **goal-setting**.

Defining performance by setting goals

Goal-setting is much advocated in the literature, particularly that which is practice-oriented (e.g., Ainsworth and Smith 1993; Armstrong 1994, 1995; Costello 1994; LGMB 1993; Lockett 1992; Moores 1994), and it has a strong theoretical underpinning. What is typically proposed is a cascading process, very reminiscent of management by objectives (MbO) – Figure 4.1, taken from Moores, provides one illustration. This cascading process is commonly seen as the means by which individual goals and objectives are aligned with organizational goals. For example, in Hewlett-Packard individuals have to achieve key job-relevant results, with these key result areas being related to the overall business objectives: these are expressed in a performance plan.

| Figure 4.1 | **Cascading goals** |

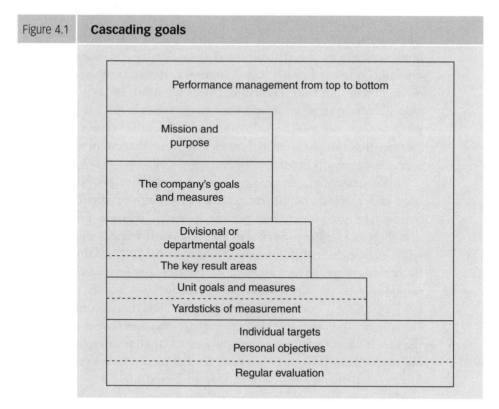

Source: Moores 1994

Performance planning is widely advocated and typically happens once a year as part of a joint discussion between job holder and manager.

In keeping with today's interest in business processes, many (e.g., Rummler and Brache 1995) advocate that individual goals must be consistent not just with departmental or functional goals, but also with process goals. To the extent that processes may be seen in horizontal terms in organizations, this then implies both horizontal and vertical integration of goals.

Though organizational goals may serve many functions (as Table 4.2 illustrates) the approach is far from being trouble-free. The mission statement may contain a statement of the organization's goals, perhaps in rather vague and general terms. Indeed, the mission statement may contain several goals and in an ideal world these will be wholly consistent with one another: but this will not always be the case, especially as different stakeholders have different expectations of performance – the discussion of the balanced scorecard in Chapter 3 illustrated this. Moreover, the deeper we dig within an organization the more we are likely to find several and different goals across its subunits. Lower-level goals, according to the theory of performance management, ought to be

Table 4.2	**Functions of goals**

- Goals provide a standard of performance. They focus attention on the activities of the organization and the direction of the efforts of its members.
- Goals provide a basis for planning and management control related to the activities of the organization.
- Goals provide guidelines for decision-making and justification for actions taken. They reduce uncertainty in decision-making and give a defence against possible criticism.
- Goals influence the structure of the organization and help determine the nature of techology employed. The manner in which the organization is structured will affect what it will attempt to achieve.
- Goals help to develop commitment of individuals and groups to the activities of the organization. They focus attention on purposeful behaviour and provide a basis for motivation and reward systems.
- Goals give an indication of what the organization is really like, its true nature and character both for members and for people outside the organization.
- Goals serve as a basis for the evaluation of change and organization development.
- Goals are the basis for objectives and policies of the organization.

Source: Mullins 1996: 293

consistent with those set at the top – Rummler and Brache (1995) refer to this as a 'performance logic' – but such goal consistency cannot be assumed. In setting goals members of departments, work teams and so on may set goals consistent with their interests as they see them. Ensuring consistency of goals thus becomes one of the main challenges for performance management systems – a participative and involving approach may help to bring this about.

Goal-setting often is presented in the literature as a top-down process and seems commonly to be practised as such. For example, Swale Borough Council has an objectives-based system of performance management. It starts at council level, passing down through committees and services and on to sections and individuals. Each service or function will have between three and seven main objectives each year, as well as specific performance targets (Audit Commission 1995a).

Whilst these sorts of structures and systems provide the framework for individual performance management, line management and the appraisal process are the key means by which performance requirements are communicated, and this communication is more commonly one-way (downwards) rather than the two-way communication that often is advocated. Though some writers see a place for a bottom-up contribution to goal-setting, in practice it seems likely that the extent of employee **involvement** or **participation** is limited to reaching **shared agreement** about their own particular job goals. An illustration is provided by the Royal Borough of Windsor and Maidenhead:

> Within the broad framework set by the corporate plan and by more specific unit business plans, every employee is asked to identify the core elements of his/her job. The outcome is identification of 'key accountabilities' for each post-holder; based on these accountabilities, performance objectives are determined for all members of staff. This is done by post-holders in collaboration with their managers. This way, each employee has 'ownership' of the performance management process, since they are all involved in establishing their own individual objectives.
>
> *(Audit Commission 1995b: 5.74)*

The absence of such ownership was found to be a barrier in the three performance management systems examined by Stiles *et al.* (1997) – targets were seen as being imposed.

What is agreed often finds expression in some sort of written **action plan**, sometimes referred to as a **performance agreement** (Armstrong

1994) or **performance contract** (Lockett 1992), as described in Box 4.3. Such a statement communicates both the **what** and the **how well** of performance (Rummler and Brache 1995).

BOX 4.3 **The performance agreement or contract**

A performance agreement, also known as a performance contract, defines expectations – the work to be done, the results to be attained and the attributes (skills, knowledge and expertise) and competences required to achieve these results. It also identifies the measures used to monitor, review and assess performance (Armstrong 1994: 46).

The contract is between two parties and consists of two elements – the clarification of performance requirements and the agreement of the corresponding support in terms of resources, training and direction from the manager. ... *The performance requirements in a performance contract are for the whole job and not just selected parts of it.* (Lockett 1992: 42).

In Mercury Communications the Performance Contract is a mandatory part of their 'Contribution Management' approach to performance management. Amongst other things it includes a statement of the job purpose, what sort of inputs (skills and abilities) the employee brings to the job, how the employee will contribute to Mercury values, agreed accountabilities (outputs to be achieved), as well as details of the review process (such as when reviews will take place) and what Mercury will contribute (e.g., by way of training).

In Zeneca Pharmaceuticals they have a 'performance management discussion record' which covers the following four areas:

- **Business role**: ensures that the job description reflects business objectives.
- **Performance planning**: targets are set by joint agreement between the employee and the appraising manager.
- **Performance development**: define what skills, knowledge and experience needed and plans the required training.
- **Performance measurement**: evaluates performance against targets.

As noted at the start of this chapter, we also find that the term 'goal' is typically defined broadly – task, objective, etc. In addition, different types of goals are distinguished in the literature. For example, it is common to find at least two types of goals, namely **work objectives** (relating to the main task areas of the job and results expected) and **developmental objectives** (personal learning objectives for improving skills and job performance) (e.g., Armstrong 1995). The Zeneca example in Box 4.3 provides one illustration. Others include Mercury Communications, where employees have a personal development plan which specifies how an employee's future career is expected to develop – both short- and medium-term training plans are included. At Standard Life a development plan supports the performance plan by setting out the development or training needed by job holders to produce their outputs.

Some writers take a still broader view. Thus, Spangenberg (1994) cites the five types of objectives identified by Warrick and Zawacki (1987), as shown in Table 4.3. The inclusion of developmental goals is certainly consistent with the developmental orientation that is claimed for many performance management systems. Moreover, we would expect that development goals would be related to business needs as well as being for the benefit of the individual, as shown by the examples given.

Characteristics of work goals

The incorporation of individual goals within some system of performance management is hardly a new idea, so we should expect

Table 4.3	**Types of objectives**
1	**Routine objectives**, which represent regular duties and responsibilities that are part of a job.
2	**Problem-solving objectives**, which are related to specific problems.
3	**Innovative objectives**, which pertain to new ideas, services or ways of doing things.
4	**Personal development objectives**, which are related to an individual's personal and professional development and growth.
5	**Organizational development objectives**, which are objectives for the development of the entire organization or a specific department.

Source: Warrick and Zawacki 1987, cited in Spangenberg 1994: 85

that by now there is some consensus about the characteristics of 'good' work goals. This is indeed the case, and McConkie (1979), analysing the views of nearly forty authorities on MbO, identified near-universal agreement on three aspects of goals within the context of MbO:

- goals and objectives should be specific;
- they should be defined in terms of measureable results;
- individual and organizational goals should be linked one to another.

On other aspects of goals there was rather less agreement, but half or more of authorities agreed on the following points:

- Objectives should be reviewed periodically.
- The time period for goal accomplishment should be specified.
- Wherever possible, the indicator of the results should be quantifiable; otherwise, it should be at least verifiable.
- Objectives should be flexible; changed as conditions warrant.
- Objectives should have an accompanying plan of action for accomplishing the results.
- Objectives should be assigned priority weightings.

These principles are reflected in much of today's conventional wisdom about goals, as in '**SMART**' goals, for example. Box 4.4 illustrates several variations on this basic theme.

The functions of work goals

One of the most robust of research findings in the behavioural sciences is that goal-setting has a beneficial effect on employees' work performance (Locke and Latham 1990). Positive findings have been reported from real-life studies in the workplace and from experimental studies in the laboratory. Studies have been carried out on a range of jobs and into quality as well as quantity goals. The main findings of the research are as follows:

- Difficult, challenging goals lead to higher performance than do easy goals, **provided that** the job holder accepts and is committed to the goals. In simple terms, the harder the goal, the higher the performance (given goal acceptance).

Box 4.4	**SMART goals**

Specific or **S**tretching
Measureable
Attainable or **A**chievable or **A**greed or **A**cceptable or **A**ssignable
Results-oriented or **R**ealistic or **R**elevant
Time-bound

For example, in Legal & General (Life and Pensions) **SMART** means:

Specific – define the work involved precisely
Measureable – to assess achievement
Agreed – both parties committed
Realistic – an acceptable but stretching challenge
Timed – specify the deadline and review date

A variation on this theme is **FRAME** (Whetten *et al.* 1994):

Few
Realistic
Agreed
Measured
Explicit

- Specific goals lead to higher performance than do vague, general 'do your best goals' or no goals at all.

These benefits derive, in part, from clarity over what is expected of employees, a point stressed by Ainsworth and Smith: 'Each person knows what is expected of him or her' and 'Everybody knows how they fit into the bigger picture' (1993: 17). Indeed, such clarity may be seen as a requirement for performance management to work, and may help to avoid the 'activity trap' – that is, losing sight of what job activities are for. This was seen to be a major benefit of a new performance management system introduced in the London Borough of Haringey's Housing Services – the aim was to create a new perception of effectiveness, one based on results rather than completion of tasks (Harris 1995). In this way, goals do provide one basis for measurement, although this is not without problems, as I shall come on to consider in just a moment. Goals may also serve to increase task interest and relieve boredom (Locke and Latham 1990). And in evaluating the operation of a performance management system we might ask employees about these aspects of role clarity.

How do goals and goal-setting work?

According to the theory of goal-setting (Locke and Latham 1990), it seems likely that goals work through several mechanisms:

- By directing the job holder's attention and action towards the desired end result – the acceptable level of performance: this is more likely to be the case when goals are specific rather than vague as a specific goal makes clear to the job holder what is meant by effective performance; vague goals, on the other hand, allow the individual to interpret pretty well any performance as effective. The mechanism involved here is one that has been described as **orientation** (Robertson *et al.* 1992).
- By mobilizing effort, in other words energizing the job holder; this is likely to be the consequence of a challenging rather than easy goal. Put simply, people try harder when faced with a task that is more rather than less difficult.
- By encouraging persistence over time; people seem more likely to stick at a hard rather than easy goal.

The above mechanisms all are believed to operate in a more or less automatic fashion (Locke and Latham 1990). But effort, action and persistence may not always be sufficient to bring about goal-accomplishment. When faced with a complex or novel task the individual will need to develop ways of (strategies for) achieving the goal(s). Furthermore, it is clear that feedback is also required.

Feedback (knowledge of results) is necessary in order to heighten the performance enhancing effect of goals. Feedback can serve to keep people on track; it provides a signal that a particular goal is still important (which may be particularly critical in cases of under-achievement) and may help to guide the individual towards ways of achieving the goal – in other words, it has **informational** and **learning** value. And when the goal is achieved feedback provides recognition.

Aspects of the goal-setting process

Gaining commitment

As we have seen, in order for goals to have the performance effects desired of them job holders have to accept and be committed to the goals. There are a number of aspects to commitment (Naylor and Ilgen 1984; Locke and Latham 1990; Earley and Shalley 1991): the job holder's attachment to the goal; its significance or importance in the eyes of the job holder; its perceived achievability/attainability (including controllability by the individual and difficulty); and the individual's determination and perseverance in achieving it, particularly when faced with obstructions and setbacks. It seems probable that more highly committed people will actually do what they say they will do.

Goal-commitment is taken to be a *sine qua non* so far as performance is concerned. The effect is particularly marked for hard goals, as the less committed job holder is more likely to give up such goals in favour of easier ones. Given this, what then can be done to enhance goal commitment? Two things would seem to be necessary: convincing job holders that it is possible for them to achieve the goal; and convincing them that the goal is important or appropriate.

- **Supervisor authority, support and explanation**. Job holders may accept a goal out of deference to the authority of the supervisor. However, it should not be assumed that the use of authority guarantees acceptance and commitment. Various supervisor behaviours, such as providing support, can help to persuade job holders of the importance and attainability of goals. Moreover, explanation, both of **why** the goal/task is important and perhaps of **how** it might be done, contributes to goal accomplishment. Such behaviours all help to create a good impression of the manager/supervisor in the eyes of the job holder (Huber *et al.* 1989).
- **Participation**. The role of employee participation in the goal-setting process remains controversial. Some authorities (e.g., Locke and Latham 1990) are of the view that it is not an absolutely necessary condition to bring about goal acceptance; explanation may be sufficient for this. Yet various case reports – the study of three performance management systems by Stiles *et al.* (1997), for example

– continue to indicate that top-down goals are received as imposed rather than owned. However, it may be that participation is important where the task is complex (Wood and Locke 1990), in which case employee participation does seem to enhance acceptance of the goal. And this seems particularly to be so if the goal has initially been rejected by the employee on the grounds that it is unreasonable or too difficult. However, the value of participation seems to be less to do with goal acceptance than, as we saw earlier, with a range of broader benefits.

- **Peer influence**. The supervisor isn't the only source of persuasive influence: peers, like supervisors, can serve as role models. Moreover, the power of peers and the work group to set norms of behaviour has long been recognized, as, for example, in the Hawthorne studies (Roethlisberger and Dickson 1939), which revealed, amongst other things, the existence of group norms about acceptable levels of production – typically below management's desired level and below the level that the workers were capable of delivering. Thus, it is important to recognize that co-workers have expectations of what a given employee should do.

- **Incentives and rewards**. Money may have a part to play here provided that the amount on offer is large enough and provided that the goal is not too difficult. If the goal is seen as impossible to achieve, the prospect of monetary reward, such as a bonus, is unlikely to bring about commitment because the reward is likely to be seen as unattainable (Locke and Latham 1990). This, of course, has important implications for appraisal-related pay, an issue that I will come back to later.

Expectancy, self-efficacy and ability

This last point introduces the notion of expectancy, or **subjective probability of success** (SPS): does the individual expect to succeed in achieving the goal? This rather depends on the difficulty of the goal. Robertson *et al.* sum up the position in these terms:

> In situations where goals are easy it seems likely that SPS is high for all performers, and therefore a link between SPS [and performance] is unlikely to appear. When goals are difficult, as predicted by expectancy-valency

theory, there should be, and is, a relationship between SPS and performance.

(Robertson et al. 1992: 43)

Expectancy is closely related to another important psychological concept – self-efficacy. The latter is the broader concept and 'may be defined as the belief that one can perform successfully the behaviour required to produce designated types of performance' (Sadri and Robertson 1993: 139). In a review of studies Sadri and Robertson found a positive, albeit modest, relationship between self-efficacy and performance.

Self-efficacy, then, is perceptual – that is, the individual's perception of their ability. But it is not enough for people to perceive themselves as being able to accomplish the goal; they must actually have the requisite ability. Once the limit of an individual's ability has been reached, his or her performance is likely to level off, perhaps even decline (Locke and Latham 1990). Hence, the goal-setting process needs to have regard for individuals' capabilities and, more broadly, performance management needs to be concerned with the management of self-efficacy (Huber *et al.* 1989).

Another factor which influences perceived performance capability is past experience. Job holders' past experience of goals may have an impact on subsequent goal-setting. If previous goals were easy to achieve, employees seem to be prepared to choose more difficult goals the next time around. But if the goals were difficult to achieve on the previous occasion, then next time the job holder seems likely to choose an easier goal (Locke and Latham 1990). The organization, on the other hand, might see goal accomplishment in one year as a reason for setting higher goals the next. However, the employee might simply see this as 'ratcheting up', leading to potential problems in the longer term (Mitchell, Thompson and George-Falvy 2000).

Problems and difficulties with goals and goal-setting

Though there is considerable evidence pointing to the value of goals and the goal-setting process, there are, not surprisingly, a number of problems, including practical difficulties and theoretical weaknesses.

First, the notion that individual goals should be integrated with organizational and unit-level goals requires that such higher-level goals have in fact been established. But as we saw earlier, there are difficulties with the organizational goal-setting process. It doesn't necessarily proceed in the rational, ordered way that is often advocated, and where higher-level goals are set out there also is the possibility of conflict amongst them – a problem that the balanced scorecard attempts to tackle. But all this does mean that the framework of organizational goals/objectives can be very complex. The integration idea also requires that the higher-level goals be communicated, and, as we saw in Chapter 1, not all organizations, including those professing to practise performance management, actually communicate their mission statement etc.

Second, there is a problem of **subjectivity**. It may seem strange to identify this as a problem with goals as these are typically regarded as substantially more objective than subjective. However, the process of setting individual goals is a very subjective one, as is the process of **interpreting** goal accomplishment. This is true whatever level of analysis we are concerned with, from the individual right up to the organizational. As Campbell puts it:

> an objective criterion is a subjective criterion once removed. For example, one might think that the number of units produced is an objective measure of an automobile assembly plant's effectiveness. However, a specific volume of production means nothing until some metric or standard is applied that informs us what numbers are good and what numbers are bad. Many subjective judgements go into the development of such standards
>
> *(Campbell 1977: 45)*

This highlights the distinction between measurement (as a counting activity) and evaluation, which involves making **judgements** about effectiveness.

Furthermore, much of the writing on goals advocates the setting of a relatively small number of goals, and this necessarily involves choice.

> Often to choose and emphasize a limited number of performance dimensions is to fail to appreciate the subtlety of organizational life, and to risk shattering subtle structures of tacit but critical employee commitment by substituting a simplistic set of objectives. It carries the

danger that if the system does 'work', in the sense that people focus on those elements of performance that have been selected and highlighted by the organization, the results may be not at all desirable: a pre-existing pride in skill and work may be replaced by a contractual focus on the rules.

(Mabey and Salaman 1995: 193)

Third, as Macdonell asks, 'Is "joint" goal-setting between a manager and subordinate ever going to be a practical possibility?' (1989: 706). Macdonell is alluding here to the boss–judge/friend–helper dilemma. There's also the added difficulty that stems from others', for example co-workers', expectations. Thus, there is the prospect of conflict amongst an individual's goals, suggesting that the idea of the balanced scorecard may be relevant at the individual level as it is at the organizational.

Fourth, there is the problem of turbulence. Mabey and Salaman describe this difficulty:

Identifying desirable aspects of performance which will be measured and rewarded may be possible in an organization which enjoys a relatively stable internal and external environment, but where greater turbulence is experienced it is possible that objectives and hence performance dimensions targeted today may be inapplicable tomorrow.

(Mabey and Salaman 1995: 194)

In similar vein Macdonell asks, 'How do you recognize when conditions are changing and what account needs to be taken of them?' (1989: 706).

Fifth, the effects of goal-setting seem to be weaker for complex tasks than they are for easier tasks – paradoxically, though, the goals-based approach is more common for complex jobs. A participative approach would seem to be particularly relevant in the case of complex goals so as to help develop performance strategies as well as enhancing self-esteem.

Finally, there must surely be the temptation (to which both manager and managed may be susceptible) to focus on that which is measured easily and to express required performance levels as minimum standards but with the consequent risk that these become the maximum levels, which are attained but not exceeded. There may also be the related temptation to concentrate on the easily accomplished. Then there's the difficulty that not all aspects of jobs may be specified in terms of goals, certainly not relatively objective, quantitative ones. Those measures that are used thus become deficient as performance indicators (for the whole

Box 4.5	**Implications for practice**

There's no one best way of expressing what employees are expected to accomplish in their jobs: use means that are appropriate to the job. It may be necessary to use more than one method to fully express performance requirements.

Where goal-setting (objective-setting; target-setting) is used set relatively few goals. Make sure that priorities and linkages (including possible conflicts) amongst the goals are clear. Remember that there may be work objectives and developmental objectives. Ensure that so far as possible the goals have the characteristics of 'good' goals that were set out earlier. Take care to avoid the dangers of both the 'activity trap' and 'goal deception'.

Employ a participative and involving approach as widely as possible so as to engender acceptance, commitment and ownership. At the very least seek the individual's agreement to what is expected of them. Encapsulate the performance requirements in a written performance contract or agreement.

Have regard for the individual's capabilities and their sense of self-efficacy. Only set goals for activities over which individuals themselves have substantial control.

Feedback (which may arise from the job itself or be self-generated) is necessary for goals to have their performance enhancing effects.

Bear in mind that integration of goals across different levels (and laterally) will not always be straightforward. Implementing and operating goal setting is complex.

job) and employees' attention may become misdirected on the measurable at the expense of other important aspects of performance. In other words, in the same way that there is the problem of the 'activity trap', so there is this problem of 'goal deception' (Henderson 1984).

A concluding comment

The output-oriented conception of performance tends to view jobs as collections of tasks to be completed to meet defined objectives/goals.

Compelling though the evidence is about work goals, we certainly should not see goal-setting as a panacea. As noted above, there are a number of practical difficulties.

It also is important to recognize how demandingly complex a process goal-setting is to implement and operate. As Mitchell *et al.* put it, 'Goal setting requires lots of work to implement successfully. There has to be coordination across people and organizational units as well as up and down the organizational hierarchy. Monitoring has to take place to assess goal progress and when attainment or progress is achieved, feedback, rewards and bonuses need to be delivered' (2000: 241). In addition, an organization's goal-setting process necessarily has to be dynamic because of the ever-changing environments – social, economic, political, etc. – in which the organization exists.

There's also the issue of how much of an individual's output is actually attributable to the particular performer. I will develop this point further in Chapter 6, but for the present it is sufficient to note that output may in some part be determined by factors that are outside the individual's control. This is one consideration that has led some writers to prefer a behavioural conception of performance. Moreover, as implied above, undue concentration on results – on the **what** – may lead to insufficient attention being paid to the **how** of performance. I will take up these points in the next chapter.

5 Individual performance II: Behaviour and competencies

The view that performance should be equated with task accomplishment, goal achievement, results, outputs, etc. is one that has been challenged in much of the psychological literature. Common today is a behavioural view of performance, one of the themes in which is that performance is *not* output or results. This is not to say that there is no place for goals in such a behavioural conception, as Murphy's definition makes clear: '*The performance domain is defined ... as the set of behaviours that are relevant to the goals of the organization or the organizational unit in which a person works*' (1990: 162; italics in original). Other examples of this approach are shown in Box 5.1.

Central to the argument that we should not regard performance as task accomplishment or goal achievement is the fact that for many jobs results aren't necessarily the product of what individual employees do – there may be other contributory factors that are nothing to do with the person doing the job (Cardy and Dobbins 1994; Murphy and Cleveland 1995). Moreover, workers do not have equal opportunity to perform, nor is everything that people do whilst at work necessarily task-related (Murphy 1989). There are also the points, alluded to in the previous chapter, that an over-concentration on outputs ignores important processual and interpersonal factors and undue focus on outputs may misdirect employees as to what is required.

Thus, we have two different views of performance – results/outputs and behaviours. Defining performance as both, particularly at the same time, would seem to be unhelpful. One of the reasons for this is that doing so confounds the relationship between behaviours and outputs. Typically (e.g. Cardy and Dobbins 1994; Waldman 1994), behaviour is regarded as one of the *causes* of output, with output being one of the means by which the *effectiveness* of performance (that is, behaviour) may

| Box 5.1 | **Conceptions of performance as behaviour** |

'Performance is what the person or system does' (Ilgen and Schneider 1991: 73).

A performance consists of a *performer* engaging in *behaviour* in a *situation* to achieve *results* (Mohrman *et al.* 1989: 48).

Performance is ... defined as synonymous with behaviour. It is something that people actually do and can be observed. By definition, it includes only those actions or behaviours that are relevant to the organization's goals and that can be scaled (measured) in terms of each individual's proficiency (that is, level of contribution). Performance is what the organization hires one to do, and do well. Performance is *not* the consequence or result of action, it is the action itself. ... performance consists of goal-relevant actions that are under the control of the individual, regardless of whether they are cognitive, motor, psychomotor, or interpersonal (Campbell *et al.* 1993: 40).

be judged. In other words we make judgements about the effectiveness of employees with reference to what they accomplish – the results they achieve, the output they produce. An illustration of this is provided by Campbell *et al.*: '*Effectiveness* refers to the evaluation of the results of performance' (1993: 41). And Ilgen and Schneider write in similar terms: 'Performance is what the person or system does. Performance measurement is the quantification of what was done, and performance evaluation is the attachment of a judgment of the value or quality of the quantified performance measurement' (1991: 73). All three are, of course, needed in performance management: the necessary first step is the expression of performance requirements.

In everyday practice, however, the term performance tends to be used in a loose way to embrace both outputs and behaviour. This may be a convenient shorthand, but from a practical point of view it is likely to be more useful to be precise about what is meant as managing performance as outputs may require different interventions from the management of performance as behaviours. For example, the production of output may well involve many factors beyond the individual's control, such as the design of the work system. Behaviour, on the other hand, though not free from extraneous influence, might be expected to be much more within the direct control of the individual. Though behaviour and results/output are different entities they both are important and both require appropriate management systems and processes.

Performance is behaviour, but is *all* behaviour performance?

What is implied in these behavioural views (and in some cases is explicit) is the idea that whilst performance is behaviour not all behaviour is performance – only behaviour that is goal-relevant counts as performance. However, some writers have drawn a distinction between the aspects of jobs that are formally required and expected and those expectations which arise, perhaps as part of the *psychological contract*, in a more informal way. Thus, Borman and Motowidlo (1993) distinguish between *task performance* (i.e., activities that contribute to the technical core of the organization, e.g. selling policies in an insurance company) and *contextual performance* (which supports the broader social/psychological environment of the organization). Some examples of what they mean by the latter are given in Table 5.1.

Table 5.1	**Examples of contextual performance and organizational spontaneity**

Contextual performance
- Volunteering to carry out task activities that are not formally a part of the job.
- Persisting with extra enthusiasm or effort when necessary to complete own task activities successfully.
- Helping and cooperating with others.
- Following organizational rules and procedures even when personally inconvenient.
- Endorsing, supporting and defending organizational objectives.

Organizational spontaneity
- Helping co-workers.
- Protecting the organization.
- Making constructive suggestions.
- Developing oneself.
- Spreading goodwill.

Source: Borman and Motowidlo 1993: 73; George and Brief 1992

This class of behaviours also has been referred to as *organizational citizenship behaviour* (e.g., Bateman and Organ, 1983), *prosocial organizational behaviour* (Brief and Motowidlo, 1986), *organizational spontaneity* (George and Brief, 1992), or *extra-role behaviours* (Van Dyne, Cummings and Parks, 1995). As Murphy (1999) notes, these terms are not interchangeable and the last is broader in scope than the others. However, there are elements of similarity as illustrated by the examples of organizational spontaneity and contextual performance in Table 5.1 (see Motowidlo and Schmit (1999) for a fuller explication of points of similarity).

What is important to recognize about contextual performance is that though these behaviours are to the benefit of the organization they are not always a formal part of the job and to that extent they are much more heavily volitional or discretionary than are formally prescribed behaviours (Van Dyne, *et al.*, 1995). Of course, we might hope that all employees would help and co-operate with others, endorse the organization's objectives, and so on, but the point being made here is that these sorts of behaviours aren't normally expressed as a formal job requirement even though they may implicitly be expected. However, there are reasons for supposing that they *should* be expected require-ments of many or all jobs – take 'developing oneself', for example. As London and Mone (1999) put it, 'The rapid pace of change in job requirements due to organizational, competitive, and technological development means that employees must constantly show the capacity to engage in new learning as they cope with change' (124–5). And Hesketh and Neal (1999) make the same point, 'The rapid pace of change in job requirements arising from technological innovations places employees in a situation where they constantly need to demonstrate a capacity to engage in new learning and cope with change. Under these circumstances, one is no longer assessing absolute performance; rather, the focus is on responsiveness to changing job demands' (p. 47).

Also, the shift in emphasis towards quality and customer-orientated service may mean that for many jobs such behaviours are more explicitly expected these days (Bowen and Waldman, 1999; Waldman, 1994). Interestingly, some North American research (MacKenzie, Podsakoff and Fetter, 1991, 1993) indicates that managers of sales personnel attach great weight to organizational citizenship behaviours (OCBs) when making performance evaluations. They examined such OCBs as altruism (voluntarily helping others), civic virtue (e.g., attending meetings that aren't formally required as part of the job) and conscientiousness and concluded that 'a salesperson's overall performance evaluation was determined more by his or her citizenship behaviour – including altruistic acts . . . and conscientiousness – than by his or her actual sales success'. Motowidlo and Schmit (1999) note other studies showing that contextual performance influences supervisor ratings of overall performance and some studies show an association between contextual performance and indicators of organizational effectiveness. If such behaviours are important for organizational performance then it is important that they are set out as explicit requirements.

One of the interesting questions raised by these findings is whether the sales agents concerned were aware that OCBs were influencing their performance evaluations. If not, then this might be one factor which would help to explain perceptual differences in performance – sales staff seeing themselves as doing well because of a high volume of sales but getting a lower than expected evaluation from their managers because the latter have also been taking OCBs into account. Moreover, under such circumstances we might regard the managers' evaluations as at least unfair, if not downright dishonest.

This discussion of extra-role behaviours indicates one of the difficulties with the performance-as-behaviour view, namely mapping the behavioural domain. One attempt to do this has been made by Campbell (Campbell 1990; Campbell *et al.* 1993; Campbell *et al.* 1996) in his theory of performance. He presents a factor model of the components of performance and speculates that job performance can be described in terms of eight general factors, as shown in Table 5.2, with each factor containing a number of sub-factors.

Campbell argues that 'three of the factors – core task proficiency, demonstrated effort, and maintenance of personal discipline – are major performance components of *every* job' (Campbell *et al.* 1993: 49), although the others vary in the extent to which they apply to different jobs. Campbell suggests that other behavioural models can be accommodated within this framework – forms of organizational spontaneity and OCBs fit within various of the factors, for example (although they would, of course, cease to be voluntary behaviours if they were formally required). Also, much of the research on job behaviour can be related to the model.

However, there has been some recent questioning of the sufficiency of the model. As noted earlier, Hesketh and Neal (1999) and London

Table 5.2	**A taxonomy of major performance components**

1 *Job-specific task proficiency.* The first factor reflects the degree to which the individual can perform the core substantive or technical tasks that are central to the job. They are the job-specific performance behaviours that distinguish the substantive content of one job from another. . . .

2 *Non-job-specific task proficiency.* This factor reflects the situation that in virtually every organization, but perhaps not all, individuals are required to perform tasks or execute performance behaviours that are not specific to their particular job. . . .

3 *Written and oral communication task proficiency.* Many jobs in the workforce require the individual to make formal oral or written presentations to audiences that may vary from one to tens of thousands. For those jobs the proficiency with which one can write or speak, independent of the correctness of the subject matter, is a critical component of performance.

4 *Demonstrating effort.* The fourth factor is meant to be a direct reflection of the consistency of an individual's effort day by day, the frequency with which people will expend extra effort when required, and the willingness to keep working under adverse conditions. It is a reflection of the degree to which individuals commit themselves to all job tasks, work at a high level of intensity, and keep working when it is cold, wet, or late.

5 *Maintaining personal discipline.* The fifth component is characterized by the degree to which negative behaviour such as alcohol and substance abuse at work, law or rules infractions, and excessive absenteeism are avoided.

6 *Facilitating peer and team performance.* Factor six is defined as the degree to which the individual supports his or her peers, helps them with job problems, and acts as a de facto trainer. It also encompasses how well an individual facilitates group functioning by being a good model, keeping the group goal-directed, and reinforcing participation by other group members. . . .

7 *Supervision/leadership.* Proficiency in the supervisory component includes all the behaviours directed at influencing the performance of subordinates through face-to-face interpersonal interaction and influence. Supervisors set goals for subordinates, they teach them more effective methods, they model the appropriate behaviours, and they reward or punish in appropriate ways. The distinction between this factor and the previous one is a distinction between peer leadership and supervisory leadership. Although modelling, goal-setting, coaching and providing reinforcement are elements in both factors, the belief here is that peer versus supervisor leadership implies significantly different determinants.

8 *Management/administration.* The eighth and last factor is intended to include the major elements in management that are distinct from direct supervision. It includes the performance behaviours directed at articulating goals for the unit or enterprise, organizing people and resources to work on them, monitoring progress, helping to solve problems or overcome crises that stand in the way of goal accomplishment, controlling expenditures, obtaining additional resources and representing the unit in dealing with other units.

Source: Campbell *et al.* 1993: 46–8

and Mone (1999) have pointed to the importance of learning and adaptability for today's ever-changing conditions of work. Hesketh and Neal propose *adaptive performance* (e.g., 'ease of learning new tasks, confidence in approaching new tasks, and flexibility and capacity to cope with change') as an additional factor of performance. Continuous learning, innovation and improvement are features of the EFQM Excellence Model and a developmental orientation to performance management is wholly consistent with fostering continuous development.

However, the model remains speculative because specific tests are rare. The work of Viswesvaran (e.g., Viswesvaran and Ones 2000), which led to an empirically-derived classification of ten performance dimensions, shows some consistency with the Campbell factors. But there are some differences also: for example, the Viswesvaran dimensions clearly point to the importance that organizations attach to output/results (in both quantitative and qualitative terms) as a factor of performance. The Viswesvaran research by no means invalidates the Campbell model – really, the only point that is being made is that we don't yet have a general model of performance as behaviour.

In the meantime, from a practitioner point of view the Campbell factors (with the addition of adaptive performance) may have value in serving as a kind of general framework to ensure that important aspects of job performance are not overlooked. For example, in designing a behaviourally based performance management system the dimensions that are identified might be compared with the Campbell framework to check that all important aspects are represented.

Positive and negative behaviours

In their fifth factor (maintaining personal discipline) Campbell and his colleagues refer to the avoidance of certain kinds of negative behaviours. The idea of negative behaviours features rather more prominently in another performance-as-behaviour model (Murphy 1989, 1990; Murphy and Cleveland 1995), which identifies four main clusters of behaviours:

- task-orientated behaviours;
- maintaining interpersonal relations;

- down-time behaviours (e.g. absenteeism, alcohol and drug abuse);
- destructive/hazardous behaviours (e.g. safety violations, sabotage).

The last two categories clearly comprise counter-productive behaviours that are to be avoided. Other kinds of (possibly) negative behaviour that need to be considered are identified by Van Dyne *et al.* (1995) in their discussion of extra-role behaviours. These are **whistle-blowing** and **principled organizational dissent**, the latter being defined as 'a protest and/or effort to change the organizational status quo because of a conscientious objection to current policy or practice' (Graham 1986; cited in Van Dyne *et al.* 1995: 228).

Recognition of these sorts of behaviours immediately points to one of the flaws with the conceptualizations of performance so far advanced, namely that they view performance solely through the eyes of the organization. In the same way that it is possible to adopt a stakeholder approach to considering organizational performance, one can see individual performance through many different sets of eyes. In recognition of this Ilgen and Hollenbeck (1991) refer to **job elements** (formally defined) and **role elements**. The latter arise out of negotiation/discussion/interaction between the job holder and another stakeholder (or stakeholders), such as a colleague or customer. The point here is that a job incumbent will be at the centre of a particular role set and it should not be assumed that the members of that role set will have the same expectations of the job holder's performance. This is a consideration to be borne in mind in using 360° feedback instruments – different evaluations of performance may be the result of differing expectations of what is required, not just different perceptions of what was done.

Competences and competencies

In Britain we have come to associate job behaviours both with competences and competencies. There is much confusion about these terms. As accounts (e.g. Tuxworth 1989) of their origins show, this confusion seems to have been there right from the early days and it has been compounded by lack of definitional rigour (Collin 1989) and by loose use of terminology in much of the literature. This has been further exacerbated by the use of such terms as **core competence** and

distinctive competence as properties of the organization, as discussed in Chapter 2 (see also Sparrow 1994, 1996).

So, we find the term **competences** being used to refer to distinctive features of the organization and to properties of jobs. Thus, in the UK we have come to associate competences with National Vocational Qualifications (NVQs) and the Management Charter Initiative (MCI) National Standards. The term **competencies**, on the other hand, more usually is interpreted in a person-related sense – but still with substantial disagreement. There seem to be two main conceptualizations.

Competencies as behaviours

In contemporary UK practice a popular interpretation of a competency is that it is 'a dimension of overt, manifest behaviour that allows a person to perform competently' (Woodruffe 1992: 17). Some examples of competencies as defined by Woodruffe are given in Table 5.3. As Fletcher (1993) notes, Woodruffe's definition is very reminiscent of terminology that we have long associated with assessment centre

Table 5.3	**Examples of Woodruffian competencies**

Drive to achieve results
Prepared to compromise to achieve a result; installs solutions within time frame; innovates or adapts existing procedures to ensure a result; takes on problems; suffers personal inconvenience to ensure problems are solved; comes forward with new ideas; sets challenging targets; sets out to win new business; sets own objectives; recognizes areas for self-development; acquires new skills and capabilities; accepts new challenges.

Incisiveness to have a clear understanding
Gets a clear overview of an issue; grasps information accurately; relates pieces of information; identifies causal relationships; gets to the heart of a problem; identifies the most productive lines of enquiry; appreciates all the variables affecting an issue; identifies limitations to information; adapts thinking in light of new information; tolerates and handles conflicting/ambiguous information and ideas.

Sensitivity to others' viewpoints
Listens to others' viewpoints; adapts to other person; takes account of others' needs; shows empathy in oral and written communications; aware of others' expectations.

Source: Woodruffe 1992: 18

practice: 'By *dimensions* we mean a cluster of behaviours that are specific, observable, and verifiable, and that can be reliably and logically classified together' (Thornton and Byham 1982: 117) – Table 5.4 gives some illustrations. Though this definition doesn't make any explicit reference to such ideas as job-relatedness, performance or effectiveness, all these are features of the job analysis procedure that Thornton and Byham advocate for identifying dimensions. For example, within their 'model job analysis procedure' they include the use of the critical incidents method (Flanagan 1954) for identifying behaviours 'associated with job success and failure' (Thornton and Byham 1982: 132). Thus, it is clear that dimensions are behaviours used in task accomplishment.

Hence, we could take the view that this behavioural interpretation of the term **competencies** is simply a replacement (or synonym) for **dimensions**. Indeed, it is hard to see how a strictly behavioural view of a competency differs to any significant extent from Campbell's definition of performance as behaviour! On the face of it, it looks as though there is at least one redundant concept in here somewhere. There is, however, another interpretation of what a competency is. To explore this we need to go back to the earlier literature which first brought the term to prominence.

Competencies as underlying characteristics of the person

What brought the term competency into popular use, particularly in the management development world, was *The Competent Manager*, the book authored by Richard Boyatzis (1982), although the term was in

Table 5.4	**Behavioural dimensions**
Sensitivity	Actions that indicate a consideration for the feelings and needs of others.
Initiative	Active attempts to influence events to achieve goals; self-starting rather than passive acceptance. Taking action to achieve goals beyond those called for; originating action.
Analysis	Identifying problems, securing relevant information, relating data from different sources, and identifying possible causes of problems.

Source: Thornton and Byham 1982: 139–40

use for some years previously. This is the conceptualization that we associate with the McBer consultancy and, as the definition in Box 5.2 makes clear, we are very much in the realm of fundamental properties of the person – traits, motives and the like – in other words, what people *are*, not simply what they do. Moreover, it is not just any underlying characteristics that we are concerned with – rather, ones that are **causally related** to superior job performance (this being defined in terms of results/outputs). (Box 5.3 gives an illustration of how this sort

---

Box 5.2 | **Definition of a competency as an underlying characteristic of the person**

A competency is an *underlying characteristic* of an individual that is *causally related* to *criterion-referenced effective and/or superior performance* in a job or situation.

- *Underlying characteristic* means the competency is a fairly deep and enduring part of a person's personality and can predict behaviour in a wide variety of situations and job tasks.
- *Causally related* means that a competency *causes* or *predicts* behaviour and performance.
- *Criterion-referenced* means that the competency actually predicts who does something well or poorly, as measured on a *specific criterion* or standard. Examples of criteria are the dollar volume of sales for salespeople or the number of clients who stay 'dry' for alcohol-abuse counsellors. [Note the results/outputs view of performance that is taken here]

(Source: Spencer and Spencer 1993: 9)

Competencies can be motives, traits, self-concepts, attitudes or values, content knowledge, or cognitive or behavioural skills – any individual characteristic that can be measured or counted reliably and that can be shown to differentiate significantly between superior and average performers, or between effective and ineffective performers. The following definitions of the above characteristics may be given:

- *Motive:* the underlying need or thought pattern that drives, directs and selects an individual's behaviour; e.g. the need for achievement. ▶

- *Trait:* a general disposition to behave or respond in a certain way; for instance with self-confidence, self-control, stress resistance or 'hardiness'.
- *Self-concept:* (attitudes or values) measured by respondent tests that ask people what they value, what they think they do or are interested in doing.
- *Content knowledge:* of facts or procedures, either technical (how to trouble-shoot a defective computer) or interpersonal (techniques for effective feedback), as measured by respondent tests.
- *Cognitive and behavioural skills:* either covert (e.g. deductive or inductive reasoning) or observable (e.g. active listening skills).

(Source: Hooghiemstra 1992: 28)

Box 5.3	**An example of a McBer competency**

Information seeking
An underlying curiosity, a desire to know more about things, people or issues drives Information Seeking. Information Seeking implies making an effort to get more information, not accepting situations 'at face value'.

Information-seeking scale
Level Behavioural Description

0   *None.* Does not seek additional information about a situation, other than what has been given.
1   *Asks questions.* Asks direct questions of immediately available people (or people who are directly involved in the situation even if not physically present), consults available resources. . . .
6   *Uses own ongoing systems.* Has personally established ongoing systems or habits for various kinds of information gathering (may include 'management by walking around', regular information meetings, etc., if these are specifically to gather information).
7   *Involves others.* Involves others who would not normally be involved and gets them to seek out information.

(Intermediate points 2 to 5 also are similarly defined.)

(Source: Spencer and Spencer 1993: 34–5)

of a competency is expressed in terms of 'a narrative definition plus three to six *behavioural indicators*, or specific behavioural ways of demonstrating the competency in the job' (Spencer and Spencer 1993: 19).) In other words, competencies, according to this conception, are a determinant or cause of performance, not performance (that is, results/outputs) itself.

The **criterion-referenced causality** element of the definition lends this conceptualization of competencies some distinctiveness. We should note, however, that at least two levels of criteria are applied: this is illustrated by the distinction drawn by the McBer group between **threshold competencies** and **differentiating competencies**. The latter distinguish between average and superior performers, whereas the former are competencies that everyone needs to do the job to a minimally adequate standard; they don't differentiate, in other words. A similar distinction is drawn by Schroder (1989) between **basic** and **high-performance** competencies. Some (Warr and Conner 1992) also identify a third, more **elementary**, level of criterion-referencing and this leads them on to an elaborated definition of a job competency as: 'A set of behaviours, knowledge, thought processes, and/or attitudes, which are likely to be reflected in job performance that reaches a defined elementary, basic or high-performance standard' (1992: 99).

The Warr and Conner and McBer definitions share a number of features in common. First, both are criterion-referenced: whereas Warr and Conner are more explicit about different criterion levels, the McBer approach specifies the definition of performance as outputs/results. This has implications for practice – if we adopt this model we need to distinguish different levels of performance (output) when we carry out our studies to determine what competencies are required to perform a job or, more probably, a family of jobs. Second, both include the idea of causality, although this is expressed in a stronger way in the McBer definition. Third, both refer to underlying characteristics of the person as well as to behaviours.

It is this last point which sets this definition apart from the seemingly behavioural approach taken by Woodruffe. Woodruffe objects to the McBer definition on the grounds that it 'seems to cover pretty well anything' (1991: 30). Indeed so, and mixing up traits, attitudes, thought processes and behaviours would seem to be unhelpful, particularly from a theoretical point of view. Thus, Woodruffe sees behaviourally defined competencies as offering 'a chance to get away from the muddle of traits and motives' (1991: 30). However, if we look at some of Woodruffe's competencies (Table 5.3) we see that the more basic characteristics of the person are implied: 'preparedness to compromise' – true enough we recognize this in behaviour that is displayed, but surely this implies a dispositional characteristic. 'Takes on problems', 'suffers personal inconvenience', 'shows empathy', 'gets to the heart of a problem', 'identifies limitations to information' – here again, these all imply dispositional, attitudinal and similar underlying characteristics of the person. Thus, when we look at examples of Woodruffe's competencies it is clear that they include more than is conveyed by his definition: they are not so exclusively behavioural after all.

Cooper and Robertson develop this as a general point by drawing attention to the non-behavioural nature of many competencies: 'Behaviour needs to be defined unambiguously and it must be observable. Most of the commonly used competencies are not sufficiently specific or observable to be classed as behaviours' (1995: 26). Of course, we might see this as a criticism of the short narrative definitions of competencies that are typically used – and many of the examples throughout this chapter indicate that the criticism is well founded. However, we should note that there are instances of more specific behavioural scales being used, as we saw in Box 5.3, and later in the chapter I will give examples of positive and negative behavioural indicators. That said, it is clear that many competency definitions mix up behaviours and personal attributes as well as referring to desired results.

In Chapter 4 I drew attention to the danger of an undue focus on outputs/results, for example detracting from the means by which results are accomplished – the behaviours that may contribute to a sale. Similarly, undue focus on behaviours runs the risk of denying the importance of what the person is. On these grounds the broader view of competencies, whether that of the McBer group or that of Warr and Conner, might be preferred. It recognizes that aspects of the person, such as personality, are important for job performance, whether one defines this as behaviour or results.

One of the advantages of this broader conception of job competencies has to do with what Warr and Conner refer to as 'syndromes' or 'important combinations' of characteristics. Thus, competencies more broadly defined may be seen as such 'syndromes'. In other words, though we might recognize a competency such as 'drive to achieve results' through its behavioural manifestations, those behaviours are a reflection of some important combination of personal attributes which we would run the risk of ignoring if we were to concentrate solely on behaviours. Moreover, the broader definition of a competency gives added meaning which may help to distinguish the term competencies from the term behaviours. The elements of **causality** and **criterion-relatedness** may also give the term some distinctiveness.

However, it is far from clear that the term is used at all consistently: it has 'a variety of meanings and no accepted consensus on its definition has emerged' (Cockerill 1995: 86). Cockerill's own definition, therefore, muddies the waters even more: 'the relatively stable behaviours which create continuously the processes that enable the organization to learn, adapt to new environmental demands, and change the environment so that it is better suited to the needs of stakeholders' (1995: 86). This brings us back to an organizational perspective – the idea of a distinctive capability possessed by the organization.

Expressing performance requirements as behaviours

If we were to trace the history of appraisal practice we would see that a behavioural interpretation of performance has long been evident. Though this is true of the UK it is even more so for North America, as evidenced, for example, by the decades of research and practitioner interest in behavioural forms of performance rating – behaviourally anchored rating scales (BARS), behavioural observation scales (BOS), behavioural expectation scales (BES). (For descriptions of these see any one of Bailey 1983; Fletcher 1993; Fletcher and Williams 1992; Cardy and Dobbins 1994; Murphy and Cleveland 1995; Latham and Wexley 1994). These sorts of scales seem not to have been especially popular in British appraisal practice, although examples of behaviourally anchored scales are to be found in assessment/development centres.

Indeed, given the results emphasis in performance management practice in the UK today we might expect there to be relatively little interest in the behavioural aspects of performance. Some evidence suggests that this might be so, although the position isn't completely clear. For example, the IMS survey of performance management practice (Institute of Personnel Management 1992) revealed that relatively few organizations use lists of behavioural competences for expressing performance requirements. And the Industrial Society (1994) found that fewer than 10 per cent of the thousand or so respondents to their survey claimed to use competencies. The later IPD survey (Armstrong and Baron 1998) showed just under a third of respondents as using competence assessment, and the Industrial Society (1998) reported the assessment of competencies in 41 per cent of responding organizations.

If these figures truly reflect the extent of interest in behavioural aspects of performance, then performance management practice surely is seriously deficient in ignoring the essence of what people contribute to their jobs. To illustrate the point, here are some examples of research that has highlighted the importance of job behaviours.

Identifying behavioural dimensions of performance

First, let's consider the now substantial body of work carried out by the McBer group. This work is important, if only because of its extent, although, as I will show below, it is open to challenge on methodological grounds. Much of it is summarized by Spencer and Spencer (1993), who present the McBer Competency Dictionary – essentially a catalogue of twenty-one generic competencies common to the several hundred jobs/ professions/occupations studied by McBer consultants over the years. Also included are competency models for a range of jobs, e.g. salespeople, helping and human service workers, managers. Taken as a whole, then, what we have here is a statement of the competencies (and their behavioural manifestations) linked with effective/superior performance (output/results) in a wide range of jobs. By way of illustration, Table 5.5 summarizes the generic competency model for helping and human service professionals. As we saw in Box 5.3, each of these competencies has a narrative definition with one or more scaled behavioural indicators.

One of the important features of the McBer model is the criterion-relatedness of the competencies. But this cannot go unquestioned. Remember that the McBer conception of performance uses measures of outputs/results as criteria of effectiveness. The identification of these is crucial:

> The first and most important step in a competency study is to identify the criteria or measures that define superior or effective performance in the

Table 5.5   **The McBer generic competency model for helping and human service workers**

Weight	Competency
XXXXX	Impact and influence
XXXXX	Developing others
XXXX	Interpersonal understanding
XXX	Self-confidence
XXX	Self-control
XXX	Other personal effectiveness competencies (e.g. accurate self-assessment, affiliative interest – genuinely likes people)
XXX	Professional expertise
XXX	Customer service orientation
XXX	Teamwork and cooperation
XXX	Analytical thinking
XX	Conceptual thinking
XX	Initiative
XX	Flexibility
XX	Directiveness/assertiveness

'Weight' refers to the relative frequency with which each competency distinguishes superior from average performers.

Source: Abbreviated from Spencer and Spencer 1993: 186–7

job to be studied. Ideal criteria are 'hard' outcome measures, such as sales or profit data for business managers, or patents and publications for research scientists. For military officers, good criteria would be unit performance outcomes, such as combat inspection scores or reenlistment rates. For human service workers, the best criteria are *client* outcomes. For example, for alcoholism counselors the best measure of performance is percentage of clients who are still 'dry', regularly employed, and have had no arrests for drunkenness in the year following counseling.

(Spencer and Spencer 1993: 94)

These criteria are then used to identify:

a clear group of superstars and a comparison group of average performers. A third group of poor (ineffective or incompetent) performers can also be identified if the purpose of the study is to establish competency levels that predict minimal success in a job.

(Spencer and Spencer 1993: 96)

The other steps in the McBer method are summarized in Figure 5.1.

Figure 5.1 | **The McBer job competency assessment process**

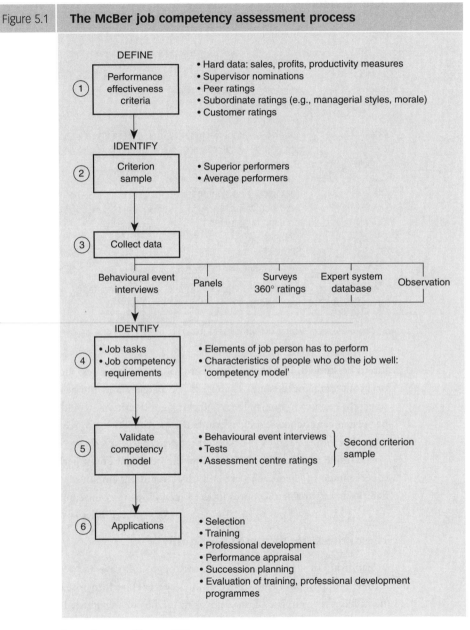

DEFINE

(1) Performance effectiveness criteria
- Hard data: sales, profits, productivity measures
- Supervisor nominations
- Peer ratings
- Subordinate ratings (e.g., managerial styles, morale)
- Customer ratings

IDENTIFY

(2) Criterion sample
- Superior performers
- Average performers

(3) Collect data

Behavioural event interviews | Panels | Surveys 360° ratings | Expert system database | Observation

IDENTIFY

(4) • Job tasks
• Job competency requirements
- Elements of job person has to perform
- Characteristics of people who do the job well: 'competency model'

(5) Validate competency model
- Behavioural event interviews
- Tests
- Assessment centre ratings
} Second criterion sample

(6) Applications
- Selection
- Training
- Professional development
- Performance appraisal
- Succession planning
- Evaluation of training, professional development programmes

Source: Spencer and Spencer 1993

But are the sorts of examples given by Spencer and Spencer really 'ideal' or 'good' criteria? Such criteria attribute to individual performers outputs or results which may not be wholly within their control. So, in the case of counselling it is of course possible that the behaviour of the counsellor has some impact on the result of the counselling process – but so do characteristics of the person being counselled, as well as the circumstances in which they find themselves. This is a general point about results and, as we saw earlier, it is used as part of the argument against regarding output as performance. Is it proper, therefore, to use such criteria as indicators of individual effectiveness? On the other hand, can we *not* use them? We might take the view that we have no choice in the matter. Schmidt (1993) draws attention to this difficulty in his critique of Campbell's behavioural model. The essence of Schmidt's argument is that it is often difficult to interpret the significance or meaning of behaviour in itself – there are times when we need results in order to do this:

> Campbell, McCloy and Oppler correctly state that consequences and results are often not fully under the control of the individual. That is true. But we may have to use results and consequences anyway; we may have no choice. In many cases, the best we can do is try to make intelligent judgements about the extent to which specific individuals are responsible for observed outcomes.
>
> *(Schmidt 1993: 504–5)*

So, from a conceptual point of view we might reasonably choose to define performance in terms of behaviour, and doing so helps to distinguish the relationship between behaviour and results. But it is obvious that we can't dispense with outputs and results. As is evident from the behavioural models, results provide the context – they make clear what behaviour should be directed towards. And in so doing they help to avoid the **activity trap** that I referred to in the previous chapter.

But as we saw earlier, it is equally clear that an excessive focus on outputs is undesirable. So, in managing performance we need *both* results *and* behaviour.

However, in using results/outputs as criteria we must be sure that they satisfy the requirements of 'good' criteria (Table 5.6): this is partly an issue of measurement accuracy and partly an issue of fairness. The determination of output-based criteria for jobs is far from problem-free; not only does this present a difficulty in using outputs for performance

Table 5.6	**Requirements for good performance criteria**
Reliable measurable	Should measure behaviours and outcomes in an objective manner
Content valid	Rationally related to the job performance activities
Defined specific	Cover identifiable behaviours and outcomes
Independent	Important behaviours and outcomes should be included in a comprehensive criterion
Non-overlapping	Criteria should not overlap
Comprehensive	No important behaviours or outcomes should be omitted
Accessible	Criteria should be phrased and named in a way that is comprehensible
Compatible	Criteria should fit in with an organization's goals and culture
Up to date	Criteria should be regularly reviewed in reponse to organizational change

Source: Altink *et al.* 1997: 293

management purposes but it also represents a threat to the methodo-logical adequacy of competency research. Competencies identified via the McBer method will only be as good as the criteria that are used: if these are deficient, then the competencies will be deficient too.

As another illustration of research showing the importance of a behavioural perspective on performance let me give an example from a high-involvement work organization using advanced manufacturing technology (Parker *et al.* 1994). I have included this example because it is methodologically rigorous, and, though it uses methods different from the McBer approach, the end result is a set of dimensions which are very similar in kind to McBer competencies. Box 5.4 describes the company briefly, explains how the dimensions of performance effectiveness were identified and illustrates their nature.

In this approach we have no independent criterion or criteria of effectiveness – the dimensions themselves are what is meant by effective performance. More precisely we might see the dimensions as 'mental models', that is, constructions of operator characteristics which are perceived to be effective. We should also note that in this case the perceptions are those of managers and supervisors. Shop-floor operators may or may not share these perceptions. A fuller picture would be

| Box 5.4 | **Dimensions of performance effectiveness in a high-involvement work organization** |

The company

An electronics company 'which designs, manufactures and installs equipment to measure, regulate, and control operations in such process industries as chemicals, nuclear power, and oil'.

How the dimensions of performance effectiveness were identified

The study was carried out in the assembly department and sought to identify dimensions of performance effectiveness for shop-floor staff.

The researchers used the repertory grid method with shop-floor operators as elements. The grids were administered to seven staff in managerial and supervisory roles. The usual method of triads was used to elicit constructs. After elicitation participants were asked to rate their elements (operators) on each construct (on a five-point scale ranging from high to low performer) and on an overall performance scale. The grids generated 129 constructs.

Grids were subjected to principal components analysis to identify 'those constructs which were most closely associated with elements of performance effectiveness'. A 'grounded theory' approach then was used to classify into dimensions the eighty constructs deriving from the principal components analysis. Finally, the dimensions identified were validated by feeding back to and discussing with production management staff. This led to certain of the dimensions being merged.

Dimensions of performance effectiveness

The process described above led to four higher-order dimensions being identified, certain of which contained several dimensions of performance effectivenes. These are summarized below:

Process ownership
1 Ownership of the production process
2 Goal/task-oriented
3 Multi-skilled/broad knowledge of the process ▶

Social skills
1 Social confidence
2 Effectiveness of communication with and across group boundaries
3 Team-working and co-operation

Personal style
1 Flexibility/adaptability
2 Systematic/planful

Loss prevention
1 Loss prevention: characterizes an individual who is organized; keeps a tidy work area and knows where everything is; shows good attention to detail; is consistent in quality and output; and exhibits good housekeeping skills.

Each of the dimensions of effectiveness is defined in the manner shown above for 'loss prevention'.

(Source: summarized from Parker et al. 1994: 5, 8, 11)

obtained by including operators as study participants, as Parker *et al.* (1994) themselves recognize. This is important from a practical point of view in the context of 360° appraisal, for example – though it may be helpful to involve others in measuring performance, the value of doing so may be reduced if those others have not had a hand in defining what performance is to be measured in the first place.

Forward-looking requirements

Let me give one more example which adopts different methods from the previous two but which shares the feature of methodological rigour. Though the context in this example was selection, the approach taken is no less relevant for performance management. Box 5.5 summarizes what was done. At heart, the approach exemplifies the traditional approach to job analysis – study the job and deduce required person characteristics. But a major difficulty with this is that is backward-looking – at best it takes jobs as they are today. Schneider and his co-workers attempt to anticipate what might be required for the future.

From the point of view of performance management the comparative analysis of present-day and future job tasks may reveal differences which

| Box 5.5 | **A future-orientated approach to identifying behavioural dimensions of performance** |

Task analysis

Based on interviews/group discussions with incumbents and supervisors and through observation. This ascertains '(1) the goals of the job and (2) the tasks that need to be accomplished for the goals to be met'. These tasks are adminstered in a survey to gather quantitative information on the criticality/importance of each task and the relative amount of time spent on each. The tasks are the basis of line manager ratings of employee effectiveness.

Personal attributes analysis

What attributes of the person are required to carry out the tasks that have been identified? Again, interviews/group discussions (with incumbents/supervisors) are used to identify required knowledge, skills and abilities, which are used to compile a questionnaire. The administration of this requires each attribute to be rated, amongst other things, on its importance for effective job performance.

Anticipating the future

The foregoing steps are typical of much job analysis practice as advocated in North American literature. But a distinctive feature of the approach adopted by Schneider and his co-workers is the attempt to anticipate future strategic demands and incorporate these in the specification of person attributes:

> To incorporate strategic issues into a 'present' job analysis we first gather information about the kinds of issues in the job, the company, and/or the larger environment that may affect the job in the future. This is accomplished in a workshop composed of subject matter experts (e.g., job incumbents, supervisors, managers, human resource staff, strategic planners) and job analysts. The participants might also include experts in a relevant technical field, economists, demographers, and so forth, depending on the specific job of interest.

In the light of this information the tasks identified earlier are re-rated in terms of importance and time spent. Also, new tasks ▶

> may be added. The personal attributes similarly are re-rated, again with the possibility of new ones being added.
>
> Comparative analysis of the present and future profiles is likely to reveal points of similarity and points of difference. This may necessitate changes to personnel procedures, such as selection or training.
>
> *(Source: summarized from Schneider and Konz 1989: 53 and Schneider and Schechter 1991: 221)*

will require a range of responses. For example, changes to job design or work organization, or perhaps even more substantial structural reorganization, may be required. Where new skills are indicated there may be implications for selection or training; it also is possible that a developmental approach to performance management will allow at least some needed personal attributes to be developed through the job itself.

The account by Schneider and Konz (1989) is one of the few descriptions that we have of a future-oriented approach. Sparrow and Boam (1992) and Shackleton (1992) discuss forward-looking competency profiles and refer to various tools, such as visioning workshops and business scenarios, which may play a part in identifying such profiles. These sorts of activities involve substantial effort – the equivalent of two person years went into the development of scenarios used by British Airways to inform their business planning (Moyer 1996) – so they are unlikely to be used simply to identify skills etc. required for the future.

Though anticipating the future is highly speculative, the application of structured tools may help to bring some rigour to the process. Even so, there must be some threat to the validity of forward-looking profiles. But we need to balance against this the threat to validity that comes from an over-reliance on traditional backward-looking approaches to job analysis – the risk I mentioned above, that of ending up with a picture of jobs (and associated behavioural requirements) as they are today or, worse, as they were.

A number of important practical points arise from the three examples that I have given. One is that they all illustrate rigorous, systematic methods to identify the behaviours that are relevant to the job(s) in question. For any performance management system which seeks to incorporate behaviours this is essential. Second, the examples show that many methods are available for use – indeed it is essential to adopt

Table 5.7	**Competencies for job families in changing environments I: new managerial roles**

Competencies for new managerial roles

I *Achieving results*
- Planning and organizing
- Focus on outcomes
- Continuous improvement
- Monitoring and evaluating

II *Analysing and deciding*
- Broad-based thinking
- Analytical thinking
- Understanding business
- Objective decision-making

III *Working with people*
- Rational persuasion
- Team-oriented working
- Interpersonal effectiveness
- Flexible management style

As well as a brief definition of each competency there are more specific positive and negative behavioural indicators, for example:

Continuous improvement: constantly seeks and brings about better/improved ways of working in both short and longer term.

Positive indicators
- Seeks advice from others, e.g. team, customers, suppliers, service departments
- Proposals aimed at permanent solution not just quick fix
- Involves team at all stages
- Sees potential for reaching and maintaining higher standards

Contra-indicators
- Proposes short-term solutions without considering long-term consequences
- Fails to consult others or to build on their contributions
- Focuses on only one or two opportunities for improvement
- Does not recognize alternative ways of tackling problems, e.g. special project team, quality circles

Source: Pearn 1992

multiple methods. Third, it is no less essential to draw on multiple sources – at the very least, job incumbents and supervisors, and others (e.g. customers, co-workers) may have a part to play too. Such involvement is important on two grounds. One is that it is consistent with the participative philosophy advocated for performance management. The other is that a participative approach generally is seen as having many process benefits (e.g. Sparrow 1994), such as generating ownership of the behaviours that are identified. Fourth, the examples have not illustrated the analysis of single jobs but, rather, categories or families of jobs.

Many of the case studies that have been published in recent years have been of models of competencies for job families. For example, in Glaxo Manufacturing Services (Pearn 1992) the interest was in three new managerial roles; Shackleton (1992) describes the development of competencies required for the future by partners in an accountancy organization – these models are shown in Tables 5.7 and 5.8. A feature of both these models is an organizational context of change.

Table 5.8	**Competencies for job families in changing environments II: partners in an accountancy practice**

1 *Identifying selling opportunities.* Being alert to and acting on indications of opportunities for expansion of existing business into new areas of the client company and/or diversification into new categories of business.

2 *Understanding the client/colleague in their own terms.* Active listening, clarifying, reflecting back the content and feeling behind statements, avoiding jargon and misinterpretation.

3 *Commercial awareness.* Using questions and statements to indicate an understanding of the totality of the business, i.e. strategy, marketing, competition, etc., as well as its financial structure.

4 *Flexibility.* Modifying own approach or style in order to achieve set goals.

5 *Communicating persuasively and effectively.* Clear and fluent oral communication of ideas with persuasive impact on the listener; clear, concise written communication.

6 *Goal-setting.* Setting realistic targets, quantifiable or behavioural, that are well defined, specific and measurable.

7 *Encouraging and building on ideas.* Assessing ideas objectively and building on them; encouraging (verbally and non-verbally) others to contribute; avoiding irrational criticism.

8 *Giving feedback.* Commenting on both the negative and positive aspects of others' behaviour and performance in a clear, balanced and constructive way.

9 *Delegating.* Effective use of colleagues, knowing when, how and to whom to delegate responsibility.

10 *Leadership.* Ability to guide and direct individuals or groups towards the achievement of objectives; taking the initiative.

11 *Helping groups to achieve consensus.* Looking for common ground; mediating between opposing views; being prepared to compromise on own views (after full discussion) for sake of group

Source: Shackleton 1992: 165–6

Box 5.6	**Implications for practice**

Competences; competencies; dimensions; factors; aspects of performance – the language doesn't matter, but performance management requires attention both to behaviour (what people do) and results (what they are expected to accomplish). A performance management process which places undue emphasis on results is likely to be deficient.

In identifying desired behaviours an empirical approach (using a range of methods and drawing on a range of sources) is preferable to armchair theorizing in the Personnel/Human Resources Department. Try to anticipate behavioural requirements of jobs/roles and the organization as they might be in the future. If future-oriented methods are used as part of the business planning process, draw on these to extrapolate behaviour requirements.

Be explicit about the behavioural dimensions that people will be expected to engage in and on which their performance will be assessed.

A concluding comment

This, and the preceding chapter, have illustrated the ambiguity of the term performance: there is far from unanimous agreement about what it means. Competencies only add to the confusion. In everyday parlance the word performance is used in a loose way to embrace both outputs and behaviours. This is unhelpful from a theoretical point of view because it fails to recognize the causal relationship between behaviours and results; it also fails to recognize that it is not just the contribution of the individual that brings about results. Loose use of the term is also unhelpful because outputs and behaviours may require different kinds of performance management interventions.

The term competencies has come to be widely used in recent years but here again there is enormous confusion. Partly this stems from the existence of another term – competences. Often it is far from clear how the one term or the other is being used in everyday organizational parlance. Sometimes the two terms are simply used as synonyms. However, some attempts have been made to distinguish different meanings. Thus we find that 'competences' is used in two senses, denoting distinctive properties of the organization or job requirements. So far as 'competencies' are concerned, one meaning places emphasis on the personal attributes which underlie behaviour – what people are; a second interpretation concentrates on the clusters of related behaviours – that is, what people do. But if we define competencies in behaviour terms, how, then, does this usage differ significantly from the earlier term 'dimensions'? Indeed, does this behavioural interpretation differ all that much from the conception of performance as behaviour? I'll explore this issue a little more in the next chapter in considering the causes of performance.

6 Individual performance III: Determinants

So, we have two interdependent conceptions of individual performance. We need to embrace both if we are to manage what employees do and achieve at work. Hartle (1995) refers to this as the 'mixed model' approach to performance management, reflecting the importance of both the 'how and what' of performance. We also need to understand the causes or determinants of employee performance as these have implications for performance management interventions. This is far from straightforward and in many respects our present understanding remains decidedly rudimentary.

Early models were vague as to the nature of performance but saw it as a function of the individual's ability and motivation, and this idea remains prominent in contemporary theories. However, recent theories have considerably elaborated the basic proposition. One important illustration of this is the theory of performance put forward by Campbell (Campbell 1990; Campbell *et al.* 1993; Campbell *et al.* 1996) and his colleagues.

A theory of performance as behaviour

We have already seen in Chapter 5 that Campbell defines performance in terms of goal-relevant behaviour and he proposes that this may be categorized into eight main factors or components. But what determines behaviour? In Campbell's view there are three major **determinants**:

1 Declarative knowledge, that is, knowledge about facts and things (knowing *what* to do).

2 Procedural knowledge and skill.
3 Motivation – defined as choice behaviour, that is:
  • the choice to perform (expend effort);
  • choice of level of effort to expend;
  • choice to persist over time in the expenditure of that level of effort.

These determinants are portrayed diagrammatically in Figure 6.1.

So, what is being proposed here is that the *direct* cause of what people do (their performance) is some function of knowledge, skill and motivation. The precise combination is unknown as the effects of personal factors are difficult to disentangle (Viswesvaran and Ones 2000).

Underlying these three determinants are certain **predictors** or **antecedents**. Campbell does not elaborate on these but it is clear that

Figure 6.1	**Determinants of job performance: knowledge, skill and motivation**

$$PC_i^a = f \left[\begin{array}{ccc} \text{Declarative} \\ \text{Knowledge (DK)} \times \end{array} \quad \begin{array}{c} \text{Procedural Knowledge} \\ \text{and Skill (PKS)} \quad \times \end{array} \quad \text{Motivation (M)} \right]$$

Declarative Knowledge (DK)	Procedural Knowledge and Skill (PKS)	Motivation (M)
Facts	Cognitive skill	Choice to perform
Principles	Psychomotor skill	Level of effort
Goals	Physical skill	Persistence of effort
Self-knowledge	Self-management skill	
	Interpersonal skill	

$i = 1,2, \ldots , k$ performance components

Predictors of Performance Determinants[b]

$DK = f$ [(ability, personality, interests), (education, training, experience), (aptitude/treatment interactions)]

$PKS = f$ [(ability, personality, interests), (education, training, practice, experience), (aptitude/treatment interactions)]

$M = f$ (whatever independent variables are stipulated by your favourite motivation theory)

Note: This entire scheme can be repeated for educational performance, training performance and laboratory task performance.
[a] Obviously, performance differences can also be produced by situational effects such as the quality of equipment, degree of staff support or nature of the working conditions. For purposes of this model of performance, these conditionals are assumed to be held constant (experimentally, statistically or judgementally).
[b] Individual differences, learning and motivational manipulations can only influence performance by increasing declarative knowledge or procedural skill or by influencing the three choices (that is, influencing motivation).
Source: Campbell *et al.* 1993

he is referring to three distinct sets of antecedent – attributes of the individual, their prior learning experience and interactions between the two. In other words, the knowledge and skill that employees have are a function of factors that are internal to the person (their abilities and traits, etc.) and of factors external to them, such as their education, the training they have received, etc. These antecedent factors thus are seen as having an **indirect** influence on performance (behaviour). Aspects of the work context also come into this category of indirect factors, as I shall come on to discuss in a moment.

Individual differences as antecedents

The role of individual difference variables in relation to performance remains controversial in some respects. Though there is some agreement (Eysenck 1994; Cooper and Robertson 1995) that intelligence and personality are the two main domains of individual difference that are of most interest to psychologists, there is considerable disagreement as to the nature and scope of the two terms.

Intelligence

What is intelligence? Cognitive ability – such as reasoning – remains at the heart of many theories but some writers have put forward wider-ranging models; Gardner (1983), for example, has proposed a theory of multiple intelligence which includes, as well as more traditional ideas, such notions as musical intelligence and interpersonal intelligence. Moreover, as Sternberg (1990) has shown, the lay person also sees an element of social competence in intelligence. Such broadening is reflected in some of the more modern theories through ideas like **practical intelligence** (which emphasizes competence; Sternberg and Wagner 1986) and **tacit knowledge** (e.g., Sternberg 1994; Sternberg *et al.* 2000) – in terms of Campbell's model, of course, both of these concepts would be seen as determinants rather than antecedents. Also, in recent years interest has developed in such aspects of intellectual functioning as cognitive style (e.g., Streufert and Nogami 1989; Warr and Conner 1992), and we have seen the label 'emotional intelligence' applied to a constellation of personality and other characteristics: all this blurs the distinction between personality and intelligence. However, for the most part these newer ideas about cognitive abilities have yet to have much impact in practice. The long-standing **factor theories** of general mental ability and more specific abilities continue to dominate.

We have evidence that ability tests (when properly constructed, chosen and used) do predict job performance (as measured using a range of indicators) across a wide range of jobs (see Cooper and Robertson 1995 for a brief review). What remains a matter of dispute is *why* such tests predict. One explanation (e.g. Anderson 1992) contends that what intelligence tests measure is the speed with which individuals process information. Though theoretically interesting, this notion does not take us very far as, for practical purposes, we don't really have direct measures of information processing. At best, therefore, conventional tests are some proxy measure of underlying processing capability. Indeed, many tests of very specific abilities are in effect measures of declarative or procedural knowledge (skill). If, for example, we consider the sorts of paper and pencil test that may be used in clerical selection then we find tests of spelling, grammar, arithmetic, etc. In other words, with these sorts of tests we measure what people know and their knowledge of how to do things.

Personality

Still more controversial is the nature of personality. One of the problems here is that there are many conceptions of personality, although, as with intelligence, in work settings it is the factor or **trait** conception which predominates. So, if we go to a test publisher wanting to buy a personality questionnaire the likelihood is that we will be offered something that measures traits. But this concept is itself controversial. What exactly is a trait? How broadly is the concept to be defined? How many traits do we need to be able to describe personality? Are traits simply descriptions or do they have explanatory value as well? These issues continue to rage (for recent reviews, see Hogan 1991; Mount and Barrick 1995; Schneider and Hough 1995; Hough and Schneider 1996).

For example, some (e.g., Digman 1990; Goldberg 1993) claim that there is today a general consensus that the structure of personality may be described in terms of five factors:

- neuroticism (emotional stability) – emotional, tense, insecure, nervous, easily upset (at the negative end of the factor);

- extraversion – sociable, talkative, energetic;
- openness to experience – imaginative, curious;
- agreeableness – good-natured, co-operative, caring, courteous;
- conscientiousness (sometimes referred to as **will to achieve** or **dependability**) – hardworking, achievement-oriented, persevering, planful, responsible, careful.

The adequacy of the five-factor model (FFM) is a matter of some dispute and some authorities (e.g., Hough and Schneider 1996) have argued for different classification schemes with a slightly larger number of factors. For present purposes, however, I will use the FFM to illustrate something of the demonstrated relationships between personality and performance. To take just one example, various studies (Mount and Barrick 1995; Schneider and Hough 1995) have shown an association between measures of **conscientiousness** and different indicators of job performance, such as employee reliability, personal discipline and effort. The conscientiousness factor is of particular interest because it is linked with motivational determinants of performance. In the same way that the boundaries between the intelligence and personality domains have become blurred, so too have those between personality and motives. If we take a broad view of personality as comprising dispositional characteristics generally, then motives (such as the need for achievement, goal-orientation, the need for power, etc.) and other attributes such as values, interests, self-efficacy, etc. fall within this domain.

For the most part the interest in personality–performance relationships continues to fall within the selection area; in other words, the interest is in using measures of personality to predict job performance. This has had rather a chequered history. Numerous reviews (e.g., Guion and Gottier 1965; Adler and Weiss 1988) drew somewhat unoptimistic conclusions about personality–performance relationships. In the 1990s, however, several studies have appeared which take a more positive line and today there is considerable advocacy of a construct-oriented approach (e.g., Schneider and Hough 1995; Robertson 1994):

> when investigators carefully conceptualize the role of personality vis-à-vis the criterion domain(s) of interest, when they select appropriate, construct valid measures based on a job analysis, or when they

systematically develop new measures built around a construct model of effectiveness, personality attributes are found to be relevant and potent predictors.

(Klimoski 1993: 112–13)

Examples of new work-related measures that have been developed in recent years include 'integrity' or 'honesty' tests (Ones *et al.* 1993) and 'customer service orientation' (see Schneider and Hough 1995). Such tests measure 'compound personality variables' (Hough and Schneider 1996) – that is, contructs that have been synthesized from some combination of personality traits that are believed to predict the work-related criterion of interest. Courtesy, helpfulness, co-operativeness and pleasantness, for example, all are qualities that we might wish to measure in assessing service orientation.

As well as measures of such trait syndromes, research shows that certain aspects of performance (for example such behaviours as demonstrating effort and contextual performance) may be susceptible to prediction by questionnaire measures of personality traits, con-scientiousness in particular (Viswesvaran and Ones 2000). But even when a construct-related approach is taken, the magnitude of the association (as indicated by correlation coefficients) between personality measures and performance indicators remains of a modest order (e.g., Robertson and Kinder 1993; Schneider and Hough 1995). In part, this may be because of deficiencies in our measures – both personality questionnaires and the independent criterion measures (such as a line manager's ratings). And, as with intelligence, there is the question of what is actually being measured. Many personality questionnaires use behavioural statements as their items – to this extent, therefore, we are merely using one representation of behaviour to predict actual behaviour in the workplace.

The problem of competencies

The problem, which stems from the ambiguity of the concept, has to do with where, if at all, competencies fit within a theory of performance. If we take a behavioural view, like Woodruffe's (1992), then the fit is apparently straightforward: competencies are job-relevant behaviours and as such they seem to be no different from Campbell's conception of performance, that is: performance ≡ behaviour ≡ competencies. Yet, as we saw in the previous chapter, there are reasons for questioning the behavioural view – not least of which is that the definitions of many competencies imply much more than behaviours.

The Spencer and Spencer (1993) and Warr and Conner (1992) definitions, on the other hand, do see a place for personal characteristics. This is illustrated by the flow diagram (from Spencer and Spencer 1993) shown in Figure 6.2. This model doesn't distinguish between antecedents (predictors) and determinants in the way that Campbell does. Rather, personal characteristics generally are seen as direct predictors of behaviour, the one exception to this being skill, which seems to be regarded as synonymous with behaviour in the McBer model. All this reinforces the indistinct nature of competencies. We might take the view that it may be helpful to see competencies as a middle-order variable of some kind – that is, as clusters of behaviours

Figure 6.2	**Competency causal flow model**

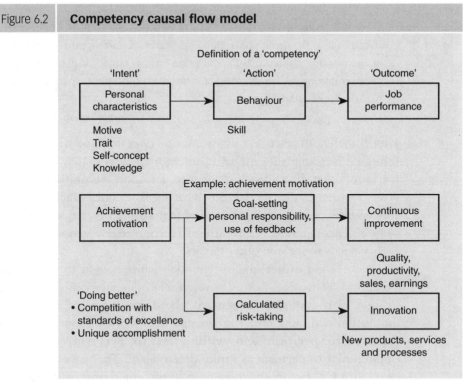

Source: Spencer and Spencer 1993

signifying some syndrome of personal characteristics (rather like the compound traits mentioned earlier, but embracing a wider range of attributes) that are required to achieve some defined level of output. But do we really need this extra term, especially when our lexicon of person- and behaviour-related terms is already more than replete?

Irrespective of this issue of where (if at all) competencies fit within a theory of performance, it remains the case that the person-centered explanations are deficient because they pay insufficient attention to factors outside the person, that is **system** or **contextual** factors. These too have an influence on what people accomplish and on how they behave.

Job context as a determinant of performance

Campbell's model (Figure 6.1) makes just a small reference to contextual factors:

> Obviously, performance differences can also be produced by situational effects such as the quality of equipment, degree of staff support, or nature of the working conditions. For purposes of this model of performance, these conditionals are assumed to be held constant (experimentally, statistically, or judgmentally).
>
> *(Campbell* et al. *1993: 43)*

Unfortunately, in practice, this assumption does not hold true. Valuable though it is, Campbell's model is not enough even to fully describe all the factors that determine performance, let alone explain them. This is not to criticize the model for what it is – one which explicitly concentrates on the individual level of analysis and which does not claim to be all-encompassing – but rather to recognize that a more complete theory needs to include other factors.

As one might expect, the early models which sought to incorporate situational/contextual factors were rather rudimentary. Blumberg and Pringle, for example, recognized the importance of ability and motivation (although rather broadened their scope by using the terms **capacity to perform** and **willingness to perform**) but added **opportunity to perform** as a third determinant. They gave as examples of opportunity factors the following: 'tools, equipment, materials, and supplies; working conditions; actions of coworkers; leader behaviour;

mentorism; organizational policies, rules, and procedures; information; time; pay' (1982: 562). They saw such factors as either **enabling** or **constraining**. In similar vein, Guzzo and Gannett (1988) write of facilitators (driving performance towards the maximally attainable level) and inhibitors (restricting performance towards the minimally acceptable level).

Two models of employee work performance which incorporate person and situational factors are those of Cardy and Dobbins (1994) and Waldman (1994). The Cardy and Dobbins model is of particular interest because it seeks to incorporate both the output view of performance and the behavioural one. However, it does not capture interactions among the various determinants; these are better brought out by Waldman, who takes a behavioural view of performance and draws on total quality management ideas.

Whereas Waldman adopts a behavioural definition of performance, Cardy and Dobbins distinguish between what the worker accomplishes, produces or delivers (referred to as **work outcomes**) and job-relevant behaviours, seeing these as two categories of performance – the distinction drawn in the two previous chapters, in other words. Work outcomes are seen as being *jointly* determined by system factors and job-relevant behaviours – the relationship of person factors to work outcomes is not direct, in other words, but operates via job-relevant behaviours. These relationships are shown diagrammatically in Figure 6.3, which derives from the models presented by Campbell *et al.* (1993, 1996), Cardy and Dobbins (1994) and Waldman (1994).

Person factors

Though Cardy and Dobbins see person factors as having a direct effect on job-relevant behaviours, Campbell, as indicated above, takes a two-tier approach to the treatment of person factors – knowledge, skill and motivation are seen as the direct determinants of job-relevant behaviour, and other characteristics of the person (such as personality traits) are seen as underlying antecedents of those determinants. The importance of person factors for performance management lies in the fact that they are what employees bring to the job and they may be capable of being enhanced or inhibited.

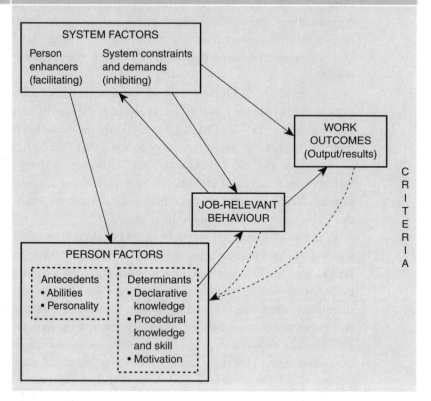

Figure 6.3 | **Determinants of job performance: person and system factors**

Source: adapted from Campbell *et al.* 1993; Cardy and Dobbins 1994; Waldman 1994

System factors

What are system factors? Contemporary literature (e.g., Waldman 1994) takes a broad view of what is meant by system factors, regarding them as existing at 'multiple levels within an organization' (Waldman 1994: 517) – system-wide, department, work unit, team, etc. But as with the performance construct, mapping the domain or boundaries of system factors remains a difficulty. Schneider and Hough (1995) note this in offering what they refer to as an 'heuristic catalogue' of situational factors, which they do not claim to be comprehensive, but which clearly illustrates that the domain of system factors is very broad. An abbreviated version of their list (showing only extra-individual factors) is given in Table 6.1. Taken together, system factors comprise the 'performance environment' (Cummings and Schwab 1973).

What influence do system factors have? Though some research (e.g., Peters and O'Connor 1980) has focused on the constraining effect that system factors may have, the prevailing view today (e.g., Guzzo and Gannett 1988; Waldman 1994) recognizes that there may be either facilitating/enhancing/enabling effects or inhibiting ones. Thus, following Waldman, the category of system factors includes **person enhancers** and **system constraints and demands**.

Constraining and inhibiting factors

Under this heading we have 'characteristics of technological and work processes, as well as organizational policies, structure, and culture' (Waldman 1994: 523). More specific examples of factors identified as constraints would include those investigated by Peters and O'Connor (1980) for example, such as tools and equipment, time availability, and the work environment. Evidence pertaining to certain of the last of these has been reviewed by Baron (1994). Many of the findings are unsurprising. For example, conditions that are too noisy, too hot or too cold have been shown to have deleterious effects; level of illumination, air quality and crowding are examples of other such environmental factors. Baron sees these factors as having an indirect effect on performance (and other outcomes, such as work attitudes). Environmental factors are presented as having their impact 'on a wide range of mediating mechanisms and processes occurring within individuals' (Baron 1994: 34). Summarizing Kane (1993), Bacharach and Bamberger note that 'constraints may have a negative impact on the performance of particular job functions by making it more difficult for individuals to take maximum advantage of their job-related knowledge, skills and abilities, and by reducing their overall level of task effort' (1995: 80).

The idea that aspects of the situation may have a constraining effect on aspects of the person is far from new. Mischel (1977), for example, argued that 'strong' situations have a constraining effect in that they inhibit the expression of individual differences – in other words, in 'strong' situations people tend to behave in a similar way regardless of their different personalities or a particular individual will behave in a required way because the situation demands it rather than because it is

Table 6.1	**Potential situational (or system) factors**

Task characteristics
- Consistency of task
- Stage of skill acquisition with respect to task
- Amount of task structure
- Time on task
- Amount of time pressure to complete task
- Skill variety, task identity, task significance, autonomy and feedback

Goal characteristics
- Specificity
- Complexity
- Difficulty
- Rewards associated with goal attainment
- Conflict with other goals
- Performance versus mastery goal

Characteristics of physical environment
- Ambient conditions (e.g. light, noise, heat)
- Time of day
- Danger of bodily harm
- Workplace layout (e.g. open-plan office versus non-open-plan office; amount of privacy at workstation)
- Work locus (home versus office)

Characteristics of work role
- Role ambiguity
- Role overload
- Role conflict

Characteristics of social environment
- Personality of co-workers (supervisors, subordinates and peers)
- Management style of immediate supervisor (e.g. autocratic versus democratic)
- Cohesiveness of work group
- Amount of social support from co-workers, friends and family
- Work primarily in groups versus work primarily independently

Characteristics of organization
- Organizational values
- Organizational reward systems
- Level of employee ownership in organization
- Amount of organizational instability (e.g. rapid changes in leadership, downsizing, growth)
- Nature of administrative policies and procedures (e.g. level of bureaucracy)
- Organizational structure (e.g. matrix versus hierarchical)

Source: abbreviated from Schneider and Hough 1995: 119

his or her 'natural' predisposition. More recently, Adler (1996) has taken up this theme in his exploration of the linkages amongst personality and work behaviour, and he points out the 'complex mutual influence of personality and situations'.

Facilitating and enhancing factors

Waldman refers to certain system factors as 'person enhancers' which 'affect performance indirectly by first influencing aspects of the individual. ... Person enhancers are proposed to involve aspects of HR systems, leadership processes, and job design that may develop and motivate individuals' (1994: 519). Campbell *et al.* take a similar view and regard system factors as antecedents which have an indirect effect on performance (behaviour) by first changing the employee's declarative knowledge, procedural knowledge and skill, and/or motivation. In other words, person enhancers may have multiple effects – that is, they simultaneously affect several person factors. For example, goals, goal-setting and feedback have motivational and informational (that is, knowledge-related) effects.

Various narrative (e.g., Kopelman 1986) and meta-analytic reviews are helpful to us in identifying interventions which may have enabling effects. Of particular interest is the work of Guzzo and his colleagues (Katzell and Guzzo 1983; Guzzo *et al.* 1985; Guzzo 1988). This examined the impact of various behavioural science/human resource interventions on performance (variously defined) and identified the following as generally having positive effects: training, socio-technical interventions, goal-setting, work redesign, supervisory methods, and appraisal and feedback. Certain of those listed – particularly goal setting and feedback – remain very much at the heart of employee-centred approaches to performance management, and these have been the subject of more recent meta-analyses and other reviews. The benefits of goal-setting, for example, were summarized in Chapter 4, where it was noted that feedback is necessary also. Some (e.g., Rodgers and Hunter 1991) argue the case for participation: in their view, both theory and research evidence support the positive productivity effects of all three activities.

Though a role for employee participation has been much advocated in the performance management literature, the evidence for its performance enhancing effects is a matter of some debate. An important meta-analytic review by Wagner (1994) concluded that participation does have positive effects on performance (and satisfaction) but suggested that the magnitude of these effects was so slight as to be of limited practical significance. However, Ledford and Lawler (1994) noted the narrowness of Wagner's definition of participation and argued that negligible positive effects were an inevitable consequence: 'Limited participation has limited effects'. Elsewhere, Lawler (e.g., 1991) has advocated a broader conceptualization of participation as 'high involvement' – essentially a pervasive organization-wide strategy. Also, a later meta-analytic review of participation in the context of performance appraisal (Cawley, Keeping and Levy 1998) concluded that participation (of various kinds) is positively associated with a range of performance appraisal outcomes.

The thorough meta-analytic review of feedback interventions by Kluger and DeNisi (1996) supported the linkage as between goals and feedback. More generally, they found that feedback does improve performance but they also found considerable variation to the extent that reduced performance may also result. The earlier quote from Kanfer (1995) referred to the possibly deleterious effects of feedback – in other words, feedback may be constructive or destructive (Baron 1988; London 1995, 1997), a facilitator or an inhibitor. I shall have more to say about feedback in the next chapter.

In similar vein, the effects of financial rewards (performance related pay is a key element in performance management in many organizations) are not uniformly positive. This was noted in the meta-analytic review by Guzzo et al. (1985): of all the work psychology-based interventions they examined this was the one where they found the greatest variability in effects. And in a later review Heneman (1992) concludes, 'The results to date on the relationship between merit pay and subsequent motivation and performance are not encouraging'. This may be because particular systems that have been implemented may have been poorly designed and operated in practice. However, it may be that performance-related pay (PRP) fails because it does not meet the requirements that psychological theory (e.g., expectancy theory) suggests – in other words, at least some applications of PRP will have been doomed from the outset. I shall return to this theme in Chapter 8.

Even at its most basic performance management isn't a single intervention. Though we know a certain amount about the effect on performance of single interventions, this only takes us so far as interventions interact with one another (DeNisi 2000). But we know relatively little about the impact of interventions in combination; interrelationships amongst them remain poorly understood. Moreover, the relationship between individual and higher levels of performance also is complex: as DeNisi notes, there is much more to be learned about 'the processes that link individual-level practices to firm-level practices' (2000: 137).

That said, according to Guzzo and Gannett (1988) there is at least suggestive evidence that the use of multiple interventions has positive impact over and above that achieved by single interventions. We naturally would hope that this would be the case: given the multiplicity of influences on organizational performance it is likely that any one intervention will have only limited positive impact (although even this is a presumption). It remains the case that there is little research on the effect of multiple interventions although the recent literature on 'high performance' or 'best practice' human resource management systems is of some relevance here.

Some studies have examined the impact of particular sets of HR practices and positive associations have been found with various measures (objective and perceptual) of organizational performance (DeNisi 2000; Ostroff and Bowen 2000). However a difficulty here is that there's little agreement as to the so-called 'best practice' practices. For example, Becker and Gerhart (1996) note that there is disagreement about variable pay and internal promotions – included in some lists but not in others. Also, as was noted earlier in the discussion of the association between culture and performance, there are many methodological difficulties with this body of research in general (discussed by Marchington and Grugulis 2000). For example, various measures of organizational performance have been used and such research tends to ignore aspects of organizational context, such as strategy, which some research suggests is important (Ostroff and Bowen 2000). A contingency approach may therefore be preferable (Ostroff and Bowen 2000; Schneider, Smith and Sipe 2000). This provides a counter-balance to the one-best-way implication of the 'best practice' idea: unfortunately, however, interrelationships amongst contingency factors (such as strategy), HR practices, and the several indicators of organizational performance remain poorly understood.

That there is evidence of a positive association between a range of human resource management practices and measures (objective and perceptual) of organizational performance is an encouraging finding, although it needs to be regarded with some caution because of the reasons given above. Also, the findings to date are of only limited assistance to practitioners. From the point of view of performance management, however, they bring with them the implication that a narrow set of interventions focused on the individual will have only limited impact (and it should be borne in mind that practices do not always operate in the way intended). Though an organization might choose to see a particular set of core activities as comprising performance management, it is important to take a systems perspective (DeNisi 2000) and recognize that these core activities not only interact with each other, but also with other HR activities and with various of the system factors that comprise the performance environment.

Direct or indirect effects

Thus far system factors have been presented as having indirect effects on work behaviour, that is, person factors are seen as mediators – constraints and facilitators alike are seen as operating in this way. However, the way in which constraints operate remains a matter of some debate. On the one hand, Campbell *et al.* (1993) take the view that constraints have an indirect effect on work behaviour – they influence motivation first. Against this, Guzzo and Gannett contend that inhibitors may also have direct effects: 'Barriers to performance such as shortages of tools and too little time can make it physically impossible to complete tasks effectively' (1988: 38). So, individuals may have the motivation and the requisite knowledge and skill, but are constrained by some aspect of the work system from doing what is expected of them – as when rain stops play, for example.

When we turn to the work system perspective on performance we also find the argument that system factors may have a more direct effect. Thus, we find claims (in particular in certain of the early quality management literature) that system factors account for as much as 95 per cent of the variation in work output. Yet, as various commentators (e.g., Cardy 1998; Masterson and Taylor 1996) note, there is little hard evidence to support these claims; rather, they are more of an assumption than an established fact (Cardy and Dobbins 1994). Though we might wish to dispute how much of work output is attributable to system factors as compared to employees' behaviour there is no doubting the direct effect of the former, and Hesketh and Neal (1999) recently have argued that technology (broadly defined) 'can be both a determinant and an antecedent of performance'. For example, the quality of output produced by tool-makers will partly be a function of the machines in use, not just the facility with which it is operated by the worker. And in sales jobs the number of units sold will be subject to the influence of buyer behaviour, the price and other attributes of what is being sold, etc. All this, of course, merely echoes the arguments put forward earlier for not regarding output as performance.

Distinct entities or opposites

Another matter of some dispute is whether facilitators and inhibitors should be regarded as distinct entities or as opposites. If we take the **'opposites'** perspective, a deficit in a system factor would be seen as a constraint, whereas sufficient presence of the same factor would be taken as facilitating. Guzzo and Gannett (1988) prefer the **'distinct entities'** perspective. So, for example, the absence of needed tools is likely to be a constraint, restricting performance towards the minimally acceptable level. But having the required tools doesn't guarantee maximum performance – this is still dependent on the worker's knowledge, skill and motivation. Facilitators, on the other hand, are those situational factors which enhance performance.

But this issue is far from resolved. Surely it is possible for certain system factors, albeit manifested in different ways, to have both facilitating and constraining effects? Job design and supervisory behaviour are two illustrations. As I will discuss in Chapter 7, there are supervisory behaviours which are supportive and performance-enhancing in their effect. But then there are other behaviours which may be damaging in their effect; as noted already, for example, negative feedback. Thus, the distinction between enhancing and constraining factors may not be so clear cut as it is sometimes presented. Moreover, the impact of system factors on person factors (and vice versa) is further complicated by interactions between them.

Person–system interaction

Earlier I gave examples of how system factors impinge upon aspects of the person and so affect their performance. But, of course, so far as work systems are concerned employees aren't passive recipients who will invariably respond in the way that management wishes. People have different values, motives, etc. and so they do not respond in the same way to a given system. A line manager with half a dozen staff may find that some prefer and respond positively to her participative management style. But others, because of their particular dispositions, find this threatening and would rather have a more directive approach – this is their idea of strong leadership.

However, not only can the system affect the person, but the person can affect the system. This is partly a matter of perception. For example, though system factors sometimes are seen as constraints (whether direct or indirect in their effect) it is possible, suggest Guzzo and Gannett, for them to be seen as 'a challenge', that is as 'an obstacle to be overcome' (1988: 38). This, then, points to the element of choice which may be found within jobs. Stewart draws attention to this in the context of managerial jobs (and certain others) in her identification of demands, constraints and choices: 'there is a core of work, **demands**, that anyone in the job will have to do; these demands are the tasks that cannot be ignored or delegated if the job holder is to survive in the job' (1991: 14). Constraints 'are the factors that limit what the job holder can do: they include resource limitations and people's attitudes' (1991: 15). Choices are the areas of opportunity within a job – what the manager decides she or he will do.

To some extent all three aspects of managerial jobs are partly a matter of perception – managers need to perceive themselves as having choice over what they do. In the same vein, Stewart refers to job holders 'exaggerating the work that they must do' (demands) and 'exaggerating the constraints' (1991: 14), both of which may be forms of impression management (Rosenfeld *et al.* 1995). But the scope for individual performers to influence their job varies also according to its design, in particular according to the extent of autonomy allowed. Waldman (1994) sees this, and hierarchical level, as factors moderating the relationship between person and system factors. Thus, managerial jobs, for example, are likely to offer greater scope for the incumbent to decide how to go about the job and, quite possibly, for deciding what the job is.

Moreover, those at the higher levels are able to influence not only the nature of their own jobs but also the design of other jobs within the work system. Though system factors may have a direct impact on the behaviour and output of those working within the system, the system itself is a product of managerial choices and decisions. It is for this reason that Deming (1986) and others see managers as having the responsibility for improving work systems so as to remove performance problems. This seems to be an implicit recognition of the importance of person factors over system factors, at least for certain jobs.

In view of the reciprocal relationship between system and person factors we might suppose that the 'person factors' and 'system factors' boxes in Figure 6.3 ought to be connected. Though system factors have a direct impact on person factors, the effect of the latter on the former is indirect in that it operates through behaviour.

The idea of reciprocal and interacting influences was mentioned earlier in this chapter and it is a theme which is found throughout the literature (e.g., Schneider 1987; Davis-Blake and Pfeffer 1989; Chatman 1989; Edwards 1991). Over and above the examples already mentioned, Kanfer notes:

> motivation and performance exert reciprocal influences on one another. Not only does motivation affect performance, but performance can affect motivation. Knowledge of how one has performed or is progressing on a task may weaken or strengthen subsequent task motivation depending on performance level, attributions about the cause of performance, and motivational conditions.

> *(Kanfer 1995: 337)*

Kanfer is referring here to the place of feedback in employee performance. Though this is a system factor I've included (in Figure 6.3) feedback loops leading from outcomes and behaviours to person factors so as to make more explicit the importance of this factor.

Person *and* system

There is no doubt that both person *and* system factors influence work behaviours and outputs. For example, if we consider a counter-productive behaviour such as absence we find research has shown that personal factors (including the individual's circumstances) are one contributory determinant, but organizational culture and policies for managing absence also are important. What is far from clear is how much of the variation in performance (whether defined as outputs or job behaviours) is attributable to one set or the other. If we subscribe to Deming's (1986) thinking our position would be that most workers (certainly those on the shop floor, that is, the direct producers or service deliverers) within an organization function or operate at about the same level and that variation in what they produce is mostly accounted for by system factors that are outside the individual's control. However, this hasn't been confirmed empirically (Cardy and Dobbins 1994). Moreover, some (e.g., Stone and Eddy 1996) have argued that system accounts of performance have underestimated the importance of person factors, almost (others have argued – e.g. Masterson and Taylor 1996) to the point of ignoring the role of the individual. As noted earlier, employees are not passive within the work system – they react (positively or negatively) to the ways in which they are treated.

Very often many system factors will be seen as fixed (and may in reality be so) and outside the control of individual performers or their line manager, and as such they may be regarded as being outside the boundaries of a performance management system. For example, once a work system has been designed it may well be difficult to change, and in consequence it may have to be taken as given. Equipment may be difficult to replace or modify. And there are invariably resource limitations of one sort or another. However, some of the more encompassing models of performance management recognize the constraining and facilitating implications of system factors. For example, Rummler and Brache (1995) refer to **job management**, which they describe as managing the **human performance system**; this is illustrated in Figure 6.4. They use the term human performance system so as to emphasize the context within which the employee performs, arguing that managers have a 'tendency to overmanage individuals and undermanage the environment in which they work' (1995: 24).

Rummler and Brache assert that, in their experience, '*about 80 percent of performance improvement opportunities reside in the environment*' (1995: 73; italics in original). As noted above, such claims have been challenged given the absence of confirmatory evidence. What seems most likely is that the extent of variation attributable to system/person factors varies from job to job (Cardy and Dobbins 1994). Key factors here would seem to be hierarchical level and the amount of autonomy that is allowed by the job (Waldman 1994). At higher levels and in jobs offering greater autonomy person factors may actually be more important than aspects of the system.

Figure 6.4 | **Factors affecting the human performance system**

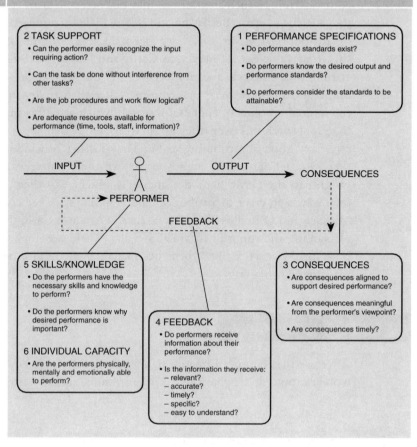

Source: Rummler and Brache 1995

Attributing cause

If we accept that job behaviour and output are caused by system and person factors we next must ask whether those different causes are actually recognized by line managers? An answer to this question might be obtained by considering how managers explain the performance of their staff. A common finding is that managers attribute the causes of performance to internal factors, that is, characteristics of the performer: this is particularly so in the case of poor performance. Job holders, on the other hand, are more likely to attribute such performance to external factors – aspects of the system outside themselves and their control. Though such attributions may be correct, it also is possible that they may be in error. Bernardin and Beatty (1984) summarize a number of attributional errors that have been discussed in the literature, as shown in Table 6.2. However, as Cardy and Dobbins (1994) note, the attributional research does not answer the question because it focuses on actors' and observers' perceptions rather than reality. In reviewing the limited amount of appraisal research which attempts more directly to grapple with this issue, they go on to conclude that appraisers are not especially good at attributing cause. They further conclude that where there are deficiencies in employee performance it appears that undue weight, to the performer's detriment, is attached to them. This in its own way is an error of attribution and is in line with the conclusion of Mitchell and O'Reilly that '*when errors occur* they occur in the direction of blaming the subordinate' (1983: 168). There are implications here both for the practice of performance management and for performance management training.

A concluding comment

If we use the term performance in a loose way it clearly embraces both work outputs and behaviours. Organizations are interested in both.

Table 6.2	**Attributional factors in assessing performance**

1 Raters may underestimate the importance of situational factors and overestimate ratee factors as causes of behaviour.
2 Raters and ratees may differ in their causal attributions, with ratees emphasizing situational factors and raters using ratee factors.
3 Raters may attribute causes to the most salient features of the environment, including novel or unique ratees.
4 Raters may tend to weight ratee behaviours that have affective consequences for the raters themselves more heavily than other behaviours, especially if these affective consequences are serious.
5 Ratees may be held more responsible for behaviour that leads to reward than for behaviour that prevents losses.
6 Attributions may be related to affective relationships. If raters like ratees, they may attribute good actions to them and bad actions to circumstances. If they dislike ratees, they may follow the reverse pattern.

Box 6.1	**Implications for practice**

Performance, whether defined in behavioural or output terms, has many determinants. Some rest within the person; others are part of the broader work system or performance environment.

Remember also that core performance management activities exist as part of a wider system having other elements – these interact and are interdependent. Ideally, they should work together in a coherent and consistent way. As part of the design and implementation process have regard for system interdependencies. Monitor, review and revise.

Remember that the performance environment contains many system factors – including the design and organization of the production/service delivery system: don't underestimate the complexity of performance management therefore. System factors may have a direct effect on production; they may also have an effect on people. In designing work procedures/structures, adopting technology, etc. pay regard to the human implications.

Other elements of the performance environment are intended to have their effects directly on people. These include HR/Personnel processes. The core of employee performance management will be some mechanism(s) for expressing performance requirements/expectations and for reviewing, developing and rewarding performance. Have modest expectations of any single intervention: interventions in combination may have greater benefit, but not necessarily more than the sum of the parts – beware of system inconsistencies. Expect employee performance to be enhanced but have regard for possible constraining effects as part of the design and implementation process. Remember, too, that systems and processes don't always operate as intended: they need to be monitored, reviewed and revised as appropriate.

Indeed, organizations also are interested in individuals' inputs – the personal attributes that they bring to a job. But it is equally clear that it is unhelpful, both theoretically and practically, to use the single term 'performance' to apply to outputs, behaviours and inputs. From a theoretical point of view, using the term as a catch-all does nothing to help us to understand the nature of performance and its causes. It is also clear that performance, whether defined as outputs or behaviours, is multiply determined.

Why do all of these theoretical issues matter for performance management? Because there are a number of implications for practice. For example, a range of interventions is needed to manage performance. Performance management is far from telling people what they have got to do. Providing direction is important of course, and from this point of view some performance management activity must be employee-focused. But as system factors have an impact on job behaviours and outputs, the context of individuals' jobs must be explicitly recognized and managed. Many of the models (especially the employee-centred ones) are largely silent on the need to manage system factors. One implication of this is that managers are likely to need training so as to focus attention on both system and person factors when work is planned and when performance is measured and reviewed. Also, for any job we would expect to see a range of criteria in use, quite possibly both output and behavioural measures. And this may mean that no single system will suit the whole of an organization. There seems to be some recognition of this in organizational practices, as evidenced by the greater prevalence of performance management systems for managerial staff and the rather different nature of those systems as compared to ones applying to those working on the shop floor.

7 Reviewing and supporting performance

When we talk about performance it is clear that in a loose way we refer to two very different things – behaviour and output/results. They necessitate different means of expressing requirements, that is, different performance criteria to serve as the basis for reviewing employee performance. Such review, an essential element in performance management, requires some sort of performance measurement, or at least the monitoring of performance, and feedback to the job holder: we commonly associate this with annual appraisal. That such review might happen only once a year under formal appraisal is, of course, one of the main criticisms of typical appraisal schemes. Within performance management, by contrast, it is advocated that review and the provision of feedback should happen much more frequently. Consequently I will pay more attention to these aspects of review and feedback than to formal appraisal, especially as the latter is dealt with in many other texts (e.g., Fletcher 1993; Fletcher and Williams 1992; Murphy and Cleveland 1995).

Though feedback may be self-generated (by the job holder) or come from peers, the line manager is commonly seen as having a key role to play. Likewise, the line manager is seen as an important agent for providing support for the job holder. This may be direct, through such activities as coaching, or indirect, via other resources that may be within the manager's control. Support for this broad view of the role of the line manager in reviewing performance and providing feedback (and providing reward – see Chapter 8) comes readily from a consideration of the research on management and managerial behaviour.

The role of the line manager

There are many models which tell us about the nature of the manager's job. For example, in the UK we have the MCI National Standards. These see the central purpose of management jobs as being 'To achieve the organization's objectives and to continuously improve its performance' (Management Charter Initiative 1990b: 14) – in other words, the function of the manager's job is seen in terms of performance management, albeit at the organizational level. The National Standards define the manager's job in terms of seven key roles: managing activities, resources, people, information, energy, quality and projects. For each of the roles a number of units and elements of competence are identified, some illustrations of which are provided in Table 7.1. In turn, for each element there are a number of performance criteria, as shown in Table 7.2. Taken together these two tables show clearly that performance management is a core feature of the MCI model of the manager's role. The National Standards also specify as a unit of competence managers' responsibility for the enhancement of their own performance, a responsibility that all employees have.

A more behavioural than functional view is found in Yukl's (1994) taxonomy of managerial practices (Table 7.3). Not surprisingly, many of these practices are directly relevant to the management of employee

Table 7.1	**Units and elements of management competence**	
	Unit	Element
	Maintain and improve service and product operations	Create and maintain the necessary conditions for productive work
	Plan, allocate and evaluate work carried out by teams, individuals and self	Set and update work objectives for teams and individuals
		Provide feedback to teams and individuals on their performance
	Create, maintain and enhance effective working relationships	Establish and maintain the trust and support of one's subordinates
		Counsel staff

Source: abbreviated from Management Charter Initiative 1990b: iii

Table 7.2	**Performance criteria for elements of job competence**

Key Role   **Manage People**
Unit   **Develop teams, individuals and self to enhance performance**

Element   **Identify, review and improve development activities for individuals**

Performance Criteria
- Development objectives and activities are based on a balanced assessment of current competence, potential future competence and career aspirations are in line with current and anticipated team/organizational requirements.
- Individuals are encouraged and assisted to evaluate their own learning and development needs and to contribute to the discussion, planning and review of development.
- Plans contain clear, relevant and realistic development objectives and details of supporting development activities.
- Development activities optimize the use of available resources.
- Plans are reviewed, updated and improved at regular intervals after discussion and agreement with the appropriate people.
- Where development activities prove inappropriate and/or the resources used are unsuitable or inadequate, realistic alternatives are discussed, agreed and implemented.

Element   **Develop oneself within the job role**

Performance Criteria
- Current competence and areas for development are identified against appropriate competence/development models.
- Objectives are achievable, realistic and challenging in terms of current and anticipated competence and updated at regular intervals.
- Where necessary, personal objectives include areas for development which are required for effective team operation.
- Sufficient and realistic amounts of time and resources are allocated to achieve set objectives.
- Progress and performance are reviewed with appropriate people at suitable intervals and results used to inform future development.
- Responsibility is accepted for achieving own development objectives.
- Feedback is compared with own perceptions of performance and used to improve future performance.

Source: Management Charter Initiative 1990b: 10–11

performance, for example 'clarifying roles and objectives', 'monitoring', 'supporting', 'recognizing' and 'rewarding'. Associated with each of these is a large number of 'specific component behaviours' (Yukl 1994) – that is, prescriptive guidelines as to what managers should do: some examples are given in Table 7.4.

| Table 7.3 | **Definitions of Yukl's managerial practices** |

Planning and Organizing. Determining long-term objectives and strategies, allocating resources according to priorities, determining how to use personnel and resources to accomplish a task efficiently, and determining how to improve co-ordination, productivity and the effectiveness of the organizational unit.

Problem-Solving. Identifying work-related problems, analysing problems in a timely but systematic manner to identify causes and find solutions, and acting decisively to implement solutions to resolve important problems or crises.

Clarifing Roles and Objectives. Assigning tasks, providing direction in how to do the work and communicating a clear understanding of job responsibilities, task objectives, deadlines and performance expectations.

Informing. Disseminating relevant information about decisions, plans and activities to people who need it to do their work, providing written materials and documents, and answering requests for technical information.

Monitoring. Gathering information about work activities and external conditions affecting the work, checking on the progress and quality of the work, evaluating the performance of individuals and the organizational unit, analysing trends, and forecasting external events.

Motivating and Inspiring. Using influence techniques that appeal to emotion or logic to generate enthusiasm for work, commitment to task objectives and compliance with requests for cooperation, assistance, support, or resources; setting an example of appropriate behaviour.

Consulting. Checking with people before making changes that affect them, encouraging suggestions for improvement, inviting participation in decision-making, incorporating the ideas and suggestions of others in decisions.

Delegating. Allowing subordinates to have substantial responsibility and discretion in carrying out work activities, handling problems and making important decisions.

Supporting. Acting friendly and considerate, being patient and helpful, showing sympathy and support when someone is upset and anxious, listening to complaints and problems, looking out for someone's interests.

Developing and Mentoring. Providing coaching and helpful career advice, and doing things to facilitate a person's skill acquisition, professional development and career advancement.

Managing Conflict and Team-Building. Facilitating the constructive resolution of conflict and encouraging co-operation, teamwork and identification with the work unit.

Networking. Socializing informally, developing contacts with people who are a source of information and support, and maintaining contact through periodic interaction, including visits, telephone calls, correspondence and attendance at meetings and social events.

Recognizing. Providing praise and recognition for effective performance, significant achievements and special contributions; expressing appreciation for someone's contributions and special efforts.

Rewarding. Providing or recommending tangible rewards such as a pay increase or promotion for effective performance, significant achievements and demonstrated competence.

Source: Yukl 1994: 69

Table 7.4	**Specific behaviours for managerial practices**

Specific behaviours for managing the work

Guidelines for defining job responsibilities
- Meet with the subordinate to mutually define the job
- Establish priorities for different responsibilities
- Explain the subordinate's scope of authority

Guidelines for setting performance goals
- Set goals for relevant aspects of performance
- Set goals that are clear and specific
- Set a deadline for the attainment of each goal
- Set goals that are challenging but realistic
- Consult with a subordinate in setting goals
- Formalize agreements in writing

Guidelines for assigning tasks
- Clearly explain the assignment
- Explain the reasons for an assignment
- Verify legitimacy, if necessary
- Check for comprehension
- Follow up to check on compliance

Specific behaviours for managing relationships

Guidelines for recognizing
- Recognize a variety of contributions and achievements
- Actively search for contributions to recognize
- Recognize improvements in performance
- Recognize commendable efforts that failed
- Don't limit recognition to high-visibility jobs
- Don't limit recognition to a few best performers
- Provide specific recognition
- Provide timely recognition
- Use an appropriate form of recognition

Guidelines for coaching and training
- Identify training needs
- Explain why additional training is needed
- Build the person's self-confidence
- Make explanations meaningful
- Sequence training content to facilitate learning
- Provide opportunity for practice with feedback
- Allow ample time for learning complex tasks
- Verify that training has been successful
- Encourage application of skills on the job

Source: summarized from Yukl 1994: 92–5, 131–3, 126–7

Research on competencies also tells us about performance-management-related activites in which managers should engage. Table 7.5 shows the McBer generic managerial competency model, that is, characteristics of individuals that are related to effective performance (i.e., results). Again, we can identify a number that would seem to have especial relevance for the management of employee performance, such as 'achievement orientation', 'developing others', 'interpersonal understanding' and 'directiveness/assertiveness'. An illustration of how one of these is defined is given in Table 7.6.

All the models described so far derive, to varying extents, from empirical research on managerial behaviour and effectiveness. Such research also points to the highly interactive nature of managerial work, much of that interaction being with subordinates. Moreover, the models together clearly point to the important role of the line manager and the tables provide several specific examples of the sorts of activities in which managers need to engage in the management of employee performance.

Performance review

Let me begin this section with a brief reminder of certain of the key points about contemporary practice in the UK. At one extreme there

Table 7.5	**The McBer generic managerial competency model**	
	Weight	Competency
	XXXXXX	Impact and influence
	XXXXXX	Achievement orientation
	XXXX	Teamwork and co-operation
	XXXX	Analytical thinking
	XXXX	Initiative
	XXX	Developing others
	XX	Self-confidence
	XX	Directiveness/assertiveness
	XX	Information seeking
	XX	Team leadership
	XX	Conceptual thinking

(Weight refers to the relative frequency with which each competency distinguishes superior from average performers.)

Source: Spencer and Spencer 1993

Table 7.6	**A managerial competency defined**

Developing others
Expresses the genuine intent to teach or to foster the learning or development of one or several other people.

Level Behavioural Description

−1 *Discourages.* Expresses stereotypical or personal negative expectations, resents subordinates, students, clients. Has a 'pacesetter' management style.

0 *Not applicable, or makes no explicit efforts to develop others.*

1 *Expresses positive expectations of others.* Makes positive comments regarding others' abilities or potential even in 'difficult' cases. Believes others want to and can learn.

3 *Gives reasons or other support.* Gives directions or demonstrations with reasons or rationale included as a training strategy; or gives practical support or assistance, to make job easier.

5 *Reassures and encourages.* Reassures others after a setback. Gives negative feedback in behavioural rather than personal terms, and expresses positive expectations for future performance or gives individualized suggestions for improvement; or breaks difficult tasks into smaller components, or uses other strategies.

7 *Creates new teaching/training.* Identifies a training or development need and designs or establishes new programmes or materials to meet it; designs significantly new approaches to teaching traditional materials; or arranges successful experiences for others to build up their skills and confidence.

9 *Rewards good development.* Promotes or arranges promotions for especially competent subordinates as a reward or a development experience; or gives other rewards for good performance.

(All of the scale points are defined as illustrated above.)

Source: abbreviated from Spencer and Spencer 1993: 54–6

are organizations where no review takes place; this is not uncommon amongst those which do not have policies for managing performance. By contrast, a healthier picture is found amongst those organizations which do have performance management policies of some sort, the core activity being a joint discussion between manager and employee. The IMS survey (Institute of Personnel Management 1992) also tells us that performance review is more frequent than annual in about 60 per cent of organizations with formal performance management systems, a finding confirmed by the Industrial Society (1994, 1998) surveys.

Performance measures

The starting point for performance reviews, particularly the more formal ones, will be the performance contract or agreement (Chapter 4). For example, in Standard Life there is a performance plan which comprises a 'job mission' statement (specifying the single main purpose of the job) and a 'performance description' – the outputs, indicators and activities to be completed in fulfilling the mission. Mercury Communications use a performance contract which includes statements of the job purpose and agreed accountabilities (outputs to be achieved), and specifies the review process. These, then, are examples of the preference, noted in Chapter 4, for organizations to use seemingly more objective means of expressing performance measures. One of the advantages of such measures is that they do lend themselves fairly readily to the collection of relevant supporting data. This is one part of performance review, namely **monitoring**.

Performance monitoring

As we saw from Yukl's definition in Table 7.3, this includes gathering information about work activities and checking on the progress and quality of work, amongst other things. Such information might be generated naturally, as it were, as part of the way in which the work system operates. But as Box 7.1 illustrates, there are in fact many ways in which monitoring may be carried out, whether by the line manager or by others – indeed, by the job holder. Quite apart from gathering information which may be used for keeping track of progress with tasks/goals or providing feedback, such monitoring behaviour in itself may carry an important message for the employee: 'the frequency with which a manager monitors a subordinate's performance may help shape that subordinate's beliefs about the relative importance of his or her various work activities' (Larson and Callahan 1990: 531).

Progress reviews

Though the very act of monitoring may have a direct impact on employee performance, as indicated above, it is more usually thought of

Box 7.1	**Performance monitoring activities**

The behaviour involved in monitoring can take many forms, including the following: (1) observation of work operations (e.g. visiting work facilities, walking around the office or plant, watching subordinates do a task), (2) reading written reports (e.g. performance summaries, progress reports, computer print-outs), (3) watching computer screen displays of performance data, (4) inspecting the quality of samples of the work, (5) holding progress review meetings with an individual or group, (6) surveying clients or customers to assess their satisfaction with organization products and services, (7) conducting market surveys to assess customer needs and preferences, and (8) holding meetings after an activity or project is completed to determine what went well and what can be improved next time.

(Source: Yukl 1994: 103)

as being linked with some other managerial behaviour, such as revising work objectives or providing feedback (Larson and Callahan 1990). Thus, there may be a review meeting of some kind between the employee and manager; such discussions are widely advocated in the performance management literature – Costello (1994), for example, describes several purposes of **progress reviews** and Whetten *et al.* (1994) describe **personal management interviews**, as shown in Box 7.2. Such reviews might take place on some regular periodic basis – in Hewlett-Packard, for example, they are monthly; quarterly formal reviews (and informal discussions as needed) are expected in Zeneca Pharmaceuticals; at least two a year are required in Legal & General (Life and Pensions) and Standard Chartered Bank; and informal reviews take place every three to six months in Standard Life with continuous feedback throughout the year. There is thus a case for saying that they should happen as and when required – to coincide with completion of a task or when a particular problem arises, for example. From this point of view, in other words, it is sensible for the review cycle to coincide with the work cycle.

Box 7.2	**Purposes of progress reviews and personal management interviews**

Progress reviews

Provide a *formal* opportunity to discuss overall performance results. Progress review meetings allow the manager to summarize informal feedback and are vital to managing performance. . . .

The overall purpose of a progress review is to:

- Progress toward goals and objectives established in performance and development plans.
- Review objectives and plans in light of business changes.
- Discuss needed changes, revisions or additions to the performance and development plan.
- Make plans for improvement, if necessary. If progress is insufficient, the manager must determine what the problems are, solicit the employee's perspective and suggested solutions, and utilize appropriate coaching skills. In some cases a formal improvement plan will need to be developed.

(Source: Costello 1994: 93)

Personal management interviews

Regular and private meetings which provide managers with the opportunity to coach and counsel subordinates and to help them improve their own skills and job performance. Meetings should focus on such items as the following: (1) managerial and organizational problems, (2) information sharing, (3) interpersonal issues, (4) obstacles to improvement, (5) training in management skills, (6) individual needs, (7) feedback on job performance and (8) personal concerns or problems.

(Source: Whetten et al. 1994: 219)

Feedback

So far as the provision of feedback is concerned, one important characteristic is that it should be timely. So, for example, good performance should be recognized when it occurs. Farr contends that 'informal or day-to-day feedback is more important than feedback that occurs during the annual or semi-annual performance appraisal session in terms of its impacts on work performance and attitudes' (1993: 177). This makes sense as we should have rather modest expectations of what can be achieved during the once-a-year event that is the appraisal interview (especially if this is the only feedback-giving activity that takes place). But positive outcomes (e.g., in terms of performance and work attitudes) may arise from the annual event where there has been more frequent review and feedback during the year. In this regard, Taylor *et al.* (1984) propose that regular feedback should bring about closer agreement over performance standards between employees and the organization (that is, the manager). Also, Ashford (1989) suggests that where there is regular feedback it may be easier to convey negative feedback when this is necessary.

A common form of providing recognition is to give credit or praise (social reward) or some more tangible reward for something that has been done well. Praise may have motivational and reinforcing consequences, although, as Lockett points out:

> Giving praise is more than a vague 'well done' or a pat on the back. An effective credit provides specific information to people about their behaviour and why it is creditworthy. This specific information gives credibility to the praise and encourages the element of performance to be repeated.
>
> *(Lockett 1992: 86)*

Thus, feedback also serves an informational purpose (Farr 1993; London 1997). But in order to be effective, feedback should possess characteristics other than timeliness, as the model depicted in Figure 7.1 illustrates.

These characteristics apply whether the feedback is positive or negative. Thus, instances of poor performance should be tackled at the time rather than being stored up for the annual appraisal or not dealt with at all. Yet we know that managers are reluctant to get to grips with performance problems. Indeed, do they provide enough feedback? Illustrative evidence of the incidence of feedback provision comes from two large-scale surveys of British Institute of Management members carried out some years ago by Nicholson and West (1988). Tables 7.7 and 7.8 show the relevant data.

Figure 7.1 **Feedback**

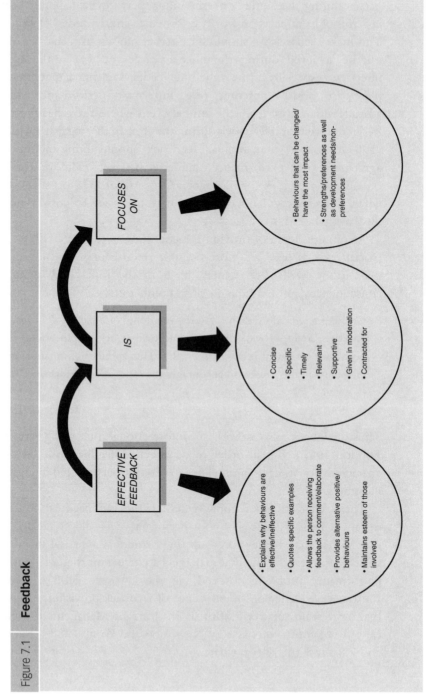

Source: Latham and Marchbank 1994

Table 7.7

Sources of feedback on performance

Have you had any feedback from the following sources on how well your superiors think you are doing in your present job?	Yes (%)	No (%)
Formal appraisal system	38	62
Informal communications from boss	79	21
Other sources	60	40
	$N = 2,061$	

Source: Nicholson and West 1988: 167

Table 7.8

Extent of feedback from different sources

How much feedback do you get in your job from . . . ?	A great deal/quite a lot (%)	Moderate (%)	Little or none (%)
Superiors	23	44	32
Colleagues	24	54	22
Clients, customers, contacts	33	45	23
Job indicators (i.e. visible results/output)	50	36	14
		$N = 1,031$	

Source: Nicholson and West 1988: 168

Sources of feedback

Nicholson and West conclude from these data that the extent of the feedback being provided by managers is less than might be desired. In their view, providing feedback 'is primarily a boss's job, and on this evidence most of our manager's bosses aren't doing this part of their jobs' (1988: 165). Of course, interpretation of these data turns on what incidence of feedback we would expect. These managers see their formal appraisal systems in an unfavourable light, whereas the provision of feedback on an informal basis is much better (but perhaps still not as much as might be desired, especially if 100 per cent is expected). The provision of feedback via informal communication is consistent with today's view of performance management as an ongoing process.

However, the increased interest these days in 360° appraisal suggests that the provision of feedback isn't the responsibility of line managers alone – there is a potential role for others, as well as oneself as a performer.

But although feedback from supervisors is valued by job holders, as is that from co-workers, it is feedback from the task and the self, Farr (1993) reports, that is regarded as the most useful. Credibility, trustworthiness, and sincerity of intent are important characteristics which influence the recipient's processing of the feedback that is delivered (Fedor 1991). And we tend to see ourselves as more credible and trustworthy as a source of feedback than external sources. Though this is none too surprising, there can be (and often is) a mismatch between self- and other perceptions, as I shall come on to shortly.

The Nicholson and West findings confirm the importance of the job itself as a source of feedback about performance. Indeed, there is the argument that job performance is actually the fundamental source of 'objective job-related feedback' (Fedor 1991: 82) and that feedback from all other sources (the manager, the self or others) is the result of some internal process of interpretation and evaluation. Certainly, the important role of feedback from the job itself has been recognized in various models of job design. For example, feedback is one of the core job characteristics in the Hackman and Oldham (1980) model, and Warr has identified the importance of feedback as 'a minimum requirement for the establishment and maintenance of personal control and for the development and utilization of skills' (1987: 261), with consequent implications for employee mental health.

However, for feedback from another to be accepted it first needs to be perceived as such by the recipient. Perception is very much a selective process, as we cannot possibly attend to all of the stimuli that bombard us. This is particularly important as feedback that is given informally will not necessarily be signalled as such by the sender. For example, the sender may be trying to give a hint, but whether the recipient takes it depends on it being perceived. Of course, rather than trying to give a hint, feedback that is clear, specific and understandable is preferable. If the feedback is perceived, it then will be processed, interpreted and evaluated by the individual (Fedor 1991). This process is likely to be influenced by our mood at the time, our past experience, our expectations, our internal standards about performance and many other factors (Ashford 1989). Thus, senders of feedback, especially of the 'hint' kind, should not assume that the message they believe they have sent will be interpreted by the recipient in the way intended. As part of their processing of the feedback recipients will decide whether the behaviour/incident/etc. that is the subject of the feedback is their responsibility. If the feedback is positive we are more likely to attribute that success to ourselves, whereas if it is unfavourable we are more likely to adopt a situational explanation.

Two points are being made here. The first is simply a reminder that factors within the performer's work situation are likely to have some influence on performance. Part of any feedback discussion has to consider this possibility. Indeed, some authorities (e.g., Bernardin, Hagan, Kane, and Villanova 1998; Cardy 1998) argue that the review of system factors and their impact on employee performance ought to be an explicit component of performance management. And for feedback to be constructive external causes need to be recognized where they have a deleterious effect; in other words, performers shouldn't be blamed for poor performance if it is outside their control (London 1997). Second, the recipient of feedback is far from passive. That we selectively attend to feedback messages implies that the sender needs to signal clearly that feedback is being provided. The sender also needs to be clear about the message that is being sent and it needs to be delivered in a supportive way, as in the model in Figure 7.1, for example.

Another implication of the idea that feedback recipients are active rather than passive is that we might actively seek out feedback from others about our performance. However, we may be apprehensive about doing so – after all, there is some risk to self-esteem, depending on how well we are doing. And those who are less self-confident or who aren't doing so well are less likely to solicit feedback. Also, our cultural background may inhibit feedback-seeking and, as Ashford points out, doing so may sometimes go against prevailing organizational norms. But even if we do not solicit feedback from others we are likely, from time to time, to reflect on our performance, and in this sense feedback may be self-generated.

Self-assessment

The self-generation of feedback necessarily involves **self-appraisal**. This might be encouraged on a formal basis within the context of performance appraisal or performance management. Survey evidence suggests the incidence of use is, however, on the low side, albeit increasing slowly. For example, Long's (1986) survey of appraisal practice reported that 28 per cent of responding organizations claimed to use self-appraisal. The IMS performance management survey (Institute of Personnel Management, 1992) reported a similar figure of 25 per cent for organizations with formal systems (and less for others). The surprising, and scarcely believable, figure is that of 71 per cent reported by the Industrial Society (1994). Unfortunately, the form of the question asked in this last survey is not reported and so we do not know if like is being compared with like, but it is hard to believe that there has been such an enormous shift in practice in the space of two years (the interval between the IMS and Industrial Society surveys), particularly as a 1995 survey by Saville and Holdsworth (quoted by Thatcher 1996) reports an incidence of use of 31 per cent amongst large organizations. The more recent (1998) surveys reveal reported incidences of use of 45 per cent (IPD) and 58 per cent (Industrial Society).

However, whatever the incidence or nature of self-appraisal on a formal basis, it nonetheless is something that we all engage in, and we may be more reliant on self-generated feedback when feedback isn't provided by others (Ashford 1989). Accurate self-assessments may also have functional value: for example, Ashford notes that 'they allow employees to correct errors and better tailor their performances to the current situation and the demands of the larger control system' (1989: 143). Furthermore, Campbell and Lee (1988) have identified the potential developmental value of self-assessments, such as helping to identify areas of disagreement. Though it might be feared that the voicing of disagreement may lead to dispute and disharmony, there is the possibility that discussion of differences will lead to benefits – at the very least, difficulties that aren't brought out into the open are likely to remain unresolved. And a range of other potential benefits of self-appraisal has been suggested, as listed in Box 7.3.

That self-assessment is naturally occurring needs to be recognized by managers as there will not necessarily be agreement between the feedback that they wish to provide and the perceptions that job holders have of their own performance. Figure 7.2 shows this diagrammatically. As the figure illustrates, some job holders may overestimate their performance (relative to the assessments made by others, such as the

| Box 7.3 | **Potential benefits of self-assessment** |

- Enhances self-raters' sense of dignity and self-respect.
- Increases employees' perceptions of the fairness of the process.
- Reduces the impact of any individual's biases by providing ratings from more sources.
- Provides a tool to increase communication in the appraisal interview.
- Highlights any discrepancies between self- and supervisor perceptions of performance.
- Minimizes halo error; self-raters see more differentiation across rated dimensions than observers.
- Helps clarify differences of opinion regarding performance requirements.
- Increases acceptance of feedback because it promotes self-reflection about performance.
- Increases commitment to development plans and goals formulated.

(Source: Atwater 1998)

line manager – this is cell 2) whereas some may underestimate their performance (cell 4). And as Campbell and Lee (1988) indicate, there may be several reasons for discrepancies between self-assessments and those made by managers. For example, there may be differing expectations as to what performance is expected, although this ought to be less of a problem where there has been discussion and there is a clear performance contract, of course. Managers might have insufficient information about what the job holder has done. The two parties may agree on what was done (or not done) but have different explanations. For example, the job holder may point to constraining factors in the work system; the manager may attach more significance to the employee's behaviours. But whatever the reasons, cells 2 and 4 may present performance management problems. Consider employees in cell 4, for example. Their perceptions of under-performance may suggest low self-efficacy. As we saw in Chapter 3, self-efficacy is associated with goal-acceptance, and so the performance management task here may be one of persuading the employee to believe in a higher level of competence. This, of course, assumes that the more accurate view of

Figure 7.2	**Possible relationships between other- and self-evaluations of goal progress**

		Self-evaluation	
		Behaviour is off track re. goal attainment (positive self-assessment)	Behaviour is on track re. goal attainment (negative self-assessment)
Other-evaluation	Behaviour is on track re. goal attainment (positive self-assessment)	1	4
	Behaviour is off track re. goal attainment (negative self-assessment)	2	3

Source: Ashford 1989

performance is the one held by the line manager. This may not be the case; the job holder's view may be the more accurate. There may, in fact, be a performance problem, although this is not to say that it lies within the employee – it may actually rest within the work system.

The issue of accuracy in performance assessment is a problematical one (Ashford 1989; Atwater and Yammarino 1997). One problem is deciding what accuracy is. In practical terms this ought to be reduced if care is taken to define performance and how it will be measured, but there can be no guarantees that there will be no ambiguity about this, especially as there may be parties other than the manager in the employee's role set who have a view about what the performers should be doing and how well they should be doing it. Where there is a performance contract it will typically be agreed between the job holder and their manager – the expectations of other interested parties most probably will not be taken into account, certainly not in a formal way. A second problem concerns the accuracy of different assessment sources. It is generally assumed that the manager will be the more accurate source (Bernardin 1986), but this assumption is very much open to question. As I shall come on to discuss in considering multiple appraisal, different sources each have their advantages and disadvantages.

Of the four cells in Figure 7.2, possibly more serious, and perhaps more difficult for the manager to deal with, would be an employee in cell 2, that is, where the employee sees him- or herself as being on track but where this view is not shared by the manager. Again, this assumes that the manager is in the right, as it were, and that the poor performance is attributable to the employee rather than (or more than) the situation. Managers' reluctance to deal with poor performance is understandable. It is likely to be time-consuming and may involve disciplinary procedures. It may also be confrontational, especially if the individual is held to be at fault. And confrontation becomes more likely the longer the problem is put off; what should be constructive feedback could all too easily become destructive (London 1995). Moreover, employees generally do not want to hear bad news, especially about themselves, as this may be ego-threatening (Ashford 1989) and this may lead to such defensive impression management behaviours as disclaimers (Eder and Fedor 1989) and excuse-making (Higgins and Snyder 1989), all of which has implications for the way in which poor performance is dealt with.

Dealing with poor performance

Much of the practical advice for dealing with poor performance advocates a problem-solving approach which recognizes that the causes of poor performance may lie within the work system (e.g., Lockett 1992). One well-established example of such advocacy is found in *Analyzing Performance Problems*, by Mager and Pipe (1990). They set out a flow diagram which serves as a model for diagnosing performance problems. Table 7.9 illustrates some of the sorts of question which need

Table 7.9	**Diagnosing performance problems**

What is the performance discrepancy?
- What is the difference between what is being done and what is supposed to be done?
- What is the event that causes me to say that things aren't right?

Is it a skill deficiency?
- Are the person's present skills adequate for the desired performance?

Is the skill used often?
- How often is the skill or performance used?
- Is there regular feedback on performance?
- Exactly how does the person find out how well he or she is doing?

Are there obstacles to performing?
- Does the person know what is expected?
- Are there restrictive policies, or a 'right way of doing it', or a 'way we've always done it' that ought to be changed?
- Can I reduce interference by
  - improving lighting?
  - changing colours?
  - increasing comfort?
  - modifying the work position?
  - reducing visual or auditory distractions?

Which solution is best?
- Have all potential solutions been identified?
- Does each solution address itself to one or more problems identified during the analysis (such as skill deficiency, absence of potential, incorrect rewards, punishing consequences, distracting obstacles)?

Source: summarized from Mager and Pipe 1990

to be asked as part of the diagnostic process.

One of the clear implications of the discussion in Chapters 4, 5 and 6 of the nature and causes of performance is that performance is multi-faceted and multiply determined. In dealing with poor performance it is especially important to identify its causes. To misdiagnose a performance problem and attribute the cause to the performer does little, if anything, to solve the problem and may even make matters worse, as the manager's response may be punishing rather than performance-improving (Bell and Tetlock 1989). Campion and Wong, for example, argue that 'There is a common tendency to blame the worker rather than the job when performance is poor' (1991: 602) and note that a performance problem is one of the situations in which the design of the job should be considered. Correct diagnosis is important, therefore, for better performance management and it is in the interests of fairness to the employee. A problem-solving approach which focuses on performance is also one of the means by which the manager demonstrates supportiveness (Whetten *et al.* 1994) and is consistent with a coaching approach, that is, 'a joint process in which manager and employee work together to find solutions to present work problems' (Anderson 1993: 141).

Answers to the sorts of questions posed by Mager and Pipe (Table 7.9) help to diagnose the cause(s) of the performance problem and possible solutions are identified. Adopting such a participative, problem-solving approach may help to reduce employee defensiveness and, in terms of procedural justice, may promote a sense of fairness about the assessment by enabling employees to put their point of view and challenge that of the manager (Greenberg 1986). After all, no single source observes so much of our behaviour at work as we do ourselves. And though our own explanations for the causes of our behaviour are sometimes suspect, allowing self-appraisal may reveal motivational or situational factors affecting performance. This kind of participation may also signal that the job holder's contribution is valued and regarded as important.

Multiple appraisal

Earlier I referred to the problem of accuracy in performance assessment. This is well documented in relation to self-appraisals, as numerous studies (summarized in Williams 1989 and more recently by Fletcher and Baldry 1999) have shown that we tend to rate our performance more highly than do our co-workers or our managers. Very often it is assumed that the assessments made by others, particularly line managers, are more accurate. This, of course, is very much open to challenge. Though line managers have a legitimate role in assessing performance this is not to say that they are necessarily the 'best' people to make those judgements. First, the manager cannot observe all that the job holder does or accomplishes – the manager, in other words, has only a partial view of performance. And this may have become a greater problem in those organizations which have experienced downsizing, delayering and the like as spans of control may have become wider. This leads to the possibility that job holders will have relatively little contact with their managers. Second, it is possible that manager- and self-assessments are based on different things. For example, given the prevalence of results-based systems of performance management we might suppose that both parties will base their assessment on the accomplishment of results. But when it comes down to it, perhaps managers actually take other factors into account as well – organizational citizenship behaviours, for example. Or the performer places more weight on the influence of system factors, particularly constraining aspects. Where the different parties observe different things or attach different weights, then discrepancies between self- and manager-assessments are likely to arise. Third, in some forms of work organization, such as matrix organizations and team-working, it isn't always clear who the manager is. So, though managers may be a necessary source of information for performance management activities they are by no means a sufficient source.

We might, therefore, want to draw on others as sources of feedback. As was shown above, there are various advantages and disadvantages with self-generated feedback, but where the purpose of performance management is developmental the advantages probably outweigh the disadvantages. In the case of managers we might also want to draw on those they manage as a source of feedback – this is sometimes referred to as **upward appraisal** reported as being used by about 20 per cent of respondents to the IPD survey. Naturally, objections to this idea have been voiced – Table 7.10 gives a list. Though we can't dismiss these objections out of hand it is clear that at least some of them may

Table 7.10	**Objections to subordinate (upward) appraisal**

1 Subordinates lack the information or skills needed to make valid ratings.
2 Subordinates are inexperienced as raters.
3 Subordinates have not been trained to make accurate ratings.
4 Subordinates will inflate ratings to avoid retaliation from managers.
5 Managers will focus too hard on pleasing subordinates.
6 The authority of managers will be undermined.
7 Managers will avoid organizations that use subordinate ratings, causing difficulties recruiting and retaining managers.
8 Subordinates will rate harshly managers who are demanding.
9 Subordinate ratings are nothing more than a popularity contest.

Source: summarized from Bernardin 1986

be tackled. Training may be provided, for example. Subordinates may be inexperienced at assessment, but so is a novice supervisor. Also, not all subordinates will be inexperienced; at least some will themselves be supervisors or managers with appraisal responsibilities. We also need to set against these objections the potential advantages. In particular, subordinates are especially well placed to assess certain aspects of managerial behaviour: Table 7.11 lists those dimensions of behaviour which managers believe can and cannot be assessed by subordinates. These, of course, are the opinons of managers and it may be that subordinates feel that they are in a position to give legitimate feedback on such matters as planning and organizing, for example. This is partly a matter of opinion; also, it is partly a matter of the opportunity to observe, and this is a general point about multi-source feedback. The different sources should be regarded as complementary to one another as each views different aspects of performance – tasks and behaviours – from his or her own distinctive perspectives. This is illustrated in Table 7.12.

Table 7.12 is intended to be only a general guide. For example, there may be circumstances where a subordinate works very closely with his or her manager such that there is frequent opportunity to observe task behaviours or results.

Notwithstanding the objections voiced by managers there is some evidence to suggest that upward appraisal may have benefits from a performance management point of view – managers' performance may

Table 7.11	**Dimensions of managerial behaviour that managers believe can and cannot be assessed by subordinates**
	Dimensions that can be assessed	Dimensions that cannot be assessed
	Leadership	Planning and organizing
	Oral communication	Budgeting
	Delegation	Goal-setting
	Co-ordination	Decision-making
	Interest in subordinates	Creativity
	Performance feedback	Quantity of work
	Providing work guidance	Quality of work
	Composure and self-control	Analytical ability
	Interpersonal relationships	Technical ability

Source: Cardy and Dobbins 1994: 161

Table 7.12	**Access to information about task and interpersonal behaviours and results**				
	Source				
	Subordinates	Self	Peers	Next level (supervisor)	Higher level (upper management)
Task					
Behaviours	Rare	Always	Frequent	Occasional	Rare
Results	Occasional	Frequent	Frequent	Frequent	Occasional
Interpersonal					
Behaviours	Frequent	Always	Frequent	Occasional	Rare
Results	Frequent	Frequent	Frequent	Occasional	Rare

Source: Murphy and Cleveland 1995: 134

rise over time. A number of studies (summarised in Fletcher and Baldry) have shown increases in ratings across successive administrations of upward appraisal. However, as Fletcher and Baldry note the changes reported are in fact changes in ratings – these are being used as a 'proxy measure of performance', and it is assumed that performance itself has actually increased. So, the findings need to be interpreted with some caution, but not dismissed out of hand. Of particular interest amongst this research is the study carried out by Walker and Smither (1999). This confirmed the finding of performance improvement (i.e., increases in ratings) – in this case across a five-year time span – and showed also that these effects were enhanced by managers discussing the feedback with those who were the sources. (It is not clear if this discussion is done collectively or individually.) This discussion is believed to increase the accountability (for taking developmental action) of the manager receiving the feedback. The discussion may also lead to managers being given further information or examples, and may contribute to a climate of sharing information and openness. The managers were given guidance in how to conduct these feedback discussions, but even if done on a collective basis there is a threat here to the anonymity of the feedback sources. I will return to this point later.

Table 7.12 indicates clearly that to obtain a more fully rounded picture of an individual's performance we should draw on multiple sources of feedback. In particular, the table suggests that some non-traditional sources ought to be drawn on much more than is common – co-workers are a case in point, especially as there is encouraging evidence about the psychometric properties of peer ratings (Fletcher and Baldry 1999). Moreover, incorporating multiple sources offers the prospect of being able to gather more extensive behavioural data, thereby doing something to redress the overemphasis on results that characterizes much of performance management practice. One further point which arises from Table 7.12 is the implication that greater weight may be attached to the more frequently encountered types of information, and this in itself may affect the judgements that are made.

In addition, there may be others over and above those shown in the Table, such as suppliers or customers/clients, who could be brought in as further sources. The involvement of the latter is, of course, highly consistent with a customer orientation and some (e.g., Cardy and Dobbins 1994) have suggested that this helps to reinforce in employees' minds the ultimate reason for their job. But if there is a role for customers in performance review, there is no less a role for them in specifying performance expectations (Cardy 1998), and Hartle (1995) sees this as an element in total performance management. On the other hand, the use of such external sources has been subject to little research and so remains poorly understood; but potential difficulties might be anticipated. For example, on what basis would the feedback be solicited from external customers? Will they be willing to provide feedback knowing that it is going to be used for performance management purposes? Also, as Bowen and Waldman (1999) note, across time any one customer may have interactions with many individual staff of an organization. And those interactions may be of a relatively fleeting kind. Also, research by Parasuraman *et al.* (1991) has identified ten dimensions used by consumers in evaluating service quality (Table 7.13) – it is possible that customers may not readily separate the system influences from employee performance. The practical issues need therefore to be very carefully thought through. None of this is intended to cast doubt on broader-based customer surveys, of course, which may serve other valuable purposes, such as product/service development, marketing and organization development.

What is explained above, in essence, is the core rationale for 360° appraisal. Though the survey evidence isn't absolutely clear-cut, there is little doubt that this practice has become more popular in recent years.

Table 7.13	**Dimensions of service quality**

- *Tangibles* include the physical evidence of the service such as the appearance of the service facilities and personnel.
- *Reliability* involves consistency of performance and dependability. It means that the firm performs the service right the first time. It also means that the firm, honours its promises.
- *Responsiveness* concerns the willingness or readiness of employees to provide service. It involves timeliness of service.
- *Competence* means possession of the required skills and knowledge to perform the service.
- *Courtesy* involves politeness, respect, consideration and friendliness of contact personnel (including receptionists, telephone operators and so forth).
- *Credibility* involves trustworthiness, believability, honesty. It involves having the customer's best interests at heart.
- *Security* is the freedom from danger, risk or doubt.
- *Access* involves approachability and ease of contact.
- *Communication* means keeping customers informed in language they can understand. It also means listening to customers.
- *Understanding the consumer* involves making the effort to understand the customer's needs.

Source: Parasuraman *et al.* 1991: 255

For example, an Industrial Society survey in 1995 showed that only 8 per cent of those responding had a system of 360° appraisal; a further 13 per cent were thinking about introducing it (cited in France 1997). On the other hand, the small scale Ashridge survey (Handy, Devine and Heath 1996), also carried out in 1995, reported 38 per cent of organizations as users. A later survey by SHL of 216 of their client organizations (Geake, Oliver and Farrell 1998) reported 47 per cent as using 360° appraisal. Somewhat confusingly perhaps the IPD's performance management survey (also in 1997) reports only 11 per cent, but it should be borne in mind that the question was asked in the context of a survey of performance management practice rather than as part of one on 360° appraisal.

Though it has become more popular today, multiple appraisal is far from a new idea. One example from some years ago is the experimental programme that was introduced in the Gulf Oil Corporation (Stinson and Stokes 1980). This was designed as a supplement to the normal annual appraisal, and the main steps are described in Box 7.4. The example is of more than historical interest for it serves to illustrate many

| Box 7.4 | **An early experiment in multiple appraisal** |

1 The participants (thirty senior executives from eight European countries) each selected between five and eight raters whom they believed to be in a position to make a useful assessment of their performance. Self-selection of the raters was regarded as important so as to increase acceptace of the feedback. The participant sent each rater a Rating Form (described below) with a covering letter requesting completion of the form and its return, anonymously, to the HR [Human Resources] Department. The rater also was told how the participant would receive feedback.

2 The completed Rating Forms were analysed by the HR Department to produce a Summary Feedback for each participant.

3 A copy of the Summary Feedback Form was sent to each participant and his or her immediate bosses (who had been briefed previously on what was to happen). Either party could go to the HR Department for clarification of any of the information on the form.

4 Each participant also completed a self-appraisal, having regard to the content of the Summary Feedback Form. The usual Corporate Appraisal Form was used for this. This was sent on to the immediate boss.

5 Based on the Summary Feedback Form, the self-appraisal and their own views, the bosses next completed a Corporate Performance Appraisal Form and then carried out an interview with the participant.

The Rating Form for the experiment had three main elements: an overall assessment of job performance; an analysis of managerial effectiveness against a seven-factor model of managerial behaviour; and a narrative assessment citing specific incidents to elaborate on the seven-factor analysis. The model of managerial behaviour was largely developed intuitively, although it drew on relevant published research and the outcome of an internal job evaluation exercise. In completing the narrative part of the form the raters had to select the two roles which they felt the participant had performed most effectively, and the two performed least ▶

> effectively, so as to identify areas in which development was needed.
>
> An evaluation of the experiment showed a high degree of acceptance, by both participants and bosses, although it was recognized that the approach could be threatening for some. The information communicated was found to be highly specific, which is clearly necessary if developmental action is to take place. Furthermore, there was no evidence that overrating had taken place as a result of multiple appraisal. It is believed that the anonymity built into the procedure was essential in encouraging greater honesty.
>
> *(Source: Stinson and Stokes 1980)*

of the features of present-day practice.

First, the multiple sources were used to supplement the normal annual appraisal. In this instance the link was quite close but the examination of systems by Ashridge Management College shows that the extent of the linkage does vary. There are systems which have a very close tie – including playing a part in salary determination (highly controversial and risky, and seen by some as counter-productive). For example, a close link with appraisal may increase resistance to feedback acceptance; raters may be less frank; there may be the element of competition amongst peers; there may be the possibility of collusion amongst some of the raters; and there is the possible risk of retaliation by the feedback recipient. Moreover, it should be remembered that traditional appraisal is to some extent a political process, particularly at higher levels (Gioia and Longenecker 1994; Folger and Cropanzano 1998) and there's no reason to suppose that such political effects wouldn't be found in the application of 360° feedback to performance appraisal. Using 360° feedback in this way is likely to require a high level of trust and openness if there is to be any chance of acceptance. In the US some organizations which were using 360° feedback systems for appraisal-related purposes have abandoned the link because of negative attitudes that were engendered and inflated ratings (Waldman, Atwater and Antonioni 1998). Where there is a looser link, multiple appraisal may be used in more of a supporting way. For example, in both Hewlett-Packard and Mercury Communications 360° appraisal is offered as an option.

Of course, 360° appraisal doesn't have to be used in conjunction with appraisal/performance management at all – the purpose may be primarily developmental. Indeed, the SHL survey reported individual development to be far and away the most common purpose. Likewise, a small survey by the IPD on 360° appraisal (cited in Armstrong and Baron 1998) reported the assessment of development needs as the most common purpose. The linkage, then, often will be to some kind of training/development programme. For example, the former Local Government Management Board's Top Managers' Programme used a 360° assessment questionnaire as one of a series of tools for diagnosing development needs. BT and Meridien Hotels both link 360° appraisal to training and development. Even in such cases as these, however, we might expect that performance improvement is ultimately an expected outcome.

Second, the multiple appraisal has both quantitative (ratings) and qualitative aspects. The use of questionnaires is probably the most common approach. For example, an organization might choose to buy an off-the-peg instrument. This has advantages to do with savings in development time and costs. But there is the disadvantage that the dimensions/competencies being measured might not fit the organization's needs. A variation on this theme is to buy a proprietary questionnaire capable of being tailored: this may increase 'fit', but at the risk of damaging the questionnaire's measurement properties. The preferable approach probably is to develop an organization-specific instrument. This could be done in-house if the organization possesses expertise in questionnaire development, but where this is lacking consultancy support will be required. The organization may already have a competency framework, in which case it makes sense to use it for the questionnaire. If the organization doesn't already have a competency model, then one will need to be developed – this then can be used for other purposes also. The framework/model thus will communicate the behaviours that are considered to be important. Bear in mind, though, that the competencies/qualities to be assessed should be capable of being developed by the individual. Whether the questionnaire is bought in or developed in-house, the reliability and validity (that is, job and organizational relevance) of the instrument need to be established (London 1997; Dalessio 1998); any vendor claiming otherwise should immediately be shown the door. Box 7.5 offers some advice about developing a 360° feedback questionnaire.

One general disadvantage of questionnaires based solely on ratings is that they may lack **specific** examples of performance – this is true of

| Box 7.5 | **Guidelines for constructing a 360° feedback questionnaire** |

Identifying competencies

- Base the questionnaire on an organization-specific competency model that is linked to other HR systems and organizational strategies.
- Establish job-relatedness through a content validation process for programmes that use generic vendor-developed competencies.

Constructing the questionnaire

- Have each item describe observable behaviour linked to job-relevant competencies.
- Limit questionnaire length to forty to sixty items if at all possible.

Choosing a response scale

- Use 'agreement', 'satisfaction', or 'extent' scales with four to seven points, bearing in mind that more research on the psychometric soundness of scales is needed.
- Avoid 'expected frequency of performance' scales, as they will not provide much information if all questionnaire items are job-relevant.

Verbatim comments

- Include verbatim comments as a supplement to ratings in most multisource feedback processes.
- Collect verbatim comments by asking raters at the end of the questionnaire to summarize strengths and areas for development.

(Source: Dalessio 1998)

questionnaires which require ratings of behavioural items as the items will be of a more generic kind. Some questionnaires, therefore, may include open-ended questions to allow specific examples to be written in. Standard Chartered Bank uses this approach in its Management Style Questionnaire for providing upward feedback.

Third, the source data are subjected to some analysis, perhaps in the Personnel/HR department or perhaps independently. Given that ratings are typically used, the analysis that is done will be of a statistical

Box 7.6	**Guidelines for presenting individual feedback reports**

Presentation of feedback report sections to facilitate interpretation

- Present overall average ratings (excluding self-ratings) for the competency categories listed from highest to lowest.
- Present from five to ten of the highest and lowest overall average rated items.
- Present average item and competency ratings for each source.
- Use graphic display to present visual comparisons among various sources at the competency level.
- Present norms for items and competency dimensions where available.
- Provide suggestions for relevant on-the-job developmental activities, readings, and seminars in the report or as a separate booklet.
- Caution participants not to rely on the midpoint as a benchmark for average performance because ratings are typically skewed, but rather use a scale value above the midpoint.

(Source: Dalessio 1998)

kind. Dalessio (1998) gives advice about this, as shown in Box 7.6. Though averages commonly are used, it is important to not simply feed back averaged ratings, as such averaging reduces the 'sensitivity' of the data (Fletcher and Baldry 1999). Part of the rationale for using 360° assessment is that it captures *different* perceptions of performance; it is important, therefore, that the variations be fed back as well as the areas of commonality. This needs to be done so as to protect the anonymity of respondents' ratings; the same point applies to feeding back narrative comments. Clearly, the raters themselves are not anonymous as they will have been chosen by the manager being assessed – this is the usual practice. Rater anonymity typically is advocated as good practice and it is clear that raters do prefer to remain anonymous: there is some risk of inflated ratings if raters are required to disclose their identities such that their assessments will be identifiable to the recipient.

Fourth, who owns the data? There is a strongly argued view that the data fed back are the sole property of the manager being assessed, are for their developmental benefit, and that there should be no obligation on the individual to share the data with any other person(s). However,

| Box 7.7 | **Potential drawbacks of 360° feedback confidentiality** |

Regarding multisource feedback as the property of the individual for developmental purposes alone may result in underutilization of the full potential of the process, argues Bracken.

Leaving feedback information solely in the hands of the ratee creates potentially serious implications for sustaining the process and realizing true behavioural change, due to the following factors:

- Ratees are not held accountable for follow-through and may lack motivation to change.
- Ratees see the feedback as supplemental information that is 'nice to have' but tangential to their real work.
- Ratees see the feedback as an 'event', happening only once or only at long intervals and lacking ongoing feedback or support.
- Raters may not see any evidence that their input is being used, and this may eventually reduce their motivation to participate and/or provide honest feedback.

(Source: Bracken 1996: 123)

disadvantages (summarized in Box 7.7) may arise from rigidly maintaining this stance, and it is common to find means of enabling recipients to discuss their data with someone else.

In the Gulf Oil example, where the 360° feedback is linked with the annual appraisal, the data are shared with the line manager and the participant does not have any choice about this. In similar vein, there is the possibility that the recipient may share the feedback with their raters, as in the earlier example from Walker and Smither (1999). This increases recipient accountability in terms of taking development action, but needs to be handled with care so as to not threaten anonymity of individual raters' assessments nor to provoke acrimony/conflict/ retaliation. In other applications, conveying the feedback may fall to an independent facilitator (that is, independent of the line, not necessarily of the organization), whether on a one-to-one basis or within the context of a workshop (see Box 7.8). Simply providing a narrative report to the recipient is unlikely to be helpful as the recipient may not know how to interpret and act on the feedback. For example, if

| Box 7.8 | **Supporting development activities** |

Facilitated feedback workshop

- Use workshop facilitators who have completed a multisource feedback process themselves, so they can speak from direct experience.
- Discuss purpose, objectives, value, and benefits of the feedback process.
- Provide background on competencies and questionnaire development.
- Discuss how rater anonymity will be maintained.
- Explain the sections of the feedback report, and how to interpret potential results.
- Provide participants with guidance on developing action plans and directing efforts to a specific goal.
- Leave participants with a workbook that covers workshop topics.

Follow-up activities

- Link multisource feedback to specific developmental pro-grammes.
- Support the multisource feedback process with on-the-job learning opportunities and coaching from supervisors or peers on strengths and developmental needs.
- Provide opportunities for follow-up administration of the process.
- Encourage participants to share their feedback results with subordinates in a group meeting.

(Source: Dalessio 1998)

the recipient is seen differently by different parties, is this because of different **observations** of performance or different **expectations** (Moses *et al.* 1993)? At the very least, then, some training will be required to sensitize the recipient to such issues; the same point applies if a narrative report is to be provided separately to an appraising manager. The issues of voluntariness, feedback ownership and anonymity/confidentiality are clearly important and complex, and need to be resolved before a scheme is launched. The agreed policy needs to

Box 7.9	**Implications for practice**

There is an important role for the line manager in reviewing and supporting performance. This by no means is a narrowly backward-looking activity – it involves the agreeing of performance requirements; it also involves monitoring performance and providing feedback – all of which are responsibilities shared with the job holder. Performers themselves have self-management and self-development responsibilities, which include the self-generation of feedback, whether from the job itself or from others.

Progress reviews should be regular – certainly more frequent than annual – but this doesn't have to mean a high degree of formality. Encourage self-review. It is likely to happen anyway for the most part. Gaps between self- and manager-perceptions may reveal misunderstandings about the performance that is expected.

Performance review should recognize that factors in the performance environment do impinge on individuals' performance. These factors may be facilitating or inhibiting. Any such impact needs to be explored, especially in cases of poor performance.

Increasing use is being made of multisource feedback, especially for developmental purposes. Where performance management has a development orientation 360° feedback may have a contribution to make, but use with care – trust and openness are required. Bear in mind that multisource feedback won't improve a poorly operating performance management process. Using 360° feedback is likely to be especially hazardous where performance management is closely tied to reward, especially if this means performance-related-pay.

be fully communicated at all stages, and enacted.

A concluding comment

That managers seem reluctant to give feedback, positive or negative, suggests that simply providing training in the skills of how to give feedback will not be a sufficient intervention. Providing feedback is not just a matter of ability; if we think back to the models of performance discussed earlier, it is clear that there is a motivational element also – in other words, there has to be a willingness to give feedback. In the broader context of performance appraisal Murphy and Cleveland (1995) discuss the need to take into account appraiser motivation (that is, goals) in designing appraisal systems, and this is true in relation to performance management also.

Similarly, training for employees might be considered. Thus, Farr notes that 'Attention also needs to be given to the topic of training work performers to receive feedback in a nondefensive constructive manner' (1993: 177). And, again, Murphy and Cleveland point to the necessity of taking into account employee goals in assessing performance, a point to which I shall return in the final chapter.

The issues involved in giving and receiving feedback become all the more complex when we consider multisource appraisal as a tool within performance management. The use of multiple appraisal is highly consistent with a participative, developmental approach to performance management. Drawing on several sources is likely to give a more rounded picture of employee performance: different sources bring different perspectives to bear (if they do not, there is not much point in having them) but this in itself is no panacea as all the sources are flawed, again in different ways. The relatively weak evidence we have so far about multiple appraisal is generally positive, but it is clear that there are many pitfalls: 360° feedback brings with it ethical, logistical, political and cost difficulties, and every potential to do more harm than good if not well implemented.

8 Rewarding performance

As the review of practice in Chapter 1 illustrated, reward within the context of performance management typically means performance-related pay (PRP; also referred to as merit pay or appraisal-related pay). This is a very narrow view which is flawed in many respects, as I shall go on to show. Reward may be derived from the job itself and, as the examination of management practices in Chapter 6 showed, the line manager has a key role to play here also.

In this chapter I will begin with a critical review of PRP before going on to consider some broader perspectives on reward. There are a number of difficulties surrounding PRP. First, there is very little evidence which confirms the positive effects desired; indeed, there is research which points clearly to possible negative consequences. Second, there is evidence which illustrates the considerable operational difficulties involved in implementing and operating PRP. Third, there is a failure to meet principles which stem from relevant psychological theory. This will lead me on to a consideration of fairness issues, not just in relation to reward but in performance management generally.

Performance-related pay

As numerous reviews (for summaries see Kessler 1994, 1995 and Brown and Armstrong 1999) have indicated, there are many different forms of PRP and in the early 1990s they became more commonplace. Though there were variations according to such factors as size and type of organization, by the mid to late 1990s the proportion of organizations apparently using some form of performance-related pay had risen to about two-thirds, with some 40 to 50 per cent linking pay with performance management. In this context the most prevalent form of PRP seems to be 'individual merit and performance-related systems based on some form of appraisal or assessment of the individual using various input (traits, skills, competences) or output (objectives) indicators. They often involve a payment which is integrated into the basic salary' (Kessler 1994: 466–7). The findings from the IMS survey (Institute of Personnel Management 1992) reported in Chapter 1 bear out this interpretation, and surveys by Price Waterhouse Cranfield (Filella and Hegewisch 1994) and by Towers Perrin (1997) demonstrate the increasing prevalence of merit pay across European countries, especially for managerial and professional jobs.

Research shows that PRP has been introduced for several reasons. Cannell and Wood (1992), for example, found six main reasons amongst UK organizations, as shown in Table 8.1. The Price Waterhouse Cranfield survey tells us that in many European countries which have introduced merit pay the reasons for doing so were often to do with responding to labour market trends and the like – although the claimed reasons may be to bring about motivational or performance improvements. Though the word performance does not specifically appear in the list in Table 8.1 it is implicit in several of the reasons, such as reward and motivation. But (as with performance appraisal) where an organization implements PRP for multiple reasons there is always the risk that none of them will be satisfactorily achieved. Based on their examination of twenty-six organizations for the IPM, Fletcher and Williams, for example, concluded that:

> it is not hard to draw the conclusion that [PRP schemes] are more concerned with managing the pay bill than with managing employee

Table 8.1	**Reasons for introducing performance-related pay**

- Problems with incremental systems
- Reward and motivation
- Promotion of cultural and organizational change
- Improving communication
- Improving recruitment and retention
- Individualizing industrial relations

Source: Cannell and Wood 1992

motivation or performance. The former is, of course, a legitimate purpose but schemes typically were not presented with this as their ostensible function.

(Fletcher and Williams 1992: 93)

Hence, conflicting messages may be conveyed to staff and there is a danger that the performance message will get lost, assuming that there is a performance message to be conveyed at all, that is.

Research on PRP

Evidence supporting PRP

Heneman reports that 'a number of studies have shown a relationship between performance ratings and changes in pay' (1992: 47), that is, higher performance ratings are associated with higher increases in merit pay. In other words, there is some evidence to suggest that organizations are able to relate PRP to past performance, and to this extent it is possible that the reward function of PRP is being satisfied (assuming, that is, that those affected do perceive a relationship between their performance and any extra pay that they receive). However, Heneman notes that 'The magnitude of the relationship between pay and performance in these studies is *not* large' (1992: 47) – the association is not strong, in other words, pointing to the possible impact of other factors (besides performance) which may affect merit pay decisions. For example, PRP guidelines (to do, say, with the size of increase available) may serve as a constraint, thus reinforcing the impression (which may be reality) that the name of the game is control of the wage bill (see Bartol and Durham 2000, Gerhart and Milkovich 1992).

Furthermore, these studies say nothing about the motivational/ incentive effect of pay. On this aspect of PRP much of the evidence seems to be negative rather than positive, as I shall come on to show. As Heneman concludes, 'The results to date on the relationship between merit pay and subsequent motivation and performance are not encouraging' (1992: 258). Indeed, there is negligible evidence of a rigorous kind which supports the positive benefits commonly claimed for merit pay.

Evidence against PRP

But can we expect PRP to work as a motivator? Can we expect it to improve performance? These questions are extremely difficult to answer, for a number of reasons. Both motivation and performance are affected by many factors, indeed they affect each other (Kanfer 1995). We should not expect to find, therefore, an association between any one intervention (in this case PRP) and a particular outcome. And even if we were to find an association, that in itself would not necessarily mean causation. Despite the difficulties, though, the questions are worth asking and at the very least we should be gathering attitudinal and perceptual data to try to answer them. In other words, what do employees and their managers believe about the effects of PRP?

Managers' opinions

We need to consider the opinions of two main sets of managers – those in central functions, such as personnel/HR, and line managers at the sharp end.

Various surveys (summarized in Brown and Armstrong 1999) show that personnel/HR managers believe that their organizations' PRP systems have had at least some positive effects, such as improving employee performance. Also, as shown in Chapter 1, there is a belief on the part of these managers that PRP is more effective in improving organizational performance when it is used as part of some broader performance management policy. However, given the lack of systematic evaluation carried out by organizations we have to recognize that this is a belief that is very much unsupported by firm evidence. Moreover, we shouldn't be too surprised at HR managers taking a positive view of systems that they themselves may have had a hand in developing.

Fletcher and Williams in their part of the IPM (1992) survey also gathered opinions about PRP, both from HR/personnel and line managers. Doing so revealed discrepant views about PRP:

> in the interviews with the HR and line representatives of the organizations visited, there was little consistency of viewpoint on the motivating power of money. The majority felt that the real motivators at management levels were professional and personal pride in the standards achieved, or loyalty to the organization and its aims, or peer pressure. On

the other hand, there were those who believed that money was the prime factor in motivating improved performance. An example of the latter view came from the Personnel department of a large retail organization; however, when line managers in the company were interviewed, they saw matters differently. As one of them said, he was self-motivated – the money came as a result of that, not as the cause of it.

(Institute of Personnel Management 1992: 117)

One of the points that this illustrates is that those at the top or centre of the organization may be proceeding on the basis of a false assumption about the motivating power of money. Thus, Murlis and Wright concluded, 'in retrospect top management, be they ministers or directors of major companies, sought to translate a simplistic motivational view into the way employees were paid and managed' (1993: 9): though there are some signs of shifts towards more sophisticated systems (Brown and Armstrong 1999), this simplistic view has by no means disappeared. Yet those affected by PRP – whether recipients or the executors of a policy that someone else has determined – clearly have views about it, and about rewards and incentives more broadly. It would seem sensible for these opinions to be discovered; Thompson, for example, reports that 'employees who have been involved in the design and implementation of a PRP scheme are more likely to perceive it to be fair and more likely to be motivated' (1993: ix).

Some evidence of line managers' views comes from a major survey carried out by Marsden and Richardson (1994) in the Inland Revenue. As well as gathering data from employees affected by PRP (shown below), they also asked those employees' line managers for their views: Table 8.2 shows what was found. Marsden and Richardson conclude thus: 'These results certainly give no comfort to those who feel that staff might understate the extent of positive motivational change. . . . Indeed, the reporting officers were, if anything, even more sceptical of the system's success in this respect' (1994: 251).

Employees' opinions

We also need to consider the views of employees affected by PRP, who may or may not be recipients of merit increases. Over the past few years some survey evidence has appeared and it paints anything but a positive

Table 8.2	**The views of Inland Revenue appraisers on the impact of performance pay on their staff**

Performance pay has	Yes (%)	No (%)
Caused many staff to work beyond the requirements of their job	15	79
Led many staff to give sustained high performance at work	14	77
Helped to increase the quality of the work of many staff	10	82
Led to an increase in the quantity of the work of many staff	22	71
Made many staff more committed to their work	12	79

Source: Marsden and Richardson 1994: 252

picture of the impact of PRP. For example, a large-scale survey by the Society of Telecom Executives (1992) showed that only 8.3 per cent of respondents ($N = 1,625$) believed that their performance had been improved by PRP. The survey of Inland Revenue employees by Marsden and Richardson (1994) tells much the same story, as Table 8.3 indicates.

As we saw above, managers were similarly unenthusiastic. Marsden and Richardson thus concluded from their findings that in this case PRP was 'very unlikely to have significantly raised employee motivation – indeed may, on balance, have been demotivating. If it did not improve employee motivation, it is hard to see how the scheme could have

Table 8.3	**Inland Revenue employees' assessment of their own motivational responses to performance pay**

Performance pay has led you to	Yes (%)	No (%)
Improve the quality of your work	12	80
Increase the quantity of your work	14	78
Work harder	9	71
Work beyond the job requirements	21	70
Give sustained high performance	27	63
Improve your priorities at work	22	64
Show more initiative	27	61
Be more effective with the public	9	68
Improve your sensitivity towards colleagues	14	63

Source: Marsden and Richardson 1994: 251

enhanced employee performance' (1994: 244). Similar conclusions are drawn by Thompson, based on his employee surveys in three organizations:

> the benefits most often claimed for performance related pay are not met in practice. Firstly, PRP does not serve to motivate (even those with high ratings) and may do more to demotivate employees. Secondly, there was little evidence to suggest that PRP could help to retain high performers and no evidence to point to poor performers seeking to leave the organizations. Thirdly, employees are negative or broadly neutral on its impact on organizational culture even in schemes that had been in operation for three or more years. Lastly, employees are unclear as to whether PRP rewards fairly (neither agreeing or disagreeing). However, high performers are likely to perceive it to be more fair than low rated performers. There is the risk that PRP may contribute to a downward spiral of demotivation for the bulk of employees and this draws into question the real costs and benefits of such schemes.
>
> *(Thompson 1993: ix)*

All this British evidence supports Heneman's unenthusiastic conclusion (mentioned earlier), drawn from his examination of North American studies. However, proponents of PRP may be tempted to dismiss the sorts of finding reported above on the grounds that in these particular cases PRP had been poorly implemented and operated. This idea may have some force, if only because there are many factors to be managed in implementing and operating PRP. However, that there are so many factors suggests that failure in implementation and operation is much more likely than success. This leads neatly to operational problems.

Operational difficulties

A substantial body of research (e.g., Cannell and Wood 1992; Geary 1992; Incomes Data Services 1985; Institute of Personnel Management 1992; Kessler and Purcell 1992; Marsden and Richardson 1994; Thompson 1992, 1993) points to the *many* potential problems which may arise in implementing and operating PRP. An illustrative list of several of these is given in Table 8.4. These all are issues which organizations will inevitably face in seeking to introduce PRP. Resolving

Table 8.4	**Operational difficulties associated with performance-related pay**

- Does PRP encourage short-termism?
- Does a focus on individual performance lead employees to place their interests ahead of those of the organization more generally?
- What effect does PRP have on team and co-operative working?
- Is PRP appropriate to all organizational cultures?
- Can performance be defined comprehensively?
- How much of performance is within the individual's control?
- What criteria should be used for measuring performance? Outputs? Inputs? Both?
- Can individual performance be measured objectively and fairly?
- What amount of pay constitutes a significant increase in the eyes of employees?
- Can PRP give rise to sex (or other unlawful) discrimination?
- Do line managers have the willingness and ability required to operate PRP?
- Does PRP create divisiveness?
- How should average performers be treated?
- Is there a climate of trust (particularly in line managers–subordinates relations)?
- Will PRP diminish the value of intrinsic rewards?

Source: derived from Cannell and Wood 1992; Geary 1992; Incomes Data Services 1985; Kessler and Purcell 1992; Kessler 1994; Pearce 1987

them successfully is hazardous to say the least; but ignoring them seems certain to lead to failure.

Another perspective on implementation and operational difficulties may be gained from considering Heneman's framework for merit pay (Figure 8.1). This illustrates the many factors – environmental, organizational and individual – that bear on the operation of PRP (indeed, reward more generally) and shows all too clearly the complexity of the task.

Psychological theory

Contributing to all this complexity are the implications of a number of psychological theories. Bartol and Durham (2000), Gerhart and Milkovich (1992), Heneman (1992) and Hume (1995) have presented helpful overviews of the several theories which may help to offer a rationale for PRP. Expectancy theory is the one that is perhaps most commonly discussed in relation to PRP (e.g., Lawler 1987; Mabey and Salaman 1995) but there are others, such as equity theory and

Figure 8.1 **Merit pay framework**

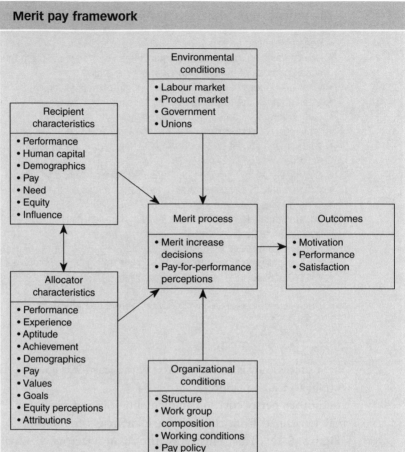

Source: Heneman 1990

reinforcement theory; Bartol and Durham and Heneman also identify a number of organizational and economic theories which have implications for PRP.

The implications of expectancy theory for PRP are quite clear. If PRP is to serve a motivational function a number of conditions must be met, as set out in Table 8.5. Certain of these conditions are supported by other theories. For example, reinforcement theory tells us that provision of the reward must be timely – a basic principle of giving feedback, as shown in the previous chapter. Reinforcement theory also supports the

Table 8.5	**Expectancy theory and performance-related pay**

Heneman sets out the following conditions which need to be met if PRP is to serve as a motivator:

- *Performance must be accurately measured.* If it is not, then employees cannot make the perceived link between effort and performance (expectancy) and performance and rewards (instrumentality).
- *Increased pay must be a valued outcome.* For employees to pursue high levels of performance, the end result of such performance must be attractive or have positive valence. Hence, pay increases must have greater valence than alternative outcomes such as leisure. If a pay increase is less attractive than leisure, then an employee will feel less motivated to perform than when promised a pay increase rather than additional time off the job.
- *The relationship between pay and performance must be clearly defined.* The relationship between performance on the job and pay associated with performance must be clearly spelled out by the organization to ensure that performance is perceived by employees as instrumental in attaining a pay increase.
- *Opportunities to improve performance must exist.* If an employee does not have the opportunity to increase or improve performance, then it is futile for that employee to expand effort at a task. If opportunity is not present, both expectancy and resultant motivation will not be present. Employees must have the time, equipment, ability and supervision required to perform a task – which translates into opportunity – before there can be expectations for performance.

Source: Heneman 1992: 27

expectancy theory performance–reward process link as pay increases must be contingent upon delivery of the desired performance, with greater increases being given for higher levels of performance. All these principles depend on performance being clearly defined – in particular, performance that is desired must be distinguished from that which is not – and clarity of definition would seem to be a precondition for accuracy of measurement. Yet, as shown in earlier chapters, coming up with a clear statement of performance requirements is no easy task – we can try to express performance requirements in terms of products or behaviours, using a range of 'objective' or subjective indicators. Moreover, we might also try to base merit rewards on skills or competencies (Armstrong and Baron 1998; Sparrow 1996). And we try to do this within a context of organizational uncertainty and complexity. Indeed, Pearce (1987) contends that under such conditions merit pay may be counter-productive as it is likely to work against the fostering of collaboration and co-operation amongst employees.

But meeting these conditions requires considerable sophistication and this is lacking in PRP schemes, which commonly seem to be applied in a universalistic way. Moreover, there is no shortage of research (see Lawler and Jenkins 1992, for one summary) which points to failure in meeting the requirements indicated by psychological theory. For example, it is assumed erroneously that the prospect of increased pay is valued by all employees as a reward. Not so; and for those who do value it, it is unlikely that they look at the prospect of a merit raise in abstract terms. This raises the question of how much of an increase will be seen as significant in the eyes of employees such that they will be motivated to improve their performance. There is no simple answer to this question, either theoretically or practically. Findings reported by Fletcher and Williams indicate organizational confusion on this matter: 'One local authority had a maximum of 15 per cent to be awarded on the basis of performance, and felt that this was insufficient.... Yet another local authority, in a not dissimilar position, had a maximum of 10 per cent of merit pay, and thought that this was too large.'

Empirical research indicates that there is no single figure – individual differences are a major factor here. This, of course, adds to the complexity of managing PRP. Furthermore, if the amount on offer is seen as too small it may be taken as insulting – hardly rewarding or motivating! This implies that where there is PRP the performance element may need to be more than organizations are currently paying. This in turn suggests that the cost may come to be too high for organizations. Indeed, there are accounts of organizations discontinuing their PRP systems because of inability to afford the (financial) cost.

Moreover, the essential process links are often not made; that is, employees may fail to see a link between their effort and their performance as measured by, say, the appraisal scheme. Likewise, they may fail to see the link between their performance (as measured, that is) and reward through pay. Such failures stem from deficiencies both in the measurement of performance and in the operation of PRP. For example, the performance–reward link may not be perceived because the performance element of pay is wrapped up with, say, a cost of living increase. For various reasons (Bartol and Durham 2000), such a 'package' may be appropriate but it doesn't help to reinforce effort–performance–reward linkages.

Faced with the accumulating evidence which indicates the operational difficulties in introducing and running PRP and which suggests that the effects are likely to be negative rather than positive, it seems clear that what is seen as one of the foundation stones of performance management simply is not working as intended. Indeed, faced with the evidence, it is scarcely credible that any sensible organization would want to have a system of PRP, certainly if the aims are to provide reward and to motivate. But, of course, these may not be the real aims. As noted earlier, the true aims may be rather different – such as managing the wage bill or individualizing the employment relationship. Both of these may be legitimate aims in themselves (if presented as such), but neither has much, if anything, to do with motivation or performance. The true reasons, then, would seem to be ideological (Storey and Sisson 1993) rather than anything else. Under such circumstances it would not be surprising if employees were to view PRP with some scepticism. For example, recent survey research into the proposed pay system for school teachers in the UK (Marsden 2000) indicates that over half of the respondents believe that the system is simply intended to get more work done and about two-thirds believe it is a device for avoiding paying more money to all teachers. Moreover, 88 per cent doubted that they could improve their performance as they were working as hard as they could anyway. And 70 per cent disagreed that linking pay with performance review will result in fairer pay allocation. This leads on to consideration of the issue of fairness in performance management.

Fairness in performance management

The fairness of performance management outcomes

It is appropriate to consider fairness in this chapter because employees' perceptions of fairness very commonly relate to the rewards or other benefits that they receive. All sorts of decisions are made about employees at work. For example, people are promoted, they are awarded merit increases or bonuses (or not, as the case may be), they receive favourable or unfavourable appraisals, they are required to achieve particular targets, etc., etc. And they have views about the fairness or otherwise of those decisions – this is what is referred to as **outcome fairness** or **distributive justice**. Some research on this that is relevant to performance management was carried out by Greenberg

(1986). He discovered that there were two distributive factors that contributed to managers perceiving performance evaluations as fair:

- the performance evaluation was based on the performance achieved;
- salary/promotion recommendations were based on the evaluation given.

As we might expect, when employees see these sorts of decisions (e.g., about rewards) as being unfair they tend to be less satisfied with them than when they see them as fair. We might suppose that these perceptions do not matter all that much – life is unfair and that is all there is to it. But perceptions of outcome fairness do have important consequences for various aspects of performance – with perceived injustice possibly leading to lowered job performance, withdrawal behaviours, decreased co-operation with co-workers, and reduced work quality (Cropanzano and Greenberg 1997; Folger and Cropanzano 1998).

The fairness of performance management procedures

Reward (and other performance-management-related decisions) are, of course, the result of some sort of process. In other words, we cannot consider the perceived fairness of the decisions themselves separately from the means by which those decisions are arrived at – this is **procedural justice**. Again, Greenberg's research on performance evaluation is relevant here. He identified five procedural factors which contribute to the perceived fairness of the evaluation process:

- employee input is solicited before the evaluation and is used;
- there is two-way communication during the evaluation interview;
- employees have the ability to challenge or rebut the evaluation;
- the rater is familiar with the employee's work;
- standards are applied consistently.

Several of these factors support the principle that employees should have a **voice** in performance evaluation if they are to have a fair hearing. Indeed, we might want to argue that the principle applies much more widely in performance management, applying not just to appraisal but also to the agreement of the performance requirements, the means by which they will be measured, and such like.

Greenberg's findings endorse other research (e.g., that performance evaluations be based on accurate and unbiased evidence) which has also identified additional procedural factors particularly relevant to performance management. For example, Landy *et al.* (1978) showed that the existence of action plans to improve identified performance weaknesses contributed to perceptions of fairness. Also, Leventhal (1976, 1980) has suggested that one rule of procedural justice is that the concerns of all interested parties be taken into account. We might see this as a principle endorsing the use of multiple appraisal, for which some support has been reported by Greenberg (in Greenberg and Lind 2000); it also backs up the case for involving all relevant parties in the design and implementation of performance management systems (Gilliland and Langdon 1998). Thompson's research, quoted earlier, lends still further support to this position.

As much as we might want to see these as ethical principles which are sufficient in themselves to guide practice, there are likely to be many who will fail to be persuaded on these grounds. However, in the same way that outcome fairness has positive outcomes for organizational performance, so too does procedural justice. For example, research has shown that when procedures are fair employees tend to be more accepting of the decisions made (even if personally unfavourable) and performance improvement may result (Gilliland and Langdon 1998).

For the most part, the procedural factors summarized above fall into two main groups – there are **structural aspects** and **social aspects** (Greenberg 1990). Examples of the former include consistency of application, freedom from bias, and the like. Social aspects are more concerned with the nature and quality of the interpersonal interaction that takes place – do people feel that they have had their say, that they have been treated with dignity and respect in the decision-making process and in the way in which the decision is conveyed to them, that they have enough information about what the procedures are and the way they work? To foster perceptions of fairness it therefore is necessary for both the structural and interpersonal features of performance management to be built on justice principles: Box 8.1 offers some guidelines.

That there is this interpersonal aspect to fairness reminds us that there is a social basis to the exchange relationship between employer and employee and we might expect this to be part of the psychological

| Box 8.1 | **Acting on justice principles in performance management** |

I. If you promise to do a performance appraisal, then do it.

II. Appraise subordinates on the appropriate criteria.

III. Have knowledgeable raters.

IV. Use a fair rating format.

Formats should provide for goal setting.

Formats should rate behaviours.

Formats should be based on good record keeping.

V. Consider the source of the ratings.

VI. Maintain interpersonal fairness in the performance appraisal interview.

Be supportive.

Be participative.

If desired, you can discuss both developmental information and the subordinate's evaluation.

Use only constructive criticism.

VII. Train subordinates to participate.

(Source: Folger and Cropanzano 1998)

contract. But employees do have formal legal contracts and these underlie the economic aspect of the exchange relationship. This brings me back to merit pay.

In the eyes of many employees the principle of merit pay is a 'good thing'; but support for that principle is by no means universal. Marsden and Richardson (1994), for example, showed that 40 per cent of their respondents disagreed with the principle. And Marsden (2000) found that nearly two-thirds of the teachers responding to his survey did not believe the principle of relating pay to performance to be a good one. Such opinions point to one reason why organizations should not assume automatically that performance and pay should be related – Lawler (1987) regards this assumption as a serious error. Another erroneous assumption is the managerial belief that pay is sufficiently valued as a reward by all employees to act as a motivator. Brown and Walsh make the point in these terms:

> There is no necessity for pay to play a central role in motivating employees. Although haphazard pay administration can have a potent

effect as a demotivator, the importance of pay as a positive incentive is greatly exaggerated.... The need for money may be the central motive for being employed at all, but it is rarely enough to ensure that work is done well.

(Brown and Walsh 1994: 450)

Hence, we need to consider rewards, and their incentive value, much more broadly. This includes accepting that individual contribution need not be a basis for determining merit increases. It is clear that there has been some reaction against individual-PRP and increasing interest is being paid to team pay. Drawing on Institute of Personnel Development (IPD) research, Armstrong (1996) identifies a number of requirements for team pay to work well, as shown in Table 8.6. But team pay is no less problematical than individual merit pay, and to adopt it in a reactive way (as happened with appraisal-related pay) is hardly a basis for a lasting system. More recently, some authorities (e.g., Armstrong and Baron 1998; Brown and Armstrong 1999) have argued for a mixed model which is consistent with rewarding both behaviours and results accomplished. This is referred to as 'contribution-related pay',

Table 8.6	**Requirements for team-based pay**

Team pay appears to work best if teams:

- stand alone as performing units for which clear targets and standards can be agreed;
- have a considerable degree of autonomy – team pay is likely to be most effective in teams that are, to a large degree, self-managed operations;
- are composed of people whose work is interdependent and where it is acknowledged by members that the team will only deliver if the members work well together and share the responsibility for success;
- are stable, where members are used to working with one another, know what is expected of them by fellow team members and know where they stand in the regard of their colleagues;
- are mature, where teams are well established, used to working flexibly to meet targets and capable of making good use of the complementary skills of their members;
- are composed of individuals who are flexible, multi-skilled and good team players, while still being capable of expressing a different point of view and carrying that point if it is for the good of the team.

Source: Armstrong 1996: 23

contribution being defined as 'what people do to bring about a result', thereby embracing results, the attributes (skills, competencies, etc.) that people possess, and how those attributes are used (Armstrong and Baron 1998). The notion certainly makes sense and it may go some way towards avoiding the drawbacks of systems that reward one and not the other. But we shouldn't assume that such a mixed model will be straightforward to operate: many of the hazards of more traditional PRP systems will remain. How real a shift there has been towards contribution-related pay presently is not clear. Moreover, we need to recognize also the contribution of rewards other than pay.

Rewards other than pay

One of the ways in which rewards may be categorized is to divide them into two main groups – intrinsic and extrinsic. The latter includes pay and many other rewards which may have remunerative consequences, such as promotion, which also brings with it other rewards like enhanced status. Some extrinsic rewards may not be financial in the way that pay is but nonetheless they incur a cost in money terms for the organization. Still other extrinsic rewards, such as recognition or praise from the boss, are wholly non-financial. And there may be other rewards that the line manager may be able to manage. For example, one of the organizations visited by Fletcher and Williams in the IPM research suggested nearly forty non-financial rewards their managers could use; importantly, this organization also trained managers in how to manage reward.

The role of the manager in rewarding and recognizing performance was noted in the previous chapter, these being two of the key managerial practices identified by Yukl (1994). He offers a number of guidelines for engaging in these activities, such as finding out what rewards people value, explaining how rewards are determined, recognizing improvements in performance, not limiting recognition to just the best performers, and providing specific and timely reward and recognition (Table 7.4 gave more examples). Wright (1996) reviews research which indicates that positive reward behaviours on the part of line managers/supervisors are associated with job holder performance – this, of course, is consistent with what we know about the importance of feedback. Other advice about giving reward comes from Dickson *et al.*

(1993); though some of this derives from educational settings, it seems no less relevant to the workplace (see Box 8.2).

Then there are intrinsic rewards – 'those that the individual provides himself or herself (e.g. feeling of accomplishment) as a result of performing some task' (Steers and Porter 1991: 478). Though the research evidence on this point is far from clear cut, one of the possible dangers of an undue concentration on extrinsic rewards, particularly those such as PRP, is that intrinsic reward and motivation may come to be diminished.

All this, then, points up the importance of the design of the job so as to make sure that intrinsic factors are present. These include, for example, opportunity for personal control (such as employee discretion, absence of close supervision, participation in decision-making), opportunity for skill use, and task variety (variation in job content, skill variety) (Warr 1996). These are features of jobs in many

Box 8.2	**Giving rewards**

Rewards seem to work best to motivate and direct when the recipient appreciates why they are being offered. If the intention is to enhance learning and performance at a certain task, then the rewarder should:

- specify the particulars of the accomplishment being praised;
- decide upon criteria for praising and preferably agree these with the recipient in advance, so reducing the chances of what is happening being constructed as the mere exercise of reward power;
- draw attainment criteria from that individual's previous levels of performance rather than those of peers;
- focus the recipient's attention on the task and his or her accomplishment at it rather than on the reward and the rewarder;
- ensure that the attribution of the cause of the positive reaction encompasses effort invested in the task and does not undermine self-beliefs in ability.

Rewards from others must be seen to be genuine and authentic, rather than manipulative, to be effective.

(Source: Dickson et al. 1993: 178–9)

contemporary 'high-performance' forms of organization (Buchanan 1994). Such factors as these have been shown to promote employee well-being and job satisfaction; a positive, although less consistent, relationship with performance also has been established (Parker and Wall 1996).

Identifying valued rewards

Though lists of non-financial rewards may be found, either in popular articles and texts or in more academic literature, there is the view that organizations should try to find out the sorts of things that their particular employees will experience as rewarding. Kerr (1988), for example, advocates a data-based diagnosis of an organization's reward system and he sets out an audit tool for discovering what employees find rewarding, discovering how they believe rewards are obtained, and such like. Table 8.7 illustrates some of the rewards that he has identified.

Rewarding the 'right' thing

Though knowing what employees find personally rewarding is important, those rewards need to be used to reinforce the 'right' thing. Problems in this area have long been recognized and they found expression many years ago in Kerr's (1975) article 'On the folly of rewarding A, while hoping for B'. This has (1995) been updated by

Table 8.7	**Examples of non-financial rewards**
	• titles
	• formal commendations and awards
	• favourable mention in company publications
	• freedom concerning job duties
	• freedom concerning working hours
	• private, informal recognition for jobs well done
	• challenging duties
	• varied, interesting work
	• important, meaningful duties and responsibilities
	• having influence in setting goals and making decisions

Source: Kerr 1988: 68

Kerr and supplemented by a survey of members of the US Academy of Management's Executive Advisory Panel.

The thrust of his article is that there exist numerous examples of 'reward systems that are fouled up in that behaviours which are rewarded are those which the rewarder is trying to *discourage*, while the behaviour he desires is not being rewarded at all' (Kerr 1995: 7). Table 8.8 shows some examples that Kerr (1995) provides, along with a number of others generated by the US Academy of Management's survey. Kerr's view is that these examples point to the need to change reward systems. Kerr (2000) also has proposed a number of principles that, if followed, will lead to improvements in reward systems. These are set out in Box 8.3. But change is easier said than done, and modifying a reward system to follow these principles will not necessarily be straightforward. For example, the US Academy of Management's Executive Advisory Panel was asked to state what it saw as the barriers to

Table 8.8	**Common management reward follies**	
	We hope for . . .	**But we often reward . . .**
	• long-term growth; environmental responsibility	• quarterly earnings
	• teamwork	• individual effort
	• setting challenging 'stretch' objectives	• achieving goals; 'making the numbers'
	• downsizing; rightsizing; delayering; restructuring	• adding staff; adding budget; adding Hay points
	• commitment to total quality	• shipping on schedule, even with defects
	• candour; surfacing bad news early	• reporting good news, whether it's true or not; agreeing with the boss, whether or not he or she is right
	• teamwork and collaboration	• the best team members
	• innovative thinking and risk-taking	• proven methods and not making mistakes
	• development of people skills	• technical achievements and accomplishments
	• employee involvement and empowerment	• tight control over operations and resources
	• high achievement	• another year's effort

Source: Kerr 1995: 12; *Academy of Management Executive*, **9(1)**, p. 15

Box 8.3	**Reward system principles**

Principle 1: Rewards should be the third thing an organization works on; measurement should be the second; clear articulation of desired outcomes should be the first.

Principle 1A: If you think you have a rewards problem that can't be solved, you're wrong; the problem is your measurements, because anything that can be measured can be rewarded.

Principle 1B: If you think you have a measurements problem that can't be solved, you're still wrong; you haven't defined and operationalized what you're trying to accomplish.

Principle 2: If a reward is unavailable, don't try to use it.

Principle 3: If you make people ineligible for a reward, you take away their motivation to strive for it.

Principle 4: For rewards to be powerful, they must be visible.

Principle 5: If you want someone to perform, you should reward them when they do perform and not when they don't.

Principle 5A: A good reward says thank you for the past, and invigorates the future.

Principle 5B: Most human beings make rotten martyrs.

Principle 5C: Never hurt your high performers.

Principle 6: A long-deferred reward loses most of its power.

Principle 7: The best rewards are those you can take back if necessary.

Principle 8: Don't underestimate the importance of non-financial rewards.

Principle 8A: Stop using the term 'reward and recognition'; it implies that 'rewards' refer to money, and 'recognition' is all that cute other stuff that organizations do. It is far better to speak about financial and non-financial rewards.

Principle 9: Get peers, subordinates and customers involved in your reward and measurement systems.

(Source: Kerr 2000)

change. Three main themes emerged, as shown in Table 8.9. However, the first step in bringing about change is recognizing the need for it, and in this regard the sort of diagnostic activity advocated by Kerr would seem to be especially helpful.

Table 8.9	**Obstacles standing in the way of dealing with the reward folly**

1 *The inability to break out of the old ways of thinking about reward and recognition practices.* In particular, there appears to be need for a new goal and target behaviour definition, including non-quantifiable behaviour and that which is system focused rather than job- or functionally dependent. Among the deterrents to change are the entitlement mentality of workers and the reluctance of management to commit to revamping or revitalizing performance management processes and systems.

2 *Lack of a holistic or overall system view of performance factors and results.* To a great extent, this is still caused by organizational structures that promote optimization of sub-unit results at the expense of the total organization.

3 *Continuing focus on short-term results by management and shareholders.*

Source: *Academy of Management Executive*, **9(1)**, pp. 15–16

A concluding comment

The survey evidence suggests that for many organizations reward is construed narrowly to mean PRP. Of course, it is possible that there is a deficiency in the evidence that we have as the surveys have not asked about other aspects of reward. That said, however, studies of managerial behaviour suggest that reward-related behaviours are not displayed by managers and supervisors to the extent that their subordinates would wish (for example, the under-provision of feedback). Not only this, the emphasis on PRP may be misconceived, in that the evidence does not strongly suggest that the positive benefits expected will be realized. Indeed, given the operational and other difficulties the more likely outcome would seem to be a negative impact – lowered morale, perceptions of injustice. The risks associated with team-based pay are no lower than those already well established for individual-PRP.

Though we might see justice as something that is valuable and proper in its own right, fairness in performance management procedures is important for other reasons as well. So, to take an instrumental view, it makes good business sense – there are positive outcomes for the organization in terms of employee commitment, performance of altruistic behaviours, positive job attitudes, and acceptance of decisions and procedures. But these benefits have to be earned – not just through the procedures themselves but also through the way in which they are designed, developed and implemented.

Box 8.4	**Implications for practice**

Take a broad view of reward. Pay is a necessary element of any reward system, but it is by no means the only one. To the extent that it is, again take a broad view – there is no one 'best' pay system. Recognize also that the pay system does not stand alone from other systems – it will interact with others. Be mindful of this during system design and development.

Expect difficulties. Take account of employee opinion. Be sure you can afford pay-for-performance systems, not just the financial cost but also be aware of the dangers of demotivation.

So far as non-financial reward is concerned, consider the adoption of a diagnostic tool to help identify suitable rewards. After all, managers might not intuitively know what others will value. Also, this is consistent with an involvement philosophy, and may help to promote perceptions of fairness.

Fairness is important in its own right. Perceived lack of fairness in performance management will have costs for the organization. Adopt a design process which is fair in itself and which seeks to build fairness into the performance management process. Remember that fairness has positive benefits.

Bear in mind that the more sophisticated and flexible the reward system becomes, the more complex it will be to operate. But beware the dangers of a simplistic, one-system-fits-all approach.

Developing and designing performance management

The development and design of a performance management system naturally depends heavily on how performance is defined and on the state and nature of the organization's existing sytems, structures, etc. In the broadest sense performance management is concerned with organizational performance but, as was shown earlier, this is a problematic concept. As Dawson points out:

> When people talk of improving organizational performance they can be referring to any one of a number of aspects, including effectiveness (goal attainment), efficiency (amount of resources used to produce a unit of output), productivity in terms of quantity or quality or timing, indicators of morale, and capacity to adapt and change to cope with the unexpected and unpredictable.
>
> *(Dawson 1996: 235)*

That organizational performance can be defined in so many terms means, of course, that the task of forging a link between individual and organizational performance is far from simple.

Indeed, defining performance at the individual level is no less complex. As we saw, there are two main conceptions – outputs/results and behaviours. But it is probable that employee inputs – their effort, for example – also fall within a loose everyday understanding of the term performance. Herein lies one of the problems of performance management, that of achieving some understanding of what is meant by performance, whether at the individual or organizational level (or anywhere in between). In this chapter I will outline a diagnostic, 'involving' approach as a means of trying to bring about the sort of understanding that is required.

Though it has several meanings, the most common interpretation of the term performance management is that it is a set of activities directed at the individual so as to channel his or her performance in support of organizational performance. That said, these activities exist within a broader framework of some kind. The integrative, holistic approach to performance management that is advocated in much of the literature sees this framework as involving the communication of the organization's mission statement, goals, etc. to all employees. The intent here is to bring individual goals into line with those expressed for the organization as a whole or, in other words, to align individual performance with organizational performance. This, of course, is a unitarist view which very often is at odds with organizational reality and which may be one of the reasons why performance management systems do not succeed as intended. It may be preferable to try to accommodate the plurality of interests that we are likely to find, at least to the extent of having different systems to suit the needs and requirements of different groups, whether they be departments, type of job or whatever.

Some accounts of employee performance management assume that the organizational framework already exists. For example, earlier I quoted Ainsworth and Smith (1993):

> This assumes that the important corporate issues of 'mission' and the setting of corporate goals have been addressed and resolved. It assumes that objectives for the sub-sections of the organization (the departments, divisions or business units) have been set within the key results areas, and that the senior management group has identified just where the competitive advantage and value added dimensions of the business lie. It further assumes that all of this has been communicated to and understood by those involved.
>
> *(Ainsworth and Smith 1993: 5–6)*

In many organizations it is likely that all of this does exist and that it operates in the way advocated. But this should not be assumed; for example, the IMS survey of performance management practices (Institute of Personnel Management 1992) revealed that communication was one aspect of their policies which organizations found to be problematical. Furthermore, the survey evidence also revealed that the organizational framework is often deficient in various respects. So, not all organizations have mission statements and even if they do there may be a failure to communicate those statements, and other relevant information, to all employees. Hence, for many organizations the starting point for performance management will have to be at the corporate/organizational level – for example, with its systems for planning, manufacturing/service delivery, employee communication, etc.

But as can be seen from earlier chapters, the predominant nature of performance management systems in UK organizations is that they are in essence evolutionary developments of performance appraisal, or as Lundy and Cowling put it, 'a logical progression' (1996: 307). This may be true of elsewhere also; for example, in the US Bernardin *et al.* (1998) note the substitution of 'performance management' for 'performance appraisal'. Being mindful of this I will outline an approach to the development and implementation of performance management which is consistent with the evolutionary stance but which allows for more radical and fundamental change. The basis of the approach comes from Mohrman *et al.* (1989). Though presented as an approach to the design of appraisal systems, it applies readily to performance management as conventionally practised in the UK and I will therefore describe it in performance-management-related terms. I shall use the Mohrman *et al.* model as a general framework within which I shall incorporate other models, including those from the broader literature on the management of change. A characteristic feature of many of the recent models of performance management system design is the strong emphasis they place on diagnosis and analysis.

Introducing performance management: evolution and iteration

One of the attractions of the approach advocated by Mohrman *et al.* (1989) is that it recognizes the organizational context of performance management – mission, strategy, structure, etc. It also recognizes that forms and procedures are commonly associated with performance management and that the core events are 'personal and interpersonal behaviours and processes' (1989: 15). In other words, the approach accommodates both the formal, procedural aspects of performance management and the informal, day-to-day aspects. All this is shown in Figure 9.1.

Figure 9.1 also depicts the design process as political, rational and participative, aspects that will become clear as this chapter proceeds. As a rational process we might view it as a more or less step-by-step sequence of activities, as in Figure 9.2.

Figure 9.1   **Designing performance appraisal: a framework for performance management**

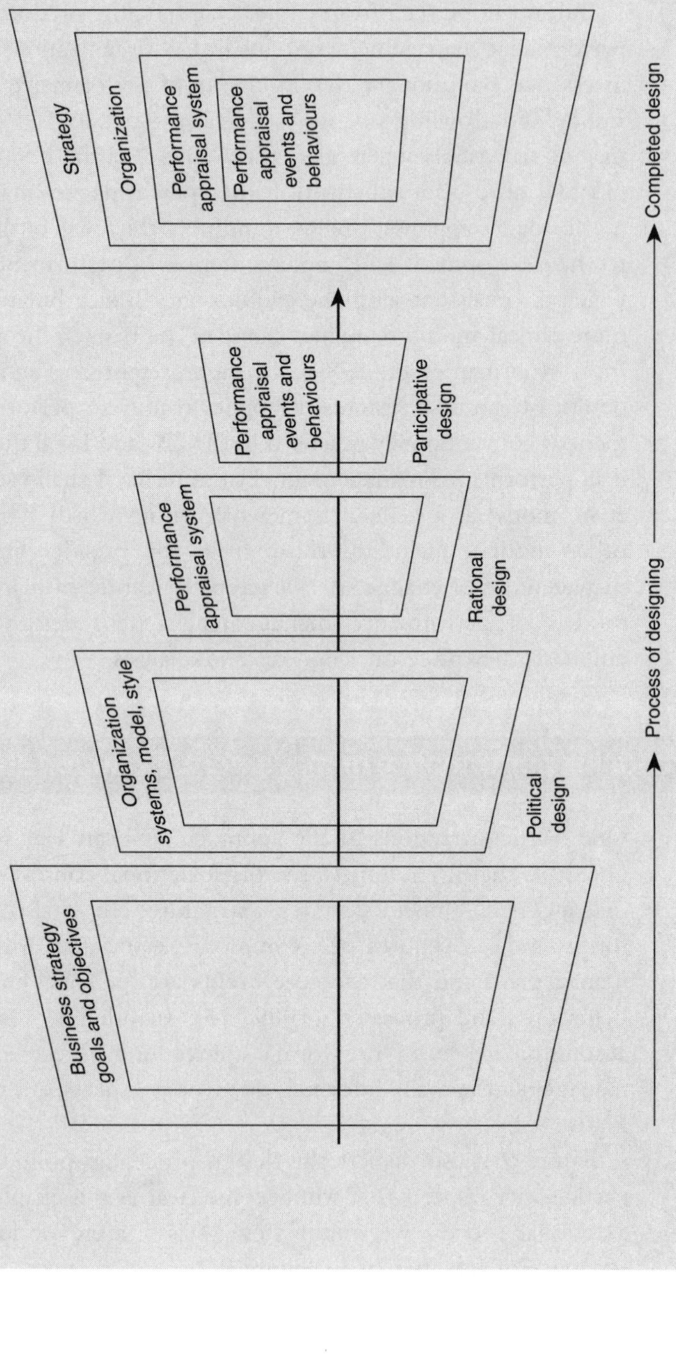

Source: Mohrman et al. 1989

Figure 9.2 **A realistic model for performance appraisal system design: a step-by-step approach for performance management**

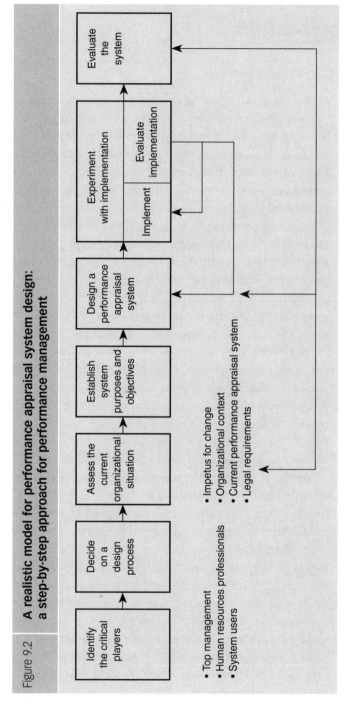

Source: Mohrman et al. 1989

The critical players

Employees and their managers

Mohrman *et al.* write of the need to 'get the right people involved': 'A cardinal rule in any type of design effort is to get the people who will be using the system involved in its design' (1989: 28). Who, then, is involved in using an organization's performance management system? Most obviously, of course, the organization's line managers and the employees who are on the receiving end of performance management. How might managers (and others) be involved? Armstrong (1994) suggests project teams, Bernardin and Beatty (1984) propose a task force comprising representatives of the groups that will be affected, and Fletcher (1993) and Yeates (1990) suggest consultative/advisory groups: 'These groups are beneficial in that they help solve real problems, investment of time in them helps demonstrate top management commitment and ensures that conflicts are aired and resolved. They also demonstrate management ownership of the scheme' (Yeates 1990: 132). Examples are to be found not just in the context of employee performance management: Standard Chartered Bank set up a committee including representatives drawn from all levels of staff; Rolls-Royce Motors set up a team comprising members from all levels (senior management to the shop floor) to investigate total quality issues; Royal Mail conducted workshops with over a thousand staff to help identify current business strengths and weaknesses.

Yet it is the groups most directly affected that are frequently conspicuous by their absence when it comes to the development and implementation of performance management, even though the sorts of consultative processes involved will be familiar to many organizations as they use them as part of their market research activities, for example as a means of keeping in touch with the customer. However, in their IPM research (1992) Fletcher and Williams found a high level of involvement in only a couple of organizations; in most it was of a low order, commonly non-existent. The development and design process more usually takes place at the centre of the organization, and where we find such a non-participatory style we would not be surprised to see it reflected in the performance management system itself – e.g. the relative absence of self-appraisal.

Customers

In earlier chapters I have referred to the potential value of the customer perspective in establishing performance standards and perhaps in assessing performance. Bernardin *et al.* (1998) argue for the linking of performance dimensions to meet internal and external customer requirements. The distinction between internal and external customers is an important one – employees and managers might not necessarily see themselves as customers in which case the process used to solicit their input will need to encourage a customer oriented frame of reference. Cardy (1998) also suggests that customers should be involved in the setting of standards of performance, and notes that: 'Failure to include customers in the vital process of criterion development may mean that workers may be applauded for performance that seems important to their functional area but is irrelevant to the customers of the product or service.'

Top management

Though the groups at the sharp end are important, the design process also has to bring in the organization's senior management and the personnel/HR function. As Mohrman *et al.* point out, the former 'set strategic and philosophical directions for the organization' (1989: 30) and these must be captured by the performance management system. The involvement of managers at the very top or in central functions such as personnel/HR was central to the changes that took place in several of the organizations investigated by Fletcher and Williams. In particular, the CEO (new in ten of the organizations visited by Fletcher and Williams) or the HR Director were key influences. Such top-level commitment needs to be broad-based. In ICI Pharmaceuticals (as it was), Sheard described the establishment of a 'group of senior, experienced business managers from across the organization' (1992: 40). Their task was to serve as a 'personnel steering group' to oversee the implementation of a company-wide initiative called the 'development of people, work and reward' (1992: 40). Such commitment and involvement are important for a number of reasons. For example, Bertsch and Williams (1994), studying the implementation of TQM, showed that the involvement of top management helped to promote the legitimacy of the planned change.

And Rodgers and Hunter (1991) have shown that the positive effects of management by objectives (MbO) are greater under conditions of high top management commitment – that is, a high level of support during implementation and active participation in operating MbO. In other words, it is not enough for top management to be involved and supportive during system development; this must continue once the new system is in operation.

Necessary though it is, the commitment of an organization's topmost management doesn't guarantee that the performance management system will be accepted by those to whom it will apply. The danger is that schemes initiated at the top and developed by the centre will simply come to be seen as having been imposed. But if performance management is to stand any chance of succeeding, the commitment of those on the receiving end is essential – involving them in the design and development process may help to bring this about.

Personnel/HR management

Personnel/HR may be users of information generated by the performance management system (depending upon its purposes and nature), but aside from this, personnel specialists may have a facilitative role to play in the development process. Fletcher and Williams encountered this in their research for the IPM:

> It is important on the one hand to be able to offer support and to give guidance where necessary, but not at the cost of taking control and ownership out of line managers' hands. . . .
>
> The role of the HR department is likely to remain very significant in effective performance management. . . . It has a strong facilitating and support role to play that is essential if the policies are to be developed and to function in an effective and equitable way. . . . In all this, the most important factor will be the ability of the HR department to balance the conflict between the need to devolve ownership and control, with the need to guide, inform and support. Without that support, it may be that the additional demands performance management places on line managers would be too great.
>
> *(Institute of Personnel Management 1992: 116)*

The apparent desire to place responsibility for performance management in the hands of line managers may be seen as part of a broader trend to devolve human resource management activities. Some research (Brewster and Söderström 1994), however, suggests that in the UK such broader devolvement is less widely practised than it is in other countries in Europe. Indeed, out of twelve countries, the UK showed the third-lowest level of devolvement.

Design process

The above remarks about the key players clearly imply a preferred approach to the design process, namely one that is participative and involving. In large organizations the direct involvement of *everyone* who will be affected by performance management is clearly unrealistic, but this need not then become an argument for involving no one! Some suggestions were made above and occasional case accounts of how particular systems have been developed provide some illustrations.

Accounts of managing change (e.g. Dawson 1996) indicate that a participative approach is only one of several which might be adopted. However, a major reason for arguing that a participative, involving approach has special appropriateness with respect to performance management is that performance management is presented as something that should be owned and driven by the line. This implies that the development process should also be driven by the line. Moreover, a number of writers associate performance management with a particular set of values – including trust, openness, free communication and involvement. To advocate such values but then not act in accordance with them when developing a new system will surely mean that the system will be received with scepticism.

This immediately brings to the surface one of the main tensions that will arise in designing a performance management system. We have already identified that there are several key groups affected by or involved in performance management on a day-to-day basis. Some of the interests of these different groups may be shared; but other interests may be in sharp conflict. This is an issue that has been taken up by Murphy and Cleveland (1995). Though they write about appraisal, what they have to say applies no less to performance management. They identify two general strategies that may be adopted in designing a new system: '(a) change participants' goals to fit the needs of the system, or

(b) change the system to fit participants' goals' (Murphy and Cleveland 1995: 381).

The former is the traditional approach and most probably is the one which remains dominant today. Thus, performance management systems are developed centrally to meet goals that have been determined centrally. The new system then is 'rolled out', perhaps supported by some training for those expected to work it. But very often the new system is not accepted, with line managers and employees failing to see it as meeting their needs.

Murphy and Cleveland therefore argue for the second approach: 'An alternative to changing the people to fit the system is to change the system to fit the people. This strategy involves assessing the goals pursued by participants in appraisal, then tailoring the system to best fit those goals' (1995: 382). The risk here, of course, is that of developing a system that will fail to meet the needs and requirements as seen by top management. As noted above, it is just as important to maintain their acceptance and commitment. Thus, as Mohrman *et al.* (1989) make clear, the design process is in part political, and it is in assessing the current situation that the interests of the different groups begin to become apparent.

Assessing the current situation

An organization which routinely carries out monitoring and maintenance of its performance management system will readily have evidence about how well it is working and in consequence will be well placed to fine tune its operation or to make more substantial changes should these be required. However, systematic data often will not be available – as we have seen, organizations commonly do little by way of monitoring and evaluation – and change is likely to come about as a result of the perception of some kind of problem. To this extent the introduction of performance management is often reactive; for example, Fletcher and Williams concluded:

> Adopting performance management has not been an entirely reactive process, forced on organizations by external circumstances. There is no doubt that some have developed policies of this kind as a result of deep thought about their values, their attitude to their employees, and their

future mission, and without any significant external pressures on them at the time. But the impression obtained from this research is that they probably are in the minority.

(Institute of Personnel Management 1992: 85)

However, in this respect the impetus for introducing performance management may be no different from that for many other changes that arise within organizations. Undoubtedly, there has to be a perception of some need for change; this point is widely recognized in the literature on organizational and cultural change (e.g. Brown 1995; Dawson 1996). Recognizing what the trigger is is an important early step in the diagnostic process. We can see this in the framework put forward by the Strategic Remuneration Research Centre (SRRC) (Table 9.1).

Factors to be analysed

One of the advantages of this framework is that it is specifically oriented towards employee-centred performance management. But there are other diagnostics which may be more or less appropriate depending on how widely the organization wishes to analyse the current situation. For example, Swanson (1994) poses questions which may be asked about performance at three levels – organization, process and individual, as shown in Table 9.2. What these frameworks illustrate is that there are many factors to be analysed in assessing the current situation; for example:

- the organization's mission etc.;
- what the organization's objectives are, whether they are generally known throughout the organization, what is generally understood by organizational performance;
- the organization's prevailing climate and culture;
- organizational structure, including decision-making processes and job design;
- the fit of performance management activities with other personnel/HR policies and practices;
- communication systems;
- reward systems.

Also, following on from what was said earlier about involving the key players, many of the questions are ones which are best answered

Table 9.1	**Strategic Remuneration Research Centre performance management diagnostic**

1 Reasons
- What has triggered a reappraisal of the performance management system or rewards at this time?

2 Objectives
- What are our strategic business goals?
- Who or what delivers critical performance with respect to business goals?
- What kind of performance contract do we want with employees?
- What is the performance system designed to do (e.g. attract, retain, motivate, control)?

3 Environment

External contingencies
- What stage of the business cycle are we in?
- What are the effects of the national/societal culture we operate in on attitudes to performance and differentials?

Internal contingencies
- What are the motivational assumptions of the relevant group(s) of employees?
- What are the relevant internal employee reference groups and how do they affect attitudes to differentials?

4 Systems
- What is the range of things we have to do to support the performance/business goals that affect employees' knowledge, capability and motivation?

5 Design

Content
- How do we define rewards?
- How do we define incentives?
- What measures are appropriate (e.g. in terms of the short, medium, and long term, financial versus non-financial measures, individual versus group)?
- Can we measure performance in the ways we want to and design rewards appropriately?
- Can people see this connection?

Process
- Are there links or disconnections through the whole reward structure?
- Do other managers involved in the design and management of the performance system buy into it?
- Is the process manageable?
- How do we communicate about performance and rewards, including feedback?

6 Outcomes
- What is the impact on behaviour (e.g. does the system reinforce the old or motivate new behaviours)?

- Retrospectively, what is the pay-off or success criterion?
- Is it possible to define or develop return on investment criteria, taking into account the costs of designing and administering the scheme, and of paying for rewards?

7 Monitoring

- What review process is in place or needs to be created?

Source: Hendry *et al*. 1997: 21

Table 9.2	**Performance diagnosis: enabling questions**		
PERFORMANCE VARIABLES	PERFORMANCE LEVELS		
	Organization level	Process level	Individual level
Mission/goal	Does the organizational mission/goal fit the reality of the economic, political and cultural forces?	Do the process goals enable the organization to meet organizational and individual missions/goals?	Are the professional and personal mission/goals of individuals congruent with the organization's?
Systems design	Does the organizational system provide structure and policies supporting the desired performance?	Are processes designed in such a way as to work as a system?	Does the individual design support performance?
Capacity	Does the organization have the leadership, capital and infrastructure to achieve its mission/goals?	Does the process have the capacity to perform (quantity, quality and timeliness)?	Does the individual have the mental, physical and emotional capacity to perform?
Motivation	Do the policies, culture and reward systems support the desired performance?	Does the process provide the information and human factors required to maintain it?	Does the individual want to perform no matter what?
Expertise	Does the organization establish and maintain selection and training policies and resources?	Does the process of developing expertise meet the changing demands of changing processes?	Does the individual have the knowledge, skills and experience to perform?

Source: Swanson 1994: 52

by systematically gathering relevant data and evidence from those who are in a position to give an informed view. This reinforces the participative and rational nature of the design process. However, certain of the factors identified above will themselves have a key influence on the nature of the design process that comes to be adopted. For example, Mohrman *et al.* argue:

> The critical variables to measure with respect to organizational climate are trust, support, openness, and amount of participation in work tasks. Without a high degree of trust and openness, it is difficult to design a performance appraisal system that meets subordinates' developmental needs. Likewise, the introduction of a participative appraisal system in an organization that is generally managed by top-down mandates will also meet with resistance. . . .
>
> Issues about the influence style of an organization are concerned with how decisions are generally made. Are they generally made quickly, from higher up, or are they made after long deliberations and consensus building from below? If the organization has a top-down mentality and expects decisions to be made quickly, then long drawn-out employee involvement in developing the appraisal system will meet with considerable resistance.
>
> *(Mohrman* et al. *1989: 36–7)*

In short, the participative philosophy being advocated here (and throughout much of the performance management literature) is likely to be a non-starter if such values are not held at the topmost levels. The issue of values leads me on to organizational culture.

Organizational culture

There are two views about culture and performance management – one is that the latter must fit with the former and the other is that performance management is a means of culture change. Whichever view is taken it is necessary first to know what the existing culture is, if indeed there is a prevailing culture for the organization as a whole – as noted earlier, the idea that an organization necessarily has a single, identifiable culture is very much open to question. Culture may exist at the surface level – 'the way we do things around here' – but the underlying values and basic assumptions may not be generally shared, nor indeed readily identifiable. So, when managers/consultants talk about performance management fitting organizational culture what most probably is meant is that performance management needs to fit the espoused culture – for example, the values that may be found in the mission statement or are otherwise articulated by the organization's top management (Legge 1995).

From this point of view we might see performance management as a mechanism for inculcating a particular culture, that is, a 'performance culture'. But what exactly is meant by a performance culture is far from clear. Armstrong, for example, associates performance management with a particular set of values – trust, openness, participation and the like. But equally we see a very strong emphasis on results, indicating that a performance culture also has to do with production and output. This is understandable but there is some risk that an overemphasis on results and the bottom line may be at the expense of employee health and well-being. A good illustration of this was provided by one of the organizations visited by Fletcher and Williams (Institute of Personnel Management 1992) – the existing performance culture overemphasized 'bottom-line' results and fear was felt to be the driving force.

Given the considerable difficulty of altering basic values it seems likely that when we talk about using performance management to change culture what probably happens is that we change the 'artifacts', and this, at best, may do no more than modify culture on the surface. In other words, systems and structure change and employee behaviour may follow suit.

The development of 'new' behaviours may be a valuable (and possibly sufficient) outcome in itself. Indeed, changing behaviour seems to be central to many culture change programmes (Williams *et al.* (1993) provide some examples). But there presumably is the intention also to change values. And underlying this may be the intention to change deeper-seated basic assumptions. But does behaviour change lead to internalization of new values? Not necessarily; Legge takes up this issue:

> in theory this internalization is only likely to occur if the individuals involved feel they have some choice and discretion over their new behaviours and that the consequences of engaging in them are positive.
> ... If the individual has no choice (other than redundancy), or is heavily 'bribed' to participate, the required behaviour may result, but even espoused values of all but senior management may remain unchanged.

> As for the taken-for-granted assumptions, it is debatable whether many of the work groups involved in culture change programmes have had sufficient time to test and be reinforced in the new espoused values for these to be absorbed into unconscious assumptions.
>
> *(Legge 1995: 197)*

Three points are being made here. The first is that deep-seated change, if it is to come about at all, will only do so in the long term. Second, there is the possibility of simply ending up with compliance rather than commitment (Ogbonna 1992). And this might not be culture change at all. Third, there is the ethical issue of the legitimacy of one group seeking to impose its set of values on another. It would seem naive to suppose that top management's values will simply be accepted. Hendry *et al.* recognize this: 'anyone designing and implementing a system must talk through their assumptions and values, plus those of the people it targets. This is the only way to persuade people to buy into it' (1997: 23).

Note that what is being suggested here is not just the analysis of the current situation but also the determination of what is desired in the future – in other words, identifying whether there is a 'performance gap' (e.g. Csoka 1994). Various tools and techniques are available, from the organizational development (OD) repertoire and elsewhere, to assist in this process, e.g. interviews/discussions with workers and managers, leaders, union officials, survey questionnaires, observation, analysis of company documentation, visioning workshops, scenario planning, business modelling (Brown 1995; Moyer 1996; Prytz 1995; Sparrow and Boam 1992).

Analysing participant goals for performance management

The widespread advocacy of initial diagnostic/analytical activity is wholly consistent with Murphy and Cleveland's (1995) argument that the goals that line managers and employees have for performance management should be identified. They draw on the ideas of Balzer and Sulsky (1990), who write about performance appraisal effectiveness in terms of satisfying the goals of the different constituencies who may be involved. That they are concerned with **effectiveness** is especially significant as the goals for performance management systems are often expressed in a rather general way, for example to motivate employees, to identify training and development needs. But what exactly do these things mean? How would we judge if a performance management scheme has been successful in identifying training and development needs? Being more specific about the criteria that we would use not only helps to assess effectiveness but also offers a basis for designing a system that is fit for its purpose. Balzer and Sulsky set out a four-step model to help determine more specific criteria, as shown in Box 9.1.

As well as the methods of analysis suggested above, another example particularly relevant to performance management is Kerr's (1988) reward-system questionnaire, discussed in Chapter 8. As part of their 'strategic human resource management (SHRM) profiling', Beer *et al.* (1995: 117) use employee task forces, interviews and feedback within their diagnostic approach, which seeks to accommodate the needs of different stakeholder groups and bring about alignment of human resource management policies and practices with organizational strategy.

As is clear from Box 9.1 each group may have several goals for performance management. Some of these goals may be shared amongst different constituencies, but others may be in conflict. I shall take up these points in the next section.

Purposes and objectives of the performance management system

As we saw in Chapter 1, performance management may be introduced to serve any one or more of several purposes – for example employee motivation, improving training and development, linking pay to performance, providing feedback on performance, improving employee performance, etc.

What we see here are tensions which have long existed in relation to performance appraisal practice. First, performance management systems are commonly multipurpose, and those purposes are predominantly to serve organizational ends. For example, it is often claimed that some purposes, such as those to do with training and development, are for the benefit of the employee. Yet it is probable that in providing training and development opportunities the organization is intending, first and foremost, to meet organizational needs. This is very reasonable, of course, but if there is also the intention that employees should benefit shouldn't they have some say in the process? Second, a given system may

| Box 9.1 | **Developing criteria of performance management effectiveness** |

Identification of constituent group(s). There will be at least three: the organization (as exemplified by top management, which may not necessarily be a homogeneous group), line managers and the employees who are subject to performance management.

Identification of constituent goal(s). Each group will have a set of goals, for example:

- **The organization**: increasing employee performance (and productivity); encouraging employee motivation; clarifying and communicating what is expected of employees (avoiding role ambiguity); planning work; identifying training and development needs; determining/contributing to administrative decisions – salary, promotion, etc.; justifying personnel decisions, e.g. in case of alleged unfair dismissal.

- **Line managers**: an easy to use system; encouraging employee motivation; clarifying and communicating what is expected of employees (avoiding role ambiguity); increasing employee performance (and productivity); avoiding interpersonal conflict; building and maintaining good interpersonal and working relationships; enhancing one's own status within the organization; managing impressions; developing employees' competence; enhancing employees' self-esteem and other aspects of well-being.

- **Employees**: feedback (especially if it is positive); avoiding interpersonal conflict; building and maintaining good interpersonal and working relationships; enhancing one's status within the organization; managing impressions; identifying and meeting development needs; knowing where one stands for the future – discussing advancement opportunities; developing personal competence; enhancing self-esteem and other aspects of well-being; defending against criticism; conveying upward feedback; having interesting and satisfying work; seeking improvements to working conditions.

Identification of specific objective(s). 'Given the distal nature and vagueness of many goals, specific objectives associated with the constituent groups' goal(s) should be clearly identified' ▶

(Balzer and Sulsky 1990: 152). Murphy and Cleveland also make the point that 'it is necessary to move from a general idea of what types of goals [the constituent groups] *might be* pursuing to an assessment of the goals they *actually are* pursuing' (1995: 389). They suggest using direct and indirect means for doing so.

Selection of criteria. Criteria are not preordained and hence need to be developed as part of the design process.

> *(Source: adapted from Balzer and Sulsky 1990;*
> *Dulewicz and Fletcher 1989;*
> *Murphy and Cleveland 1995)*

have too many purposes, with the consequent risk that none of them comes to be well served. Third, there may be conflicts between the purposes. The likelihood of conflict becomes more apparent when we recognize that line managers and employees have their own goals for performance management even if they are not an explicit feature of an organization's system. A simplified model of possible conflicts is illustrated in Figure 9.3.

Development or reward?

In their analysis of UK practice Bevan and Thompson (Institute of Personnel Management 1992: 52) concluded that the main purpose of performance management was 'to facilitate the integration of the

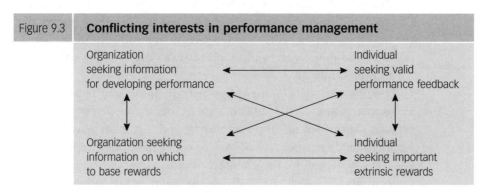

Figure 9.3 **Conflicting interests in performance management**

Organization seeking information for developing performance ⟷ Individual seeking valid performance feedback

Organization seeking information on which to base rewards ⟷ Individual seeking important extrinsic rewards

Source: Anderson 1993; adapted from Mohrman *et al*. 1989

various components of human resource management (HRM) and mesh them more closely with the business objectives of the organization' (Institute of Personnel Management 1992: 52). They identified two routes to integration, **reward-driven** and **development-driven**:

> Reward driven integration processes concentrate on the role of performance payment systems to change organizational behaviour and tend to place less emphasis on the role of the myriad of human resource policies that can also be used to pursue these objectives. In these organizations changing the remuneration philosophy and practices was seen as the main means of delivering improvements in overall organizational effectiveness. This is emerging as the dominant mode of integration among UK employers.
>
> The second approach to integration – development driven – stresses the importance of ensuring that the range of human resource activities (including training and career development) is right for the organization and that there is a sufficient co-ordination between them. The remuneration dimension is seen as complementary [to] but not dominating this process and, as a result, is not given undue weight within the organization. This approach would appear to be only undertaken by a minority of employers.
>
> *(Institute of Personnel Management 1992: 53)*

Writ large here are McGregor's Theory X and Theory Y, set out by him over forty years ago and shown here in Box 9.2. The dominant approach to performance management (a results-orientated conception of performance linked to financial reward) is a clear reflection of Theory X. An ever-increasing body of evidence points to the drawbacks of this set of values for performance management practice. For example, the evidence about PRP reviewed in Chapter 8 shows that the motivational benefits claimed for it are difficult to realize in practice, and there is every likelihood that an organization will end up with lowered morale.

Though the development–reward dilemma can't be avoided altogether, some of the difficulties may be alleviated by adopting a broader view of reward. If we do this we find that many reward-related practices and behaviours are consistent with a development perspective, e.g. jobs which allow the exercise of autonomy and which provide opportunities for skill use and enhancement, praise, providing feedback/coaching.

| Box 9.2 | **McGregor's Theory X and Theory Y** |

Theory X

1 Management is responsible for organizing the elements of productive enterprise – money, materials, equipment, people – in the interest of economic ends.

2 With respect to people, this is a process of directing their efforts, motivating them, controlling their actions, modifying their behaviour to fit the needs of the organization.

3 Without this active intervention by management, people would be passive – even resistant – to organizational needs. They must therefore be persuaded, rewarded, punished, controlled – their activities must be directed. This is management's task – in managing subordinate managers or workers. . . .

Behind this conventional theory there are several additional beliefs – less explicit, but widespread:

4 The average man is by nature indolent – he works as little as possible.

5 He lacks ambition, dislikes responsibility, prefers to be led.

6 He is inherently self-centred, indifferent to organizational needs.

7 He is by nature resistant to change.

8 He is gullible, not very bright, the ready dupe of the charlatan and the demagogue.

The human side of economic enterprise today is fashioned from propositions and beliefs such as these. Conventional organization structures, managerial policies, practices and programmes reflect these assumptions.

Theory Y

1 Management is responsible for organizing the elements of productive enterprise – money, materials, equipment, people – in the interest of economic ends.

2 People are *not* by nature passive or resistant to organizational needs. They have become so as a result of experience in organizations. ▶

3 The motivation, the potential for development, the capacity for assuming responsibility, the readiness to direct behaviour towards organizational goals are all present in people. Management does not put them there. It is a responsibility of management to make it possible for people to recognize and develop these human characterisitcs for themselves.

4 The essential task of management is to arrange organizational conditions and methods of operation so that people can achieve their own goals *best* by directing *their own* efforts towards organizational objectives.

This is a process of primarily creating opportunities, releasing potential, removing obstacles, encouraging growth, providing guidance.

(Source: McGregor 1957: 23–30)

Designing the performance management system

Deciding what the purpose of the performance management system is to be is perhaps the most important part of the whole development process as the design of the system will follow in large part from the decisions that are taken about purpose. The diagnostic frameworks suggested earlier will help decision-makers focus their attention on what they want the system to accomplish, how it will fit with other systems and how those systems might need to be changed.

As noted earlier, the design and development process is as much political as rational (Mohrman *et al.* 1989). Indeed, there is widespread recognition today that it is not just the design process that is political – appraisal (and, by extension, performance management) itself is as well (e.g. Cardy and Dobbins 1994; Murphy and Cleveland 1995; Tziner *et al.* 1996). One of the advantages of the analytical approach is that the potential conflicts of interest can be brought to the surface at an early stage. Resolving them, however, may be problematic and it may be necessary to assess the relative priorities of the different goals of the several interested parties (Murphy and Cleveland 1995). This may necessarily mean, as Fletcher and Williams (1992) have indicated, that the resulting system(s) will involve compromises. Though this may be seen as disadvantageous, the reverse perhaps is more likely to be the case in that organizational reality – the plurality of interests – is better reflected.

This particular step in the overall development process involves answering a whole series of questions about the nature, scope, content and mode of operation of performance management. The two diagnostic frameworks suggested earlier illustrate some of what needs to be asked. A fuller list of questions is offered by Armstrong (1994). Armstrong poses sixty-four questions, some examples of which are shown in Table 9.3. This list offers a very helpful and practical checklist for any organization developing a performance management system. The questions need to be answered in the context of the analysis of the organization's current and desired future state.

This more detailed design step is thus concerned with analysing the requirements and constraints (Roe 1989) associated with the proposed purpose/function. Many of the questions, in other words, focus on what the sytem specifically will be *required* to do, how it will operate. For example, if the purpose of performance management will be a developmental one – the route to improving performance is to be by developing people's capabilities – then we might expect to see behaviours or competencies feature prominently within the system. Following from this will be certain requirements concerning the validity etc. of the performance dimensions that are identified – that is, we would expect to see efforts to identify performance criteria that will meet the requirements set out in Table 5.6. This also means that in practice we would expect to see behavioural dimensions of performance being identified in the sorts of participative, research-based manners described in Chapter 5.

And then when we come to consider constraints we would need to face up to issues such as cost. For example, if an organization were to opt for a reward-driven approach would it be able to afford it? Would it be able to meet the costs of performance-related pay? As Milkovich and Wigdor (1991) have pointed out, if the organization does not allocate sufficient funds to award merit payments that people see as meaningful, then the whole system becomes pointless. But it is not just the direct financial costs that need to be considered – there are also the indirect ones resulting from lowered motivation and morale.

Having reached the point of realizing a prototypical design for the system (or systems), the organization might now be tempted to

Table 9.3	**Designing a performance management system: a checklist**

1 *General*. What are our objectives in introducing performance management?
2 *Performance agreement*. Should the approach be based on a formal performance agreement, plan or contract?
3 *Objectives*. What do we mean by objectives? Do we, for example, differentiate between short-term and standing objectives?
4 *Performance measures or indicators*. Do we include inputs as well as outputs as factors to be considered in assessing performance?
5 *Attributes and competences*. To what extent is it possible or desirable to develop generic competences?
6 *Performance and development plans*. How should we incorporate development and training plans?
7 *Managing performance throughout the year*. How do we ensure that managers are aware of their responsibilities for managing performance throughout the year and carry them out?
8 *Performance reviews*. To what extent do we incorporate self, upward or peer assessment in the review process?
9 *Performance rating*. Do we need performance rating?
10 *Documentation*. What written guidelines do we need for managers and individuals?
11 *Existing arrangememts*. What account do we take of existing arrangements for performance appraisal?
12 *Performance management for teams*. Do we want to emphasize the importance of incorporating teams into the performance management process?
13 *Performance-related pay*. If we have performance-related pay, how do we prevent this from prejudicing the motivational and developmental aspects of performance management?
14 *Reaction and behaviour of managers/reactions of other employees*. How can we generate ownership of performance management by line managers? How do we get employees to accept and understand performance management?
15 *Training and briefing*. Do we train both managers *and* their staff? What sort of briefing is required?
16 *Pilot testing and implementation*.
17 *Evaluation and quality*.

Source: Armstrong 1994: 154–7

launch into full scale implementation. However, this may be too hasty: what looks fine on paper may not work in quite the way intended. A phased approach to implementation therefore offers advantages, and I shall come on to this in the next chapter.

Box 9.3	**Implications for practice**

Recognize that designing and implementing a performance management system will be an iterative process. Also, unless the existing system is going to be cast aside completely, it is likely to be an evolutionary process.

Adopt a participative approach to system design. This is likely to take longer than non-consultation, but is likely to yield benefits in gaining acceptance/ownership and in identifying the interests of different stakeholder groups. But those interests may conflict – they might not all be satisfied equally well. Resolving any such conflicts will be a political process that may require compromises to be made.

Identify the critical players who need to be involved – the stakeholder groups that have an interest in performance management.

Assess the current situation. Use a diagnostic framework for this. As part of this process identify the goals of the different stakeholders.

Decide what the overall aim is to be. Be wary of having too many objectives for performance management. And bear in mind that different purposes may conflict with one another – will they all be achievable within a single process?

Use a checklist to guide the process of designing the system.

A concluding comment

As this chapter has shown, the process of designing and developing a performance management system is highly complex and involved. This is true even if we take a very narrow employee-focused approach to performance management.

The design process is partly rational and the diagnostic frameworks that have become more common in recent years present useful questions which help to make the process more systematic and ordered. But the process of design, as advocated here and by many others, is also a participative one. This is important for several reasons – to help create a system that is fit for its intended purpose, that will be accepted by those who are expected to use it and benefit from it, and that will be perceived as fair. But such an involving approach is likely to bring to the surface potential conflicts of interest stemming from the different goals that different parties have for performance management.

Difficult though they are to deal with, it is important that these differences be identified. Resolving them is less of a rational process than a political one. Consequently, there are no neat answers and no prescriptive solutions when it comes to system design. Inevitably, any performance management system that is developed is going to fall some way short of what might be considered ideal. It is important to accept this because it bears on the expectations that we might have of what performance management will deliver. In their IPM research Fletcher and Williams encountered organizations in which expectations were almost certainly far too high. The danger, of course, is that these expectations will not be realized, leading to disillusionment and, at worst, system decline. This reinforces the need for performance management systems themselves to be managed.

10 Implementing and managing performance management

As I noted in the previous chapter, once a performance management system has been designed it may be tempting to introduce it across the whole of the organization straight away. This may be a mistake, if only because of the likely magnitude of the task: a phased approach may therefore be more sensible. Moreover, having been introduced it cannot just be left in the hope that it will run smoothly and without any problems. This has been recognized for other approaches to managing performance – for example, TQM. One recent US survey of senior managers in TQM organizations (Longenecker and Scazzero 1996) showed that there were perceived to be various continuing problems, such as individuals not effectively performing their jobs, communication breakdowns, ineffective supervision and several others. Some sort of systematic monitoring or auditing activity is therefore required to identify these difficulties so that they can be overcome. Furthermore, Knights and McCabe (1996) identified the need, in a survey of UK financial services organizations, to manage quality initiatives. This is no less important for performance management – it needs maintenance, monitoring and management. Where possible, such activity should be built in as an integral and routine part of the system itself. All this is often underestimated or even goes unrecognized, as Fletcher and Williams discovered:

> The Chief Personnel Officer of one County Council, when asked what he would do differently if he were starting out to introduce performance management again, said that he would get across to people that the maintenance costs were high. He was referring to the fact that once it was set up, you could not afford to leave it – it was essential to talk about it and keep it as a live issue.
>
> (*Institute of Personnel Management 1992: 94*)

This is so even if there has been participation by line managers and others in designing the system. The positive effects of such participation may wear off over time if nothing is done to maintain the sense of involvement – for example within the performance management system itself. Monitoring, too, is an involving activity and shows that the opinion of employees and their managers is valued. It has as its central purpose the improvement of the performance management system: this is important as there is little point in carrying out audit and evaluation activities if nothing is done with what is found. The results need to be fed back to those who are able to act on them.

The need for auditing and other tools to improve the operation of organizational systems (of all kinds) has long been advocated. Some specific examples relevant to performance management include the Management Development Audit – a toolkit which, amongst other things, gathered information about various aspects of an organization's appraisal system, such as employee involvement, upward and downward communication. More recently, Fletcher and Williams (1992), Fletcher (1993) and Anderson (1993) provided helpful advice and examples of questionnaires that might be used. And for several decades survey and feedback methods have been part of the repertoire of organizational development tools (French and Bell 1995). The latter methods are of particular interest as they offer the prospect of integrating an audit tool as a core element of the performance management system, as in upward appraisal for example. Later in this chapter I will go on to give examples of some of these tools and techniques.

Experimenting with implementation

The implementation of performance management may well be organizational change on a large scale. The more wide-ranging the scope of the system, the greater the scale of the task. Even if the system is relatively circumscribed as an employee-focused intervention, implementation will be a big task. And it should not be assumed that the system (or systems) as designed will run as intended. A phased approach to implementation therefore offers advantages: some experimentation – a pilot test of the prototype – which is monitored systematically may be a sensible first step. Mohrman *et al.* (1989) suggest six questions which should be answered in selecting a suitable site for the piloting, as shown in Table 10.1. It is possible that answers to these questions will reveal that no single site will fit the bill, in which case pilot testing may have to extend across a number of sites. The piloting provides an opportunity to test out not just the system itself but also the accompanying support systems, such as the briefing/publicity and training that will be required. Briefing/publicity needs to cover what the system is for, why and how it has come about, and various other matters as indicated in Table 10.2.

Table 10.1	**Selecting a pilot site**

1 Is the size of the unit appropriate? Is it small enough to be studied carefully but large enough for the variety necessary to generalizability?
2 Is the structure of the unit typical of other units?
3 Is the function of the unit generalizable?
4 Is the unit politically acceptable? Will other units believe that this was a representative pilot site?
5 Does the unit have a stigma? (Is it known as the most productive, loosest, hardest, laziest?)
6 Are top managers supportive? Piloting is often arduous and disruptive. Without top managers' support, you may be asked to leave before you find out what you need to know.

Source: Mohrman *et al.* 1989: 43–4

Table 10.2	**Content of performance management briefing**

- The aims and objectives of the performance management system.
- How the system has been developed
- How it fits the business strategy.
- The links with other systems.
- Benefits to key parties – employees, managers and the organization.
- Full details of the performance management cycle, its various elements, including methods and documentation – that is, the process of the scheme, how it works, etc.
- Precisely what is expected of each party, at every stage in the performance management cycle.
- Performance management outcomes: how the performance management cycle is completed, what happens to performance management data, including confidentiality of data.
- Training provision.

Source: adapted from Anderson 1993; Yeates 1990

Though some briefing (Anderson 1993) will be required it is unlikely that this in itself will be enough. The models of performance management discussed at the start of the book all emphasize the importance of communication much more generally, and I will come on shortly to other aspects of organizational communication. But so far as implementation is concerned training will be needed for both parties most actively involved in performance management. The training that should be provided for managers depends on the specific content of the performance management system, but if we draw on what is advocated in the literature it seems likely that the sorts of things listed in Table 10.3 will need to be covered.

If logistically feasible it may be beneficial to deliver the training on a department-by-department (or similar) basis. Though 'stranger' groups have advantages, e.g. broadening participants' awareness of other parts of the organization, the benefits of 'family group' training may be preferable in this instance. In particular, a valuable team-building function may be served, and the bedding down of the new process may be more effectively facilitated. If training is to be delivered across rather than within departments, try to get together participants who have shared interests or who need to work together – again, this may help to serve a broader organizational development function.

Table 10.3	**Content of performance management training for managers**

- Goal-setting and work planning, including the establishment of performance measures – not just the 'mechanical' aspects such as characteristics of 'good' goals, but also motivational issues and the relevant interpersonal skills (Hale 1993)
- Managing the job context – helping to find ways of overcoming constraints
- Understanding of competencies/behavioural dimensions – the particular ones in use in the organization
- Gathering performance information and measuring performance – objectives/goals/results and behaviours/competencies
- Providing feedback and receiving/responding to feedback
- Reviewing/identifying causes of performance – distinguishing between system and person factors
- Coaching
- Discussing employee development
- Conducting informal and formal performance reviews
- Managing reward

Fletcher and Williams found that there were many organizations where the level of training provided was insubstantial, with only occasional examples of more wide-ranging interpersonal skill training (e.g., Wright 1996) which extended beyond the narrow confines of appraisal-related activity. Training for the 'recipients' of performance management – those to whom it is done – is advocated in some models of performance management (e.g., Masterson and Taylor's (1996) *Total Performance Management*) but occurs in practice even less than that provided for line managers. That said, we need to recognize that managers are employees too and so the training provided to them may serve a dual purpose even though this probably is not intended explicitly. But specific employee training would seem to be sensible; Table 10.4 suggests what might be covered.

The piloting may reveal that some changes are required. These may be changes to the system itself or changes to some aspect of the organizational context. In this way the design and implementation process is an iterative one – the feedback loops in Figure 9.2 illustrate this. Once any issues that need to be resolved have been sorted out, the new system may then be progressively introduced over a period of time. Fletcher and Williams (Institute of Personnel Management 1992) discovered that many performance management schemes were implemented rather hastily. But the more extensive the change, the longer the time-scale needs to be – many of the changes associated with performance management are of a long-term nature.

Those involved in the piloting could later become involved in this promulgation. For example, the use of 'line manager coaches' (as in ICI Pharmaceuticals) is one illustration.

The job of introducing and integrating performance management in departments was given to line managers throughout the business. These

Table 10.4	**Content of performance management training for employees**

- Participating in goal-setting – work and developmental goals
- Understanding competencies/behaviours – the particular ones in use in the organization
- Self-review/self-assessment
- Self-management behaviours
- Providing upward feedback
- Receiving feedback

managers, known as 'performance management coaches', were selected by their heads of department because they had legitimacy and status with their peers, good interactive skills, and welcomed involvement in the process of changing the culture.

(Sheard 1992: 42)

Mercury Communications adopted a similar approach – 120 staff were trained as occasional trainers to help implement their new system.

But once a new system has been introduced it cannot simply be left in the hope that it will run smoothly – it needs to be managed and maintained. Part of the managing of performance management requires having an infrastructure for organizational communication.

Communication

The importance of vision, mission and strategy as the framework for performance management is strongly emphasized in much of the practitioner-oriented literature (as Table 1.5 showed). Prominence is also given to organizational communication. At the very least we would expect downward communication about matters such as the nature of the corporate/business plan, productivity/efficiency, products/services, etc. However, as we saw when considering the reality of organizational practice, this is very often deficient, although organizations with formal performance management systems fare rather better than those without. Generally, though, organizations regard communications as a problem area.

Downward communication

Townley notes that:

> Management communication systems are likely to use a number of different methods, although with a preference for oral rather than written presentations. The most common form of communication with employees across all employment sectors is the systematic use of the 'management chain'. .... The most common combination of communication methods is the use of the management chain allied with newsletters.

(Townley 1994: 597)

Townley notes also that traditional methods such as notice boards continue to be widely used. The use of the management chain is especially important in the context of performance management given the key role that is seen for line managers. However, there are broader aspects to performance management – keeping employees informed about what is going on in the organization – so we might expect to see a wide range of communication media in use.

Also, downward communication is not directed solely at individuals. In particular, there has been a growth in the practice of team briefing. Though such downward communication may serve to convey information, organizations also regard it as a process of influence – persuading/ convincing the employee to subscribe to organizational goals and values (a very unitarist perspective, in other words). But if this is an entirely one-way flow there is the risk that it will be seen simply as propaganda.

Upward communication

The incidence of upward communication remains of a relatively low order, and exists most commonly in the shape of formal means such as suggestion schemes or attitude surveys. Not only that, upward communication is often of a relatively passive kind, as in the case of attitude surveys where the content and any subsequent action are firmly controlled by management. Possibly more active is the upward communication sometimes found in the context of quality management initiatives – joint problem-solving, for example; here the intention is likely to be conceived more broadly as one of employee involvement.

Two-way communication

One of the problems with means of downward and upward communication is that they are predominantly one-way. Related to this, another problem is that communication is management-controlled. For example, downward communication is typically intended to convey information that management has determined should be passed on. Similarly, when it comes to forms of upward communication such as attitude surveys it will usually be management which determines the content of the survey.

This 'one-sidedness' is evident in many of the purposes of communication programmes. Table 10.5 summarizes many of the reasons why organizational communication programmes have been introduced. A number of similarities with performance management may be discerned. First, there is a responsive aspect to organizational communication programmes; as with performance management, external pressures are a major stimulus. Second, employee communication is seen as helping to improve organizational and individual performance – this clearly is consistent with the goals of performance management. Third, although a purpose of communication may be to inform there is a broader intention to *involve*. Here again, this last theme is evident in the advocacy about

Table 10.5	**Reasons for introducing organizational communication programmes**

Educative purposes
- Encourage sense of responsibility
- Improve employees' understanding of company policy and business generally

Production benefits
- Motivate employees toward higher productivity
- Make the organization work better
- Gain acceptance of change
- Increase work flexibility

Participation and involvement
- Involve employees in company affairs – participation and involvement
- Motivate employees/improve morale

'Industrial relations purposes'
- Moderate wage demands/influence negotiations
- Reduce work disruption
- Minimize trade union influence
- Make managers manage

External pressures
- Employee pressure
- Trade union pressure
- Legal requirements
- Pre-empt expected legislation

Broader 'political' considerations
- General social trend
- Discharge responsibilities of company/'right to know'

Source: adapted from Townley 1994: 610

performance management – e.g. not just communicating the mission statement but creating a sense of mission – albeit not in practice.

It seems likely that if these broader purposes are to be served, communication must at least be two-way. As well as receiving information about matters that affect them, employees want to have the opportunity to have some say. As Marchington notes, 'employees like to have the opportunity to find out why (certain) decisions have been made, plus the potential to influence those which are felt to be within their own domain' (1995: 291).

More than this, if such purposes as the involvement of employees are to be achieved organizational action must go beyond communication. So, for example, the literature (e.g., Beaumont 1993; Hyman and Mason 1995; Marchington 1995; Ramsay 1996) shows that employee involvement and participation, which may be seen as a management philosophy or movement in its own right, may comprise direct and indirect means (e.g., task participation and consultation/representative participation) and financial involvement (e.g., Marchington 1995). Clearly, then, employee involvement practices are consistent with performance management.

Does performance management work?

The short answer to this question is that we do not really know. And one of the main reasons why we do not know is that organizations do not do much to discover systematically how their performance management systems are operating and what they are accomplishing. To be fair, though, it is difficult to test certain of the outcomes expected. For example, how effective is performance management in improving organizational performance?

The effectiveness of performance management: organizational performance

According to the IMS survey (Institute of Personnel Management 1992), improving organizational performance is the reason most commonly cited for introducing performance management. However, using a number of financial indicators the IMS researchers distinguished between high-performing and low-performing organizations but were unable to find any association with the presence or absence of formal performance management systems. But perhaps this is too much to expect. As was shown in earlier chapters, organizational performance is a very complex concept and requires multiple measures. Demonstrating an association between performance management and financial indicators may be too much to hope for. We need to use a much wider range of indicators of organizational functioning if we are to identify the contribution being made by performance management.

There is some recognition of this within organizations – the IMS survey showed that a number of indicators are used, including labour turnover, productivity, attitude surveys and salary information. Productivity measures were generally considered to be the most useful across all organizations, with formal performance management organizations attaching particular value to employee attitude surveys and salary information. Moreover, formal performance management organizations were more likely to use the outcome of their monitoring and evaluation activities to make changes to their policies and practices. However, it would seem that these indicators are used in an essentially impressionistic way as organizations commonly do not do much by way of systematic monitoring and evaluation.

Do organizations monitor and evaluate?

The IMS researchers asked organizations to give their own estimates of the effectiveness of their systems and a majority claimed that they were 'moderately effective'. However, it is far from clear that this judgement is based on any evidence – as noted above, it is very much an impression: of all organizations responding to the IMS survey, 'just over half ... conducted any monitoring and evaluation at all' (Institute of Personnel Management 1992: 48). In other words, nearly half of organizations do not!

Benefits claimed for performance management

In the light of the IMS findings about the nature of monitoring methods and the relatively low incidence of systematic monitoring we need to be sceptical about claims made for the benefits of performance management. The Industrial Society survey reports that about two-thirds of their respondents claim benefits with respect to training planning and about 60 per cent for individual motivation. But for other aspects the proportion reporting benefits is relatively low: for example, quality – 22 per cent; customer service – 21 per cent; financial performance – 11 per cent.

Other evidence about benefits comes from the case studies carried out by Fletcher and Williams (Institute of Personnel Management 1992). They found that very few organizations claimed that their performance management activities had improved organizational performance. Rather more common was the view that:

> performance management helped the individual to see his or her part in the wider enterprise with greater clarity. It conveyed a sense of corporate direction and increased identification with the broader aims and goals, with a resulting rise in commitment.
>
> *(Institute of Personnel Management 1992: 98)*

Matters such as these are, of course, susceptible to investigation by employee opinion surveys. Fletcher and Williams were able to carry out such surveys in nine of their participating organizations and discovered quite strong associations between the presence of formal performance management policies and such outcomes as goal clarity, high commitment, job satisfaction, etc.

Further evidence about the impact of performance management on staff comes from surveys carried out for the Audit Commission (1995b) in seventeen local authorities. Using a version of the questionnaire compiled by Fletcher and Williams the Audit Commission surveyed staff opinion about two sets of issues – 'know-how' and 'feel-good'. These are defined in Box 10.1. Employee opinions on these two factors were associated with a 'performance management index' (Audit Commission 1995b: 5.48). The main findings were that:

- Performance management policies contribute to staff 'know-how'; those authorities with the highest 'know-how' scores tend to have well-established performance management programmes extending to all staff.
- Staff with strong 'know-how' also tend to 'feel-good' about their work.

Box 10.1	**Performance management effectiveness: 'know-how', 'feel-good' and the performance index**

'Know-how' measures staff understanding of their role. The survey asked staff about the clarity, priority, difficulty and feedback of goals they were set, and how they thought they had contributed to these goals.

The 'feel-good' factor measures job satisfaction and commitment. The survey asked staff how they felt about the authority, in terms of personal identification, involvement and loyalty. They were also asked to assess their job satisfaction.

The 'performance index' is an indicator of the satisfactoriness of performance management systems. It derives from ratings of six main aspects of performance management: internal communication, external communication, personal appraisal, performance review, financial planning, aims and objectives.

(Source: Audit Commission 1995b)

Effectiveness of organizational communication

As with other aspects of performance management, organizations tend not to evaluate their organizational communication activities. Not surprisingly, therefore, the evidence about effectiveness suggests that management has a more rosy view than do employees at lower levels in the organization. In particular, when an organizational communication programme is newly introduced there may initially be suspicion, although employee responses may become somewhat more positive over time (Townley 1994). A loss of momentum following initial enthusiasm has also been noted (Ramsay 1996) – here again, this endorses the need for continuing management.

The Audit Commission (1995b) evidence (reported earlier) indicates the beneficial effect of good communication on employee attitudes. But the feeling on the part of employees that they do not have as much information as they would like about what is going on, the reasons for decisions and such matters persists. This may be one reason why organizational communication fails. Employees may see the communication as too one-sided – as not providing them with information of relevance or interest to them or as not providing an opportunity to have some say.

Second, employees may see themselves as having no voice or a voice that is not heard. This view may be reinforced if there is excessive management control over the means and content of communication. For example, as Hyman and Mason comment in relation to attitude surveys:

> First, the organization must encourage this method to ascertain information and views on a broad range of company activities and policies, and not just wish to hear 'what it wants to hear', no matter how negative the opinions and attitudes appear to be. And second, the organization should respond positively to generalized feelings and views, rather than just collecting and collating data to be filed away in the personnel department.
>
> *(Hyman and Mason 1995: 82)*

Third, the organization's senior management may fail to see the psychological (e.g., Williams 1991) and political (e.g., Townley 1994) nature of communication. In the latter regard the senior and other managers who design and implement organizational communication programmes may take insufficient account of the perspectives of those expected to deliver the communications. For example, the management chain is regarded as a key communication channel and particular importance attaches to it because it offers the potential for two-way communication.

As in performance management generally, therefore, the role of the line manager is highlighted (possibly with the intention of strengthening the role), with particular emphasis being placed on their interpersonal skills for conveying and gathering information (Wright 1996). Yet line managers and supervisors may not be committed to organizational communication in the way that their senior managers would wish (Marchington 1995). For example, formal communication activities, like team briefing, may be seen as burdensome, as something extra to be done on top of an already heavy workload (even though in some instances the amount of time taken up is actually very short). Moreover, some line managers and supervisors may feel threatened, particularly if the communication truly is intended to be of an involving kind. And many commentators (e.g., Hyman and Mason 1995; Marchington 1995; Townley 1994) have commented on the lack of skill on the part of managers and supervisors, and on the insufficiency of the support (such as training) provided for them.

For all these reasons, organizational communication may achieve less than organizations would hope for. As with performance management, it is important for organizations to have realistic expectations of the benefits that will be realized. Though firm evidence that organizations are getting what they want is, for the most part, lacking, the data that are available do suggest that worthwhile benefits (for organizations and employees) can be obtained. Thus, monitoring is important as a means of finding out what is being achieved as well as for helping to improve the operation of the system.

Monitoring performance management systems

Fitness for purpose

There are a number of levels of monitoring that might be attempted. At the most basic, certain procedural aspects of the performance management system might be monitored. For example, if it is expected that completed forms be returned to the personnel/HR department, does this in fact happen? Non-return clearly is an indicator of some kind of problem – for some reason(s) the system hasn't been accepted – which needs to be investigated.

A more sophisticated level of evaluation would be to carry out some analysis of what gets written on the forms. For example, training and development-related recommendations might be analysed and followed up to ensure that action is taken. This is important, as the failure to take action may lead to the system becoming discredited. If the performance management system is used for pay purposes, merit awards might be monitored by sex and ethnic groupings to ensure that there is no unlawful discrimination.

Completed forms might also be content-analysed to confirm that work objectives conform to the requirements of 'good' (SMART) objectives. Where they do not, this might reveal a training need or, indeed, a more fundamental weakness in the operation of the system. For example, if this sort of analysis was to be done by taking a vertical slice through the organization some assessment could be made of whether the goal-setting process is operating in the cascading fashion that is typically advocated. Are objectives related to key result areas? Are they related to/integrated with organizational and departmental objectives? In other words, is it possible to identify the 'performance logic' (Rummler and Brache 1995) which links the goals? This is tricky, of course, as the idea of the balanced scorecard suggests that the performance logic will not always be as logical and clear cut as we might imagine. But this sort of analytical activity is in itself a tool for diagnosing performance problems – a tool for improving and managing performance in other words. However, all these sorts of evaluative activity seek to establish how fit the system is for its purpose and how well the objectives set for it are being met.

This is problematical as measurable criteria for performance management typically are not established. The series of steps set out by Balzer and Sulsky (1990) offers a way forward here; as noted in Chapter 9, the development of criteria helps to clarify what the system is for as well as setting standards against which the effectiveness of the system will be measured. The criteria used for evaluating a performance management system will necessarily be context-specific and so absolute standards do not really apply. This is understandable given that several parties have an interest in the operation and outcomes of performance management. Hence, any evaluation must capture these several perspectives – senior managers, line managers, employees.

Senior managers

One illustration of an approach which aims to gather senior managers' (and others') perceptions of performance management activities is the 'good practice review' developed by the Audit Commission (1995b). This is outlined briefly in Box 10.2. Though designed for local government the idea (and many aspects of the questionnaire) may be adapted readily for use elsewhere. Many of the questions shown in Box 10.2 are like those suggested in Chapter 9. I made the point there that organizations which routinely carry out monitoring and maintenance activities will, as a matter of course, be assessing their current situation, an important first step in developing a performance management system. This reinforces the need to see evaluation not as something that gets tacked on at the end but rather as an integral part of managing performance management. Several of the questions in Box 10.2 also highlight the importance of capturing the experience of those most directly affected by performance management – line managers and staff.

Box 10.2	**'Good practice' review of performance management**

The objectives of the self-diagnostic good practice review are:

- to provide an assessment by members, chief officers and middle managers of the strengths and weaknesses of the authority's performance management systems
- to identify which elements of the performance managment system should be improved

Good practice review is based on a questionnaire designed to reflect respondents' views on the effectiveness of the authority's policies on managing performance. Councils should seek a separate assessment from three different groups of people:

- members
- chief officers/management team
- middle managers

The self-assessment form asks forty-two questions about six aspects of performance management:

- specification of objectives, e.g:
  - Does the authority have a clear and articulated view of its mission and core values?
  - Is there a clear set of aims (or goals) and objectives (or targets) for the authority as a whole?
- financial/business planning
- performance review, e.g.:
  - Are performance indicators used extensively to monitor inputs, outputs, service efficiency and service effectiveness?
  - Are qualitative indicators (including measures of customer satisfaction) used in situations where quantitative measures are neither practical nor relevant?
  - Does the review of performance result in actions to remedy poor performance? ▶

- individual appraisal, e.g.:
  - Is it an effective two-way process (e.g. by including self-assessment, upward appraisal and participation in goal-setting)?
- external communication
- internal communication, e.g.:
  - How effectively have corporate and departmental objectives been communicated throughout the authority?
  - Are line managers and more junior staff actively involved in the development of goals and objectives?
  - Are all staff given adequate information on how well the authority has achieved its objectives?

(Source: Audit Commission 1995b)

The impact of performance management on line managers and employees

Many writers (e.g., Anderson 1993; Armstrong 1994; Balzer and Sulsky 1990; Dickinson 1993; Fletcher 1993; Fletcher and Williams 1992; Murphy and Cleveland 1995) advocate seeking line manager and employee opinion as part of evaluation activity. What sorts of things should be covered? This depends on the specific nature of the system(s) in use but it is likely that information would need to be gathered about how procedural aspects of the system are experienced as well as feelings about what happened and opinions on the impact of the system.

As a formal system performance management commonly comprises many specific procedures and events that may merit particular attention, such as the analysis of forms that I mentioned above. Employee opinion about these events is important also. For example, the communication and review of objectives and other aspects of performance is a central part of performance management systems and some sort of formal meeting continues to be central to this. Hence, there is a place for evaluation of the kind long advocated for appraisal interviews and other aspects of appraisal systems. Such audits might concern themselves with factual matters – what was discussed and what action arose – as well as subjective and attitudinal dimensions like perceptions of accuracy and fairness. This more focused monitoring may have diagnostic value in shedding light on which procedures are working well and which need improvement.

But there is an important place, too, for broader-ranging surveys of reactions to and attitudes towards performance management in all its aspects. A checklist of the sorts of things that might be covered is given in Box 10.3.

Box 10.3	**A checklist for evaluation**

- Aspects of goals and goal-setting:
  - How involved staff feel in setting their work goals
  - How clear and specific they feel their goals to be
  - How clear people feel their work group to be about its goals
  - How clear people are about the organization's goals
  - What sense people have of how their work contributes to departmental and organizational goals
  - The perception of an emphasis on short-term goals
  - Perceptions of goal difficulty
- Other aspects of the work, e.g. job demands
- Feedback on individual peformance
- Aspects of organizational communication:
  - Communication of organizational mission
  - Communication of business plan
  - Communication about organizational performance
- Aspects of organizational climate:
  - Perceptions of openness/trust
  - Perceptions of fairness
  - Sense of empowerment
  - Sense of involvement
  - Feeling of team working/sense of co-operation
  - Perceptions of management/supervisory style
  - Perceptions of climate for learning/development
- Organizational commitment
- Job involvement/ownership
- Job satisfaction
- Employees' sense of well-being
- Perceived impact on motivation, e.g. perceived relationship between effort and reward
- Employees' sense of personal competence
- Perceived impact on performance
- Perceptions of and attitudes towards reward

Gathering the data

A range of methods may be used, including interviews, group discussions and questionnaires. Some combination is likely to be useful as each method has its advantages and disadvantages. For example, questionnaires allow the collection of quantitative data on a large scale but the format may be constraining, even if some open-ended write-in questions are included. Interviews, on the other hand, allow participants more freedom of expression. And interviews and group discussions may have a particular part to play in the process of developing a questionnaire. As suggested above, if there is no employee involvement in developing the questionnaire there is the risk that it will not be seen as an instrument of two-way communication.

Though it makes sense for organizations to tailor interview schedules and questionnaires to fit their own particular systems, this does not mean having to reinvent the wheel in every case. There are many examples available which can be adapted and modified to suit. If an organization wants to look specifically at, say, the feedback/performance review discussion, the sorts of questions set out in Table 10.6 might be asked of the job holder.

There also is a substantial body of other research on which an organization may draw in developing opinion questionnaires. For example, Fletcher and Williams (Institute of Personnel Management 1992) drew on scales from the behavioural science literature in developing a questionnaire for the IPM research on performance management. This questionnaire was further developed by Fletcher for use within local authorities by the Audit Commission (1995b) – the 'know-how' and 'feel-good' indicators described in Box 10.1. Broad-brush indicators like 'know-how' and 'feel-good' might, however, simply be *too* broad and it may be more useful to focus on more specific measures of the sorts of things listed in Box 10.3. Are staff clear about their goals and what is expected of them? Do they feel that they get enough feedback on their performance? Do they feel that they know what is going on in the organization? Do they feel that the performance management system is fair? Do they feel that their efforts are rewarded? Examples of items which might be used to answer such questions as these are given in Box 10.4. These are intended merely to be illustrative

Table 10.6	**Evaluating the performance review/feedback discussion**

- How much notice were you given that you were going to be interviewed?
- Was this enough time for you to prepare for the discussion?
- Did the interviewer mention any parts of the job that you had done particularly well?
- Was there any mention or discussion of the weaker aspects of your performance in the job during the interview?
- Were your training/development needs mentioned or discussed in the interview?
- Were you able to agree with the interviewer on what your objectives should be for the next year?
- Were factors outside your control discussed?
- Did the interview make you feel that you *wanted* to improve your performance in the job?
- After the discussion, were you any clearer in your own mind about what you could do to improve your work?
- Were you able to put forward and discuss your ideas and feelings at the interview?
- Was the discussion frank and open?
- Did you receive accurate and useful feedback on how your boss feels you are getting on in your job?
- Were follow-up actions agreed to improve your performance?

Source: drawn from Anderson 1993; Fletcher and Williams 1992

so as to make the point that scales do already exist that organizations may wish to use if they have the internal resources to search them out and carry out their own survey.

Advantages of using well-established scales are that the development work has already been carried out and (where relevant) the psychometric properties of the measures are known. There may also be normative data which would allow an organization to compare itself with others, as in the case of the work by Fletcher and Williams and the Audit Commission. Opinion surveys, using standard measures, thus have a place where organizations wish to benchmark themselves against others. But already-established measures might not capture exactly the language used in an organization and in this sense the questionnaire might not 'fit'. For this reason an organization might prefer to develop a tailor-made questionnaire and use it over a period of years as part of regular monitoring and diagnostic activity. Repeated use also helps to offset the initial development costs – organizations get a better return on their money, in other words.

Box 10.4	**Employee opinions about performance management: some specimen questions**

Aspects of goals and goal-setting

Participation in goal-setting

- I am allowed a high degree of influence in the determination of my work objectives
- I really have little voice in the formulation of my work objectives (R)
- The setting of my work goals is pretty much under my own control
- My supervisor usually asks for my opinions and thoughts when determining my work objectives

Goal specificity

- My work objectives are very clear and specific: I know exactly what my job is
- I think my work objectives are ambiguous and unclear (R)
- I understand fully which of my work objectives are more important than others; I have a clear sense of priorities on these goals

Goal difficulty

- I should not have too much difficulty in reaching my work objectives; they appear to be fairly easy (R)
- My work objectives will require a great deal of effort from me to complete them
- It will take a high degree of skill and know-how on my part to attain fully my work objectives
- My work objectives are quite difficult to attain

The above items are scored on a seven-point scale from (1) 'strongly disagree' to (7) 'strongly agree'; items marked (R) are reverse scored.
(Source: Steers 1973; in Cook et al. 1981)

Aspects of fairness in discussing and reviewing performance

Indicate the extent to which your supervisor did each of the following:

- Was honest and ethical in dealing with you

- Gave you an opportunity to express your side
- Used consistent standards in evaluating your performance
- Considered your views regarding your performance
- Gave you feedback that helped you learn how well you were doing
- Was completely candid and frank with you
- Showed a real interest in trying to be fair
- Became thoroughly familiar with your performance
- Took into account factors beyond your control
- Got input from you before a recommendation
- Made clear what was expected of you

(Source: Folger and Konovsky 1989)

Aspects of supervisory reward behaviour

- My supervisor always gives me positive feedback when I perform well
- My supervisor gives me special recognition when my performance is especially good
- My supervisor would quickly acknowledge an improvement in the quality of my work
- My supervisor commends me when I do a better than average job
- My supervisor personally pays me a compliment when I do outstanding work
- My supervisor informs his/her boss and others when I do outstanding work
- If I do well, I know my supervisor will reward me
- My supervisor would do all that he/she could to help me go as far as I would like to go in this organization if my work is consistently above average
- My good performance often goes unacknowledged by my supervisor (R)
- I often perform well in my job and still receive no praise from my supervisor (R)

Scored on a seven-point scale from 'strongly agree' to 'strongly disagree'

(Source: Schriesheim et al. 1991)

Many of the items in Box 10.4 are about supervisory behaviours. This is to be expected given the central role that line managers have to play in performance management. But what the examples illustrate is how upward appraisal/feedback can serve a dual purpose. On the one hand it is a tool to assist the personal development of line managers. But when the data are aggregated across a department or the organization as a whole they become a tool for managing the performance management system. But in order for either of these purposes to be served the data do need to be fed back and action taken.

Taking action

Surveys raise expectations and if organizations embark upon such activity without being prepared to act on what they find this is likely to cause more harm than good. It is essential, therefore, to feed back the data, partly to develop understanding further and partly to assist in solving any problems that are identified and to seek suggestions for improving those aspects of performance management which are not working well.

As noted above, an opinion survey may be used as an individual feedback instrument – as in upward (or multiple) appraisal (discussed in Chapter 7). In the present context, though, we are not so much interested in changing the behaviour of individual managers but rather in improving aspects of the system. Results, therefore, need to be reported back and it often is suggested that this be done in a cascading way, starting at the top of the organization. It is also essential that what is fed back is relevant, that is relevant to the particular department, unit, team, etc. Moreover, it is helpful if the findings are discussed with the recipients – they may be able to help interpret the data and offer explanations for what has been found. They may also be able to suggest remedial actions, should these be needed. It is important that positive, improving action (rather than punishment) happens, otherwise the reaction is going to be defensiveness and lowered trust (Hinrichs 1996). Used in this constructive way, then, surveys are a valuable tool for helping to manage the performance management system *and* for managing performance.

A concluding comment

Though the term performance management is open to a number of interpretations, in the UK it has come to take on a particular meaning. It denotes a system where the level of intervention is the individual employee and the overall intent is to align individual performance with organizational performance. This, in other words, is a unitarist perspective and as such it may represent one of the threats to performance management as it fails to recognize the plurality of interests that are so much a part of organizational reality. It is also far too simple a view – the idea of the balanced scorecard points to the complexity of organizational performance and we should not expect that it will be an easy task to align individual performance with possibly conflicting and contradictory goals.

Typically, performance management is presented as a cycle of activity in which an especially important role is seen for the line manager. Thus, performance management is commonly presented as something that is (or should be) owned and driven by the line. What is less well established, however, is the extent to which this particular aspect of advocacy is matched by reality. There is little to suggest that much is done to bring about ownership or to support managers in this task.

The core of performance management practice, for many organizations, would seem to be traditional performance appraisal, perhaps with appraisal-related pay tacked on to it. The organizational context and aspects of the work system seem, on the face of it, to be taken for granted. Core practice, then, is narrow, it reflects outmoded (Theory X) ideas about motivation and it may be overly focused on their performance at the expense of other aspects of individuals, such as their well-being. Much contemporary practice may also be too narrow in concentrating so much on the individual whilst underemphasizing the job itself and the immediate job environment. A properly holistic and integrated approach would recognize the many influences on performance and its different facets (both output and behavioural conceptualizations) and reflect this through multiple interventions operating at multiple levels. This is not to say that the management of employee performance should be ignored – quite the contrary. But we should be modest in our expectations of what narrowly focused interventions will achieve, especially if the consequences for those who are affected by them are ignored.

| Box 10.5 | **Implications for practice** |

Begin with small-scale implementation: identify a suitable pilot site in which to test a prototype of the new process. Bear in mind that subsequent modifications may be required.

Provide appropriate briefing and training for all the parties involved. Consider providing the training for 'family' rather than 'stranger' groups.

Use internal staff – trained as occasional trainers – to help implement the new process and so as to foster ownership.

Remember that the implementation of performance management involves large-scale and long-term organizational change. The new process may not work as intended: the introduction therefore should be monitored so that corrective action may be taken.

The implementation of performance management, indeed performance management itself, is a major exercise in organizational communication. Consider what can be done to make sure that communication structures and processes are fully two-way and involving.

Monitor and evaluate. This may be part of some regular employee opinion survey. Or perhaps auditing specific to the performance management process. Remember that survey activity in itself raises expectations: so, take action on the results.

Monitor at several levels: compliance with procedures (if these are important); impact on line managers and staff; impact on other HR/PM systems; test for fairness. Involve all the interested parties, and build in monitoring activity as an inherent component of the performance management process.

Have modest expectations of what an employee-centred performance management process will do for organizational performance – remember that this has multiple dimensions and multiple determinants. But be more optimistic about the impact on employee performance, especially for those jobs where performance is less subject to the influence of system factors.

To take account of the needs and interests of those who will be affected requires a more involving approach to the design and development process. This offers the prospect of a performance management system more in keeping with Theory Y than Theory X. In such a system we would expect to see the sorts of things that are advocated in the prescriptive and normative literature, for example:

- effective organizational communication;
- empowering and enriching work organization and job design;
- a broad view of performance – not just goals/outputs but also behaviours/competencies;
- participation in goal-setting;
- frequent feedback;
- a broad view of reward;
- the promotion of employee well-being.

Perhaps this is all too utopian. Certainly, the evidence we have from surveys of practice – performance management, employee involvement and the like – does not offer much comfort. But perhaps we should not be too surprised. Financial constraints in organizations are often real enough and the participative approach that is advocated in so much of the literature is time-consuming and costly. Moreover, the control-related (and other) advantages of Theory X thinking are very appealing. But this theory views people as costs and liabilities. Much-espoused today is the view that employees are assets or resources. But espousal is not enough; Pettigrew and Whipp (1993) demonstrated in their research on competitiveness that staff actually have to be valued as assets and treated as such, and this means policies and practices for information sharing, participation and involvement, skill development and a long-term perspective (Pfeffer 1994). Approached in these broader terms, performance management may have a future.

References

Adler, S. (1996) Personality and work behaviour: Exploring the linkages. *Applied Psychology*, **45 (3)**, pp, 207–24.

Adler, S. and Weiss, H. M. (1988) Recent developments in the study of personality and organizational behaviour. In C. L. Cooper and I. T. Robertson (eds) *International Review of Industrial and Organizational Psychology*, Chichester: Wiley.

Ainsworth, M. and Smith, N. (1993) *Making it Happen: Managing Performance at Work*, Sydney: Prentice Hall.

Altink, W. M. M., Visser, C. F. and Castelijns, M. (1997) Criterion development: the unknown power of criteria as communication tools. In N. Anderson and P. Herriot (eds) *International Handbook of Selection and Assessment*, Chichester: Wiley.

Andersen, B. (1995) The productivity term. In A. Rolstadås (ed.) *Performance Management: A Business Process Benchmarking Approach*, London: Chapman & Hall.

Anderson, G. C. (1993) *Managing Performance Appraisal Systems*, Oxford: Blackwell.

Anderson, M. (1992) Intelligence. In A. P. Smith and D. M. Jones (eds) *Handbook of Human Performance*, vol. 3, London: Academic Press.

Armstrong, M. (1993) *Managing Reward Systems*, Buckingham: Open University Press.

Armstrong, M. (1994) *Performance Management*, London: Kogan Page.

Armstrong, M. (1995) *A Handbook of Personnel Management Practice*, 5th edn, London: Kogan Page.

Armstrong, M. (1996) How group efforts can pay dividends. *People Management*, January, pp. 22–7.

Armstrong, M. and Baron, A. (1998) *Performance Management: The New Realities*, London: Institute of Personnel and Development.

Ashford, S. J. (1986) The role of feedback seeking in individual adaptation: a resource perspective. *Academy of Management Journal*, **29**, pp. 465–87.

Ashford, S. J. (1989) Self-assessments in organizations. *Research in Organizational Behaviour*, **11**, pp. 133–74.

Atkinson, A. A., Waterhouse, J. H. and Wells, R. B. (1997) A stakeholder approach to strategic performance measurement. *Sloan Management Review*, Spring, pp. 25–37.

Atwater, L. E. (1998) The advantages and pitfalls of self-assessment in organizations. In J. W. Smither (ed) *Performance Appraisal: State of the Art in Practice*, San Francisco: Jossey-Bass.

Atwater, L. E. and Yammarino, E. J. (1997) Self-other rating agreement: A review and model. *Research in Personnel and Human Resources Management*, **15**, pp. 121–74.

Audit Commission (1995a) *Calling the Tune: Performance Management in Local Government*, London: HMSO.

Audit Commission (1995b) *Paying the Piper . . . Calling the Tune: People, Pay and Performance in Local Government: A Management Handbook*, London: HMSO.

Audit Commission (1995c) *Paying the Piper: People and Pay Management in Local Government*, London: HMSO.

Bacharach, S. B. and Bamberger, P. (1995) Beyond situational constraints: job resources inadequacy and individual performance at work. *Human Resource Management Review*, **5(2)**, pp. 79–102.

Bailey, C. T. (1983) *The Measurement of Job Performance*, Aldershot: Gower.

Balzer, W. K. and Sulsky, L. M. (1990) Performance appraisal effectiveness. In K. R. Murphy and F. E. Saal (eds) *Psychology in Organizations*, Hillsdale, NJ: Erlbaum.

Baron, R. A. (1988) Negative effects of destructive criticism: Impact on conflict, self-efficacy and task performance. *Journal of Applied Psychology*, **73**, pp. 199–207.

Baron, R. A. (1994) The physical environment of work settings. *Research in Organizational Behaviour*, **16**, pp. 1–46.

Bartol, K. M. and Durham, C. C. (2000) Incentives: Theory and Practice. In C. L. Cooper and E. A. Locke (eds) *Industrial and Organizational Psychology: Linking Theory with Practice*, Oxford: Blackwell.

Bate, P. (1984) The impact of organizational culture on approaches to organizational problem-solving. *Organization Studies*, **5(1)**, pp. 43–66.

Bateman, T. S. and Organ, D. W. (1983) Job satisfaction and the good soldier: the relationship between affect and employee 'citizenship'. *Academy of Management Journal*, **26**, pp. 587–95.

Beaumont, P. B. (1993) *Human Resource Management*, London: Sage.

Becker, B. and Gerhart, B. (1996) The impact of human resource management on organizational performance: Progress and prospects. *Academy of Management Journal*, **39**, pp. 779–801.

Beer, M., Eisenstat, R. A. and Biggadike, E. R. (1995) Strategic change: a new dimension of human resource management. In G. R. Ferris, S. D. Rosen and

D. T. Barnum (eds) *Handbook of Human Resource Management*, Cambridge, MA: Blackwell.

Bell, N. and Tetlock, P. (1989) The intuitive politician and the assignment of blame in organizations. In R. A. Giacalone and P. Rosenfeld (eds) *Impression Management in the Organization*, Hillsdale, NJ: Erlbaum.

Bernardin, H. J. (1986) Subordinate appraisal: a valuable source of information about managers. *Human Resource Mangement*, **25**, 421–39.

Bernardin, H. J. and Beatty, R. W. (1984) *Performance Appraisal: Assessing Human Behavior at Work*, Boston, MA: Kent.

Bernardin, H. J., Hagan, C. M., Kane, J. S. and Villanova, P. (1998) Effective performance management: A focus on precision, customers, and situational constraints. In J. W. Smither (ed.) *Performance Appraisal: State of the Art in Practice*, San Francisco: Jossey-Bass.

Bernardin, H. J., Kane, J. S., Ross, S., Spina, J. D. and Johnson, D. L. (1995) Performance appraisal design, development, and implementation. In G. R. Ferris, S. D. Rosen and D. T. Barnum (eds) *Handbook of Human Resource Management*, Cambridge, MA: Blackwell.

Bertsch, B. and Williams, R. (1994) How multinational CEOs make change programmes stick. *Long Range Planning*, **27(5)**, pp. 12–24.

Bevan, S. and Thompson, M. (1991) Performance management at the crossroads. *Personnel Management*, November, pp. 36–9.

Blumberg, M. and Pringle, C. C. (1982) The missing opportunity in organizational research: some implications for a theory of work performance. *Academy of Management Review*, 7, pp. 560–9.

Borman, W. C. and Motowidlo, S. J. (1993) Expanding the criterion domain to include elements of contextual performance. In N. Schmitt, W. C. Borman and Associates *Personnel Selection in Organizations*, San Francisco, CA: Jossey-Bass.

Bounds, G., Yorks, L., Adams, M. and Ranney, G. (1994) *Beyond Total Quality Management*, New York: McGraw-Hill.

Bowen, D. E. and Waldman, D. A. (1999) Customer-driven employee performance. In D. R. Ilgen and E. D. Pulakos (eds) *The Changing Nature of Performance*, San Francisco: Jossey-Bass.

Boyatzis, R. E. (1982) *The Competent Manager*, New York: Wiley.

Brabet, J. and Klemm, M. (1994) Sharing the vision: company mission statements in Britain and France. *Long Range Planning*, **27(1)**, pp. 84–94.

Bracken, D. W. (1996) Multisource (360-degree) feedback: surveys for individual and organizational development. In A. I. Kraut (ed.) *Organizational Surveys*, San Francisco, CA: Jossey-Bass.

Bredrup, H. (1995a) Background for performance management. In A. Rolstadås (ed.) *Performance Management: A Business Process Benchmarking Approach*, London: Chapman & Hall.

Bredrup, H. (1995b) Competitiveness and competitive advantage. In A. Rolstadås (ed.) *Performance Management: A Business Process Benchmarking Approach*, London: Chapman & Hall.

Bredrup, H. (1995c) Performance measurement. In A. Rolstadås (ed.) *Performance Management: A Business Process Benchmarking Approach*, London: Chapman & Hall

Bredrup, H. (1995d) The traditional planning hierarchy. In A. Rolstadås (ed.) *Performance Management: A Business Process Benchmarking Approach*, London: Chapman & Hall.

Bredrup, H. and Bredrup, R. (1995) Performance planning to ensure business achievements. In A. Rolstadås (ed.), *Performance Management: A Business Process Benchmarking Approach*, London: Chapman & Hall.

Brewster, C. and Söderström, M. (1994) Human resources and line management. In C. Brewster and A. Hegewisch (eds) *Policy and Practice in Human Resource Management*, London: Routledge.

Brief, A. P. and Motowidlo, S. J. (1986) Prosocial organizational behaviour. *Academy of Management Review*, **11**, pp. 710–25.

Brinkerhoff, R. O. and Dressler, D. E. (1990) *Productivity Measurement*, Newbury Park, CA: Sage.

Brown, A. (1995) *Organizational Culture*, London: Pitman.

Brown, A. (1998) *Organizational Culture*, 2nd edn., London: Financial Times Management.

Brown, D. and Armstrong, M. (1999) *Paying for Contribution*, London: Kogan Page.

Brown, W. and Walsh, J. (1994) Managing pay in Britain. In K. Sisson (ed.) *Personnel Management*, Oxford: Blackwell.

Buchanan, D. A. (1994) Principles and practice in work design. In K. Sisson (ed.) *Personnel Management*, Oxford: Blackwell.

Cameron, K. S. (1986) Effectiveness as paradox: consensus and conflict in conceptualizations of organizational effectiveness. *Management Science*, **32**, pp. 539–53.

Cameron, K. S. (1995) Organizational effectiveness. In N. Nicholson (ed.) *Blackwell Encyclopedic Dictionary of Organizational Behaviour*, Oxford: Blackwell.

Campbell, A. and Yeung, S. (1991a) Creating a sense of mission. *Long Range Planning*, **24(4)**, pp. 10–20.

Campbell, A. and Yeung, S. (1991b) Brief case: mission, vision and strategic intent. *Long Range Planning*, **24(4)**, pp. 145–7.

Campbell, D. J. and Lee, C. (1988) Self-appraisal in performance evaluation: development versus evaluation. *Academy of Management Review*, **13(2)**, pp. 302–14.

Campbell, J. P. (1977) On the nature of organizational effectiveness. In P. S. Goodman and J. M. Pennings (eds) *New Perspectives on Organizational Effectiveness*, San Francisco, CA: Jossey-Bass.

Campbell, J. P. (1990) Modeling the performance prediction problem in industrial and organizational psychology. In M. D. Dunnette and L. M. Hough (eds) *Handbook of Industrial and Organizational Psychology*, Palo Alto, CA: Consulting Psychologists Press.

Campbell, J. P. and Campbell, R. J. (1988) Industrial-organizational psychology and productivity: the goodness of fit. In J. P. Campbell, R. J. Campbell and Associates *Productivity in Organizations*, San Francisco, CA: Jossey-Bass.

Campbell, J. P., Gasser, M. B. and Oswald, F. L. (1996) The substantive nature of job performance variability. In K. R. Murphy (ed.) *Individual Differences and Behaviour in Organizations*, San Francisco, CA: Jossey-Bass.

Campbell, J. P., McCloy, R. A., Oppler, S. H. and Sager, C. E. (1993) A theory of performance. In N. Schmitt, W. C. Borman and Associates *Personnel Selection in Organizations*, San Francisco, CA: Jossey-Bass.

Campion, M. A. and Wong, C. S. (1991) Improving efficiency and satisfaction through job design. In J. W. Jones, B. D. Steffy and D. W. Bray (eds) *Applying Psychology in Business*, Lexington, MA: Lexington Books.

Cannell, M. and Wood, S. (1992) *Incentive Pay*, London: Institute of Personnel Management.

Cardy, R. L. (1998) Performance appraisal in a quality context: A new look at an old problem. In J. W. Smither (ed.) *Performance Appraisal: State of the Art in Practice*, San Francisco: Jossey-Bass.

Cardy, R. L. and Dobbins, G. H. (1994) *Performance Appraisal: Alternative Perspectives*, Cincinnati, OH: South-Western.

Cascio, W. F. (1993) Downsizing: what do we know? What have we learned? *Academy of Management Executive*, 7(1), pp. 95–104.

Cawley, B. D., Keeping, L. M. and Levy, P. E. (1998) Participation in the performance appraisal process and employee reactions: A meta-analytic review of field investigations. *Journal of Applied Psychology*, 83(4), pp. 615–33.

Chakravarthy, B. (1986) Measuring strategic performance. *Strategic Management Journal*, 7, pp. 437–58.

Chatman, J. A. (1989) Improving interactional organizational research: a model of person-organization fit. *Academy of Management Review*, 14(3), pp. 333–49.

Cockerill, A. P. (1995) Competencies. In N. Nicholson (ed.) *Blackwell Encyclopedic Dictionary of Organizational Behaviour*, Oxford: Blackwell.

Collin, A. (1989) Managers' competence: rhetoric, reality and research. *Personnel Review*, 18(6), pp. 20–5.

Connock, S. (1991) *HR Vision: Managing a Quality Workforce*, London: Institute of Personnel Management.

Cook, J. D., Hepworth, S. J., Wall, T. D. and Warr, P. B. (1981) *The Experience of Work*, London: Academic Press.

Cooper, D. and Robertson, I. T. (1995) *The Psychology of Personnel Selection: A Quality Approach*, London: Routledge.

Costello, S. J. (1994) *Effective Performance Management*, New York: Irwin.

Cropanzano, R. and Greenberg, J. (1997) Progress in organizational justice. In C. L. Cooper and I. T. Robertson (eds) *International Review of Industrial and Organizational Psychology*, vol. 12, Chichester: Wiley.

Csoka, L. (1994) *Closing the Human Performance Gap*, New York: The Conference Board.

Cummings, L. L. and Schwab, D. P. (1973) *Performance in Organizations*, Glenview, Ill: Scott Foresman.

Dale, B. G. (ed.) (1994) *Managing Quality*, Hemel Hempstead: Prentice Hall.

Dale, B. G. and Boaden, R. J. (1994) A generic framework for managing quality improvement. In B. G. Dale (ed.) *Managing Quality*, Hemel Hempstead: Prentice Hall.

Dalessio, A. T. (1998) Using multisource feedback for employee development and personnel decisions. In J. W. Smither (ed.) *Performance Appraisal: State of the Art in Practice*, San Francisco: Jossey-Bass.

Davis-Blake, A. and Pfeffer, J. (1989) Just a mirage: the search for dispositional effects in organizational research. *Academy of Management Review*, **14(3)**, pp. 385–400.

Dawson, S. (1996) *Analysing Organizations*, Basingstoke: Macmillan.

Deming, W. E. (1986) *Out of the Crisis*, Cambridge, Mass: Massachusetts Institute of Technology.

DeNisi, A. S. (2000) Performance appraisal and performance management: A multilevel analysis. In K. J. Klein and S. W. J. Kozlowski (eds) *Multilevel Theory, Research and Methods in Organizations: Foundations, Extensions and New Directions*, San Francisco: Jossey-Bass.

Dickson, D., Saunders, C. and Stringer, M. (1993) *Rewarding People*, London: Routledge.

Dickinson, T. L. (1993) Attitudes about performance appraisal. In H. Schuler, J. L. Farr and M. Smith (eds) *Personnel Selection and Assessment*, Hillsdale, NJ: Erlbaum.

Digman, J. M. (1990) Personality structure: emergence of the five-factor model. *Annual Review of Psychology*, **41**, pp. 417–40.

Dulewicz, V. and Fletcher, C. (1989) The context and dynamics of performance appraisal. In P. Herriot (ed.) *Assessment and Selection in Organizations*, Chichester: Wiley.

Earley, P. C. and Shalley, C. E. (1991) New perspectives on goals and performance. *Research in Personnel and Human Resources Management*, **9**, pp. 121–57.

Eccles, R. G. (1991) The performance measurement manifesto. *Harvard Business Review*, **68(1)**, pp. 131–7.

Eder, R. W. and Fedor, D. B. (1989) Impression management: its interpretive role in the supervisor–employee feedback process. In R. A. Giacalone and

P. Rosenfeld (eds) *Impression Management in the Organization*, Hillsdale, NJ: Erlbaum.

Edwards, J. R. (1991) Person-job fit: a conceptual integration, literature review, and methodological critique. In C. L. Cooper and I. T. Robertson (eds) *International Review of Industrial and Organizational Psychology*, vol. 6, Chichester: Wiley.

Eysenck, M. W. (1994) *Individual Differences: Normal and Abnormal*, London: Erlbaum.

Farr, J. L. (1993) Informal performance feedback: seeking and giving. In H. Schuler, J. L. Farr and M. Smith (eds) *Personnel Selection and Assessment*, Hillsdale, NJ: Erlbaum.

Fay, C. (1995) The changing nature of work. In H. Risher and C. Fay (eds) *The Performance Imperative*, San Francisco, CA: Jossey-Bass.

Fedor, D. B. (1991) Recipient responses to performance feedback. *Research in Personnel and Human Resources Management*, **9**, pp. 73–120.

Feldman, D. C. (1995) The impact of downsizing on organizational career development activities and employee career development opportunities. *Human Resource Management Review*, **5(3)**, pp. 189–221.

Filella, J. and Hegewisch, A. (1994) European experiments with pay and benefits policies. In C. Brewster and A. Hegewisch (eds) *Policy and Practice in Human Resource Management*, London: Routledge.

Flanagan, J. C. (1954) The critical incident technique. *Psychological Bulletin*, **51**, pp. 327–58.

Fletcher, C. (1993) *Appraisal: Routes to Improved Performance*, London: Institute of Personnel Management.

Fletcher, C. (1994) Performance appraisal in context: organizational changes and their impact on practice. In N. Anderson and P. Herriot (eds) *Assessment and Selection in Organizations*, Chichester: Wiley.

Fletcher, C. and Baldry, C. (1999) Multi-source feedback systems: A research perspective. In C. L. Cooper and I. T. Robertson (eds) *International Review of Industrial and Organizational Psychology*, vol. 14, Chichester: Wiley.

Fletcher, C and Williams, R. (1992) *Performance Appraisal and Career Development*, 2nd edn, Cheltenham: Stanley Thornes.

Flood, P. C. and Olian, J. D. (1996) Human resource strategies for world-class competitive capability. In P. C. Flood, M. J. Gannon and J. Paauwe (eds) *Managing Without Traditional Methods*, Wokingham: Addison-Wesley.

Folger, R. and Cropanzano, R. (1998) *Organizational Justice and Human Resource Management*, Thousand Oaks, CA: Sage.

Folger, R. and Konovsky, M. (1989) Effects of procedural and distributive justice on reactions to pay raise decisions. *Academy of Management Journal*, **32(1)**, pp. 115–30.

France, S. (1997) *360° Appraisal*, London: Industrial Society.

French, W. L. and Bell, C. H. (1995) *Organization Development*, 5th edn, Englewood Cliffs, NJ: Prentice Hall.

Gardner, H. (1983) *Frames of Mind: The Theory of Multiple Intelligences*, New York: Basic Books.

Geake, A., Oliver, K., and Farrell, C. (1998) *The Application of 360° Feedback: A Survey*, Thames Ditton, Surrey: SHL Ltd.

Geary, J. F. (1992) Pay, control and commitment: linking appraisal and reward. *Human Resource Management Journal*, **2(4)**, pp. 36–54.

George, J. M. and Brief, A. P. (1992) Feeling good – doing good: a conceptual analysis of the mood at work/organizational spontaneity relationship. *Psychological Bulletin*, **112**, pp. 310–29.

Gerhart, B. and Milkovich, G. T. (1992) Employee compensation: research and practice. In M. D. Dunnette and L. M. Hough (eds) *Handbook of Industrial and Organizational Psychology*, Palo Alto, CA: Consulting Psychologists Press.

Gill, D. (1977) *Appraising Performance: Present Trends and the Next Decade*, London: Institute of Personnel Management.

Gilliland, S. W. and Langdon, J. C. (1998) Creating performance management systems that promote perceptions of fairness. In J. W. Smither (ed.) *Performance Appraisal: State of the Art in Practice*, San Francisco: Jossey-Bass.

Gioia, D. A. and Longenecker, C. D. (1994) The politics of executive appraisal. *Organizational Dynamics*, **22**, pp. 47–57.

Goldberg, L. R. (1993) The structure of phenotypic personality traits. *American Psychologist*, **48**, pp. 26–34.

Graham, J. W. (1986) Principled organizational dissent: a theoretical essay. *Research in Organizational Behavior*, vol. 8, Greenwich, CT: JAI Press.

Greenberg, J. (1986) Determinants of perceived fairness of performance evaluations. *Journal of Applied Psychology*, **71(2)**, pp. 340–2.

Greenberg, J. (1990) Organizational justice: yesterday, today, and tomorrow. *Journal of Management*, **16(2)**, pp. 399–432.

Greenberg, G. and Lind, E. A. (2000) The pursuit of organizational justice: From conceptualization to application. In C. L. Cooper and E. A. Locke (eds) *Industrial and Organizational Psychology: Linking Theory with Practice*, Oxford: Blackwell.

Guinn, K. (1987) Performance management: not just an annual appraisal. *Personnel*, August, pp. 39–42.

Guion, R. M. and Gottier, G. F. (1965) Validity of personality measures in personnel selection. *Personnel Psychology*, **18**, pp. 135–64.

Guzzo, R. A. (1988) Productivity research: reviewing psychological and economic perspectives. In J. P. Campbell, R. J. Campbell and Associates *Productivity in Organizations*, San Francisco, CA: Jossey-Bass.

Guzzo, R. A. and Gannett, B. A. (1988) The nature of facilitators and inhibitors of effective task performance. In F. D. Schoorman and B. Schneider (eds) *Facilitating Work Effectiveness*, Lexington, MA: Lexington Books.

Guzzo, R. E., Jette, R. D. and Katzell, R. A. (1985) The effects of psychologically based intervention programmes on worker productivity: a meta-analysis. *Personnel Psychology*, **38**, pp. 275–91.

Hackman, J. R. and Oldham, G. R. (1980) *Work Redesign*, Reading, MA: Addison-Wesley.

Hale, R. (1993) *How to Introduce Target Setting*, London: Kogan Page.

Hall, R. H. (1996) *Organizations: Structures, Processes and Outcomes*, 6th edn, Englewood Cliffs, NJ: Prentice Hall.

Handy, L., Devine, M., and Heath, L. (1996) *360° Feedback: Unguided Missile or Powerful Weapon*, Berkampstead: Ashridge Management College.

Harris, V. (1995) Moving ahead on cultural change. *People Management*, March, pp. 30–3.

Harrison, A. (1994) Just-in-time manufacturing. In J. Storey (ed.) *New Wave Manufacturing Strategies*, London: Paul Chapman Publishing.

Hartle, F. (1995) *How to Re-engineer your Performance Management Process*, London: Kogan Page.

Heap, J. (1992) *Productivity Management: A Fresh Approach*, London: Cassell.

Heisler, W. J., Jones, W. D. and Benham, P. O. (1988) *Managing Human Resources Issues*, San Francisco, CA: Jossey-Bass.

Henderson, R. I. (1984) *Performance Appraisal*. 2nd edn, Reston, VA: Reston Publishing Co.

Hendry, C., Perkins, S. and Bradley, P. (1997) Missed a motivator? *People Management*, May, pp. 20–5.

Heneman, R. L. (1990) Merit pay research. *Research in Personnel and Human Resources Management*, vol. 8, Greenwich, CT: JAI Press.

Heneman, R. L. (1992) *Merit Pay: Linking Pay Increases to Performance Ratings*, Reading, MA: Addison-Wesley.

Hesketh, B. and Neal, A. (1999) Technology and performance. In D. R. Ilgen and E. D. Pulakos (eds) *The Changing Nature of Performance*, San Francisco: Jossey-Bass.

Higgins, R. L. and Snyder, C. R. (1989) The business of excuses. In R. A. Giacalone and P. Rosenfeld (eds) *Impression Management in the Organization*, Hillsdale, NJ: Erlbaum.

Hinrichs, J. R. (1996) Feedback, action planning, and follow-through. In A. I. Kraut (ed.) *Organizational Surveys*, San Francisco, CA: Jossey-Bass.

Hitt, M. A. and Ireland, R. D. (1987) Peters and Waterman revisited: The unended quest for excellence. *Academy of Management Executive*, **1(2)**, pp. 91–8.

Hogan, R. T. (1991) Personality and personality measurement. In M. D. Dunnette and L. M. Hough (eds) *Handbook of Industrial and Organizational Psychology*, Palo Alto, CA: Consulting Psychologists Press.

Hooghiemstra, T. (1992) Integrated management of human resources. In A. Mitrani, M. Dalziel and D. Fitt (eds) *Competency Based Human Resource Management*, London: Kogan Page.

Hough, L. M. and Schneider, R. J. (1996) Personality traits, taxonomies, and applications in organizations. In K. Murphy (ed.) *Individual Differences and Behavior in Organizations*, San Francisco, CA: Jossey-Bass.

Hubbard, G. (1995) Core competence. In N. Nicholson (ed.) *Blackwell Encyclopedic Dictionary of Organizational Behaviour*, Oxford: Blackwell.

Huber, V. L., Latham, G. P. and Locke, E. A. (1989) The management of impressions through goal setting. In R. A. Giacalone and P. Rosenfeld (eds) *Impression Management in the Organization*, Hillsdale, NJ: Erlbaum.

Hume, D. A. (1995) *Reward Management*, Oxford: Blackwell.

Hyman, J. and Mason, B. (1995) *Managing Employee Involvement and Participation*, London: Sage.

Ilgen, D. R. and Hollenbeck, J. R. (1991) The structure of work: job design and roles. In M. D. Dunnette and L. M. Hough (eds) *Handbook of Industrial and Organizational Psychology*, Palo Alto, CA: Consulting Psychologists Press.

Ilgen, D. R. and Schneider, J. (1991) Performance measurement: a multi-discipline view. In C. L. Cooper and I. T. Robertson (eds) *International Review of Industrial and Organizational Psychology*, Chichester: Wiley.

Incomes Data Services (1985) *The Merit Factor*, London: Incomes Data Services.

Incomes Data Services (1992) *Performance Management*, IDS Study 518, London: Incomes Data Services.

Industrial Society (1994) *Performance Management*, London: Industrial Society.

Industrial Society (1998) *Performance Management*, London: Industrial Society.

Institute of Personnel Management (1992) *Performance Management in the UK: An Analysis of the Issues*, London: Institute of Personnel Management.

Kane, K. (1993) Situational constraints and performance: an overview. *Human Resource Management Review*, **3(2)**, pp. 83–103.

Kane, J. S. (1986) Performance distribution assessment. In R. Berk (ed.) *Performance Assessment*, Baltimore: Johns Hopkins Press.

Kanfer, R. (1995) Motivation and performance. In N. Nicholson (ed.) *Blackwell Encyclopedic Dictionary of Organizational Behaviour*, Oxford: Blackwell.

Kaplan, R. S. and Norton, D. P. (1992) The balanced scorecard – measures that drive performance. *Harvard Business Review*, **69(1)**, pp. 71–9.

Kaplan, R. S. and Norton, D. P. (1993) Putting the balanced scorecard to work. *Harvard Business Review*, **70(5)**, 134–47.

Kaplan, R. S. and Norton, D. P. (1996) Using the balanced scorecard as a strategic management system. *Harvard Business Review*, **73(1)**, pp. 75–85.

Karlöf, B. (1993) *Key Business Concepts*, London: Routledge.

Katz, D. and Kahn, R. L. (1978) *The Social Psychology of Organizations*, 2nd edn, New York: Wiley.

Katzell, R. A. and Guzzo, R. A. (1983) Psychological approaches to productivity improvement. *American Psychologist*, **38**, pp. 468–72.

Kerr, S. (1975) On the folly of rewarding A, while hoping for B. *Academy of Management Journal*, **18**, pp. 769–83.

Kerr, S. (1988) Some characteristics and consequences of organizational reward. In F. D. Schoorman and B. Schneider (eds) *Facilitating Work Effectiveness*, Lexington, MA: Lexington Books.

Kerr, S. (1995) On the folly of rewarding A, while hoping for B. *Academy of Management Executive*, **9(1)**, pp. 7–14.

Kerr, S. (2000) Organizational rewards: Practical, cost-neutral alternatives that you may know, but don't practice. *Organizational Dynamics*, **28(1)**, pp. 61–70.

Kessler, I. (1994) Performance pay. In K. Sisson (ed.) *Personnel Management*, Oxford: Blackwell.

Kessler, I. (1995) Reward systems. In J. Storey (ed.), *Human Resource Management*, London: Routledge.

Kessler, I. and Purcell, J. (1992) Performance related pay – objectives and application. *Human Resource Management Journal*, **2(3)**, pp. 34–59.

Kirkpatrick, I. and Lucio, M. M. (1995) *The Politics of Quality in the Public Sector*, London: Routledge.

Klimoski, R. (1993) Predictor constructs and their measurement. In N. Schmitt, W. C. Borman and Associates *Personnel Selection in Organizations*, San Francisco, CA: Jossey-Bass.

Kluger, A. N. and DeNisi, A. S. (1996) The effects of feedback interventions on performance: A historical review, a meta-analysis, and a preliminary feedback intervention theory. *Psychological Bulletin*, **119(2)**, pp. 254–84.

Knights, D. and McCabe, D. (1996) Do quality initiatives need management? *The TQM Magazine*, **8(3)**, pp. 24–6.

Kopelman, R. E. (1986) *Managing Productivity in Organizations*, New York: McGraw-Hill.

Kotter, J. P. and Heskett, J. L. (1992) *Corporate Culture and Performance*, New York: Free Press.

Landy, F. J., Barnes, J. L. and Murphy, K. R. (1978) Correlates of perceived fairness and accuracy of performance evaluation. *Journal of Applied Psychology*, **63**, pp. 751–4.

Larson, J. R. and Callahan, C. (1990) Performance monitoring: how it affects work productivity. *Journal of Applied Psychology*, **75(5)**, pp. 530–8.

Latham, C. and Marchbank, T. (1994) Feedback techniques. In G. Lee and D. Beard (eds) *Development Centres*, Maidenhead, Berks: McGraw-Hill.

Latham, G. P. and Wexley, K. N. (1994) *Increasing Productivity Through Performance Appraisal*, 2nd edn, Reading, MA: Addison-Wesley.

Lawler, E. E. (1987) The design of effective reward systems. In J. W. Lorsch (ed.) *Handbook of Organizational Behaviour*, Englewood Cliffs, NJ: Prentice Hall.

Lawler, E. E. (1991) Participative management strategies. In J. W. Jones, B. D. Steffy, and D. W. Bray (eds) *Applying Psychology in Business*, Lexington, MA: Lexington Books.

Lawler, E. E. (1995) Organizational effectiveness: new realities and challenges. In H. Risher and C. Fay (eds) *The Performance Imperative*, San Francisco, CA: Jossey-Bass.

Lawler, E. E. and Jenkins, D. (1992) Strategic reward systems. In M. D. Dunnette and L. M. Hough (eds) *Handbook of Industrial and Organizational Psychology*, Palo Alto, CA: Consulting Psychologists Press.

Lawlor, A. (1985) *Productivity Improvement Manual*, Aldershot: Gower.

Lawson, P. (1995) Performance management: an overview. In M. Walters (ed.) *The Performance Management Handbook*, London: Institute of Personnel and Development.

Ledford, G. E. and Lawler, E. E. (1994) Dialogue: Research on employee participation: Beating a dead horse? *Academy of Management Review*, **19**, pp. 633–6.

Legge, K. (1995) *Human Resource Management: Rhetorics and Realities*, Basingstoke: Macmillan.

Letza, S. R. (1996) The design and implementation of the balanced business scorecard. *Business Process Re-engineering and Management Journal*, **2(3)**, pp. 54–76.

Leventhal, G. S. (1976) Fairness in social relationships. In J. W. Thibaut, J. T. Spence and R. C. Carson (eds) *Contemporary Topics in Social Psychology*, Morristown, NJ: General Learning Press.

Leventhal, G. S. (1980) What should be done with equity theory? In K. J. Gergen, M. S. Greenberg and R. H. Willis (eds) *Social Exchange: Advances in Theory and Research*, New York: Plenum.

LGMB (1993) *People and Performance*, Luton: Local Government Management Board.

Locke, E. A. and Latham, G. P. (1984) *Goal Setting: A Motivational Technique that Works!*, Englewood Cliffs, NJ: Prentice Hall.

Locke, E. A. and Latham, G. P. (1990) *A Theory of Goal Setting and Task Performance*, Englewood Cliffs, NJ: Prentice Hall.

Lockett, J. (1992) *Effective Performance Management*, London: Kogan Page.

London, M. (1995) Giving feedback: source-centered antecedents and consequences of constructive and destructive feedback. *Human Resource Management Review*, **5(3)**, pp. 159–88.

London, M. (1997) *Job Feedback*, Mahwah, NJ: Erlbaum.

London, M. and Mone, E. M. (1999) Continuous learning. In D. R. Ilgen and E. D. Pulakos (eds) *The Changing Nature of Performance*, San Francisco: Jossey-Bass.

Long, P. (1986) *Performance Appraisal Revisited*, London: Institute of Personnel Management.

Longenecker, C. O. and Scazzero, J. A. (1996) The ongoing challenge of total quality management. *The TQM Magazine*, **8(2)**, pp. 55–60.

Luffman, G., Lea, E., Sanderson, S. and Kenny, B. (1996) *Strategic Management*, 3rd edn, Oxford: Blackwell.

Lundy, O. and Cowling, A. (1996) *Strategic Human Resource Management*, London: Routledge.

Mabey, C. and Salaman, G. (1995) *Strategic Human Resource Management*, Oxford: Blackwell.

Macdonell, R. (1989) Management by objectives. In P. Herriot (ed.) *Assessment and Selection in Organizations*, Chichester: Wiley.

MacKenzie, S. B., Podsakoff, P. M. and Fetter, R. (1991) Organizational citizenship behaviour and objective productivity as determinants of managerial evaluations of salespersons' performance. *Organizational Behaviour and Human Decision Processes*, **50(1)**, pp. 1–28.

MacKenzie, S. B., Podsakoff, P. M. and Fetter, R. (1993) The impact of organizational citizenship behaviour on evaluations of salesperson performance. *Journal of Marketing*, **57**, pp. 70–80.

McAfee, R. B. and Champagne, P. J. (1993) Performance management: A strategy for improving employee performance and productivity. *Journal of Managerial Psychology*, **8(5)**, pp. 24–32.

McConkie, M. L. (1979) A clarification of the goal setting and appraisal processes in MBO. *Academy of Management Review*, **4(1)**, pp. 29–40.

McGregor, D. M. (1957) The human side of enterprise. In *Adventures in Thought and Action*, Proceedings of the Fifth Anniversary Convocation of the School of Industrial Management, Massachusetts Institute of Technology.

McKenney, J. L. (1995) *Waves of Change*, Boston, MA: Harvard Business School Press.

Mager, R. F. and Pipe, P. (1990) *Analyzing Performance Problems*, 2nd edn, London: Kogan Page.

Makin, P. J. and Robertson, I. T. (1983) Self assessment, realistic job previews and occupational decisions. *Personnel Review*, **12(3)**, pp. 21–5.

Management Charter Initiative (1990a) *Management Competences: The Standards Concept*, London: MCI.

Management Charter Initiative (1990b) *Occupational Standards for Mangers* (Management 1), London: MCI.

Mansfield, R. (1986) *Company Strategy and Organizational Design*, London: Croom Helm.

Marchington, M. (1995) Involvement and participation. In J. Storey (ed.) *Human Resource Management: A Critical Text*, London: Routledge.

Marchington, M. and Grugulis, I. (2000) 'Best practice' human resource management: perfect opportunity or dangerous illusion? *International Journal of Human Resource Management*, **11(6)**, pp. 1104–24.

Marsden, D. (2000) Teachers before the 'Threshold'. London: London School of Economics Centre for Economic Performance.

Marsden, D. and Richardson, R. (1994) Performing for pay? The effects of 'merit pay' on motivation in a public service. *British Journal of Industrial Relations*, **32(2)**, pp. 243–61.

Masterson, S. S. and Taylor, M. S. (1996) Total quality management and performance appraisal: an integrative perspective, *Journal of Quality Management*, **1**, pp. 67–89.

Martin, J. (1995) Organizational culture. In N. Nicholson (ed.) *Blackwell Encyclopedic Dictionary of Organizational Behaviour*, Oxford: Blackwell.

Meek, V. L. (1988) Organizational culture: origins and weaknesses. *Organization Studies*, **9(4)**, pp. 453–73.

Meyer, M. W. and Gupta, V. (1994) The performance paradox. *Research in Organizational Behaviour*, **16**, pp. 309–69.

Milkovich, G. T. and Wigdor, A. K. (1991) *Pay for Performance*, Washington, DC: National Academy Press.

Mischel, W. (1977) The interaction of person and situation. In D. Magnusson and N. S. Endler (eds), *Personality at the Crossroads*, Hillsdale, NJ: Erlbaum.

Mitchell, T. R. and O'Reilly, C. A. (1983) Managing poor performance and productivity in organizations. *Research in Organizational Behaviour*, vol. 5, Greenwich, CT: JAI Press.

Mitchell, T. R., Thompson, K. R. and George-Falvy, J. (2000) Goal setting: Theory and practice. In C. L. Cooper and E. A. Locke (eds) *Industrial and Organizational Psychology: Linking Theory with Practice*, Oxford: Blackwell.

Mohrman, A. M. (1990) Deming versus performance appraisal: is there a resolution? In G. N. McLean, S. R. Damme and R. A. Swanson (eds) *Performance Appraisal – Perspectives on a Quality Management Approach*. Alexandria, VA: American Society for Training and Development.

Mohrman, A. M., Resnick-West, S. M. and Lawler, E. E. (1989) *Designing Performance Appraisal Systems*, San Francisco, CA: Jossey-Bass.

Moores, R. (1994) *Managing for High Performance*, London: Industrial Society.

Moses, J., Hollenbeck, G. P. and Sorcher, M. (1993) Other people's expectations. *Human Resource Management*, **32**, pp. 283–98.

Motowidlo, S. J. and Schmit, M. J. (1999) Performance assessment in unique jobs. In D. R. Ilgen and E. D. Pulakos (eds) *The Changing Nature of Performance*, San Francisco: Jossey-Bass.

Mount, M. K. and Barrick, M. R. (1995) The big five personality dimensions. *Research in Personnel and Human Resources Management*, **13**, pp. 153–200.

Moyer, K. (1996) Scenario planning at British Airways – a case study. *Long Range Planning*, **29(2)**, pp. 172–81.

Mullins, L. J. (1996) *Management and Organizational Behaviour*, 4th edn, London: Pitman.

Murlis, H. and Wright, V. (1993) Remuneration. *Benefits and Compensation International*, January–February, pp. 5–10.

Murphy, K. R. (1989) Dimensions of job performance. In R. F. Dillon and J. W. Pellegrino (eds) *Testing: Theoretical and Applied Perspectives*, New York: Praeger.

Murphy, K. R. (1990) Job performance and productivity. In K. R. Murphy and F. E. Saal (eds) *Psychology in Organizations*, Hillsdale, NJ: Erlbaum.

Murphy, K. R. (1999) The challenge of staffing a postindustrial workplace. In D. R. Ilgen and E. D. Pulakos (eds) *The Changing Nature of Performance*, San Francisco: Jossey-Bass.

Murphy, K. R. and Cleveland, J. N. (1995) *Understanding Performance Appraisal*, Thousand Oaks, CA: Sage.

Naylor, J. C. and Ilgen, D. R. (1984) Goal setting: A theoretical analysis of a motivational technology. *Research in Organizational Behaviour*, **6**, pp. 95–140.

Newell, S. (1995) *The Healthy Organization*, London: International Thomson Business Press.

Nicholson, N. and West, M. A. (1988) *Managerial Job Change: Men and Women in Transition*, Cambridge: Cambridge University Press.

Ogbonna, E. (1992) Organizational culture and human resource management: Dilemmas and contradictions. In P. Blyton and P. Turnbull (eds) *Reassessing Human Resource Management*, London: Sage.

Ogbonna, E. and Harris, L. C. (2000) Leadership style, organizational culture and performance: empirical evidence from UK companies. *International Journal of Human Resource Management*, **11(4)**, pp. 766–88.

Ones, D. S., Viswesvaran, C. and Schmidt, F. L. (1993) Comprehensive meta-analysis of integrity test validities: findings and implications for personnel selection and theories of job performance. *Journal of Applied Psychology*, **78**, pp. 679–703.

O'Reilly, C. (1989) Corporations, culture and commitment: motivation and social control in organizations. *California Management Review*, **31(4)**, pp. 9–25.

Ostroff, C. and Bowen, D. E. (2000) Moving HR to a higher level: HR practices and organizational effectiveness. In K. J. Klein and S. W. J. Kozlowski (eds) *Multilevel Theory, Research and Methods in Organizations: Foundations, Extensions and New Directions*, San Francisco: Jossey-Bass.

Parasuraman, A., Berry, L. L. and Zeithaml, V. (1991) Understanding, measuring, and improving service quality. In S. W. Brown, E. Gummesson, B. Edvardsson and B. Gustavsson (eds) *Service Quality*, Lexington, MA: Lexington Books.

Parker, S. K. and Wall, T. D. (1996) Job design and modern manufacturing. In P. Warr (ed.) *Psychology at Work*, 4th edn, Harmondsworth, Penguin.

Parker, S. K., Mullarkey, S. and Jackson, P. R. (1994) Dimensions of performance effectiveness in high-involvement work organizations. *Human Resource Management Journal*, **40(3)**, pp. 1–21.

Pearce, J. L. (1987) Why merit pay doesn't work: implications from organization theory. In D. B. Balkin and L. R. Gomez-Mejia (eds) *New Perspectives on Compensation*, Englewood Cliffs, NJ: Prentice Hall.

Pearn, M. (1992) A competency approach to role and career management restructuring. In R. Boam and P. Sparrow (eds) *Designing and Achieving Competency*, Maidenhead: McGraw-Hill.

Peppard, J. and Preece, I. (1995) The content, context and process of business process re-engineering. In G. Burke and J. Peppard (eds) *Examinimg Business Process Re-engineering*, London: Kogan Page.

Peppard, J. and Rowland, P. (1995) *The Essence of Business Process Re-engineering*, Hemel Hempstead: Prentice Hall.

Peters, L. H. and O'Connor, E. J. (1980) Situational constraints and work outcomes: the influence of a frequently overlooked construct. *Academy of Management Review*, **5**, pp. 391–7.

Peters, T. J. and Waterman, R. H. (1982) *In Search of Excellence*, New York: Harper & Row.

Pettigrew, A. and Whipp, R. (1993) Managing the twin processes of competition and change: the role of intangible assets. In P. Lorange, B. Chakravarthy, J. Ross and A. Van de Ven (eds) *Implementing Strategic Processes*, Oxford: Blackwell.

Pfeffer, J. (1994) *Competitive Advantage Through People*, Boston, MA: Harvard Business School Press.

Prahalad, C. K. and Hamel, G. (1990) The core competence of the corporation. *Harvard Business Review*, **68**, May–June, pp. 79–81.

Pritchard, R. D. (1990a) Measuring organizational productivity. In P. J. D. Drenth, J. A. Sergeant and R. J. Takens (eds) *European Perspectives in Psychology*, vol. 3, Chichester: Wiley.

Pritchard, R. D. (1990b) Enhancing work motivation through productivity measurement and feedback. In U. Kleinbeck, H. H. Quast, H. Thierry and H. Häcker (eds) *Work Motivation*, Hillsdale, NJ: Erlbaum.

Pritchard, R. D. (1992) Organizational productivity. In M. D. Dunnette and L. M. Hough (eds) *Handbook of Industrial/Organizational Psychology*, Palo Alto, CA: Consulting Psychologists Press.

Pritchard, R. D. (1995) Productivity. In N. Nicholson (ed.) *Blackwell Encyclopedic Dictionary of Organizational Behaviour*, Oxford: Blackwell.

Pritchard, R. D., Jones, S. D., Roth, P. L., Stuebing, K. K. and Ekeberg, S. E. (1988) The effects of feedback, goal setting, and incentives on organizational productivity. *Journal of Applied Psychology Monograph Series*, **73(2)**, pp. 337–58.

Pritchard, R. D., Jones, S. D., Roth, P. L., Stuebing, K. K. and Ekeberg, S. E. (1989) The evaluation of an integrated approach to measuring organizational productivity. *Personnel Psychology*, **42(1)**, pp. 69–115.

Prokopenko, J. (1987) *Productivity Management*, Geneva: International Labour Office.

Prytz, K. (1995) Modeling in manufacturing enterprises. In A. Rolstadås (ed.) *Performance Management*, London: Chapman and Hall.

Purcell, J. (1995) Corporate strategy and its link with human resource management strategy. In J. Storey (ed.) *Human Resource Management: A Critical Text*, London: Routledge.

Quinn, R. E., Faerman, S. R., Thompson, M. P. and McGrath, M. R. (1996) *Becoming a Master Manager: A Competency Framework*, 2nd edn, New York: Wiley.

Ramsay, H. (1996) Involvement, empowerment and commitment. In B. Towers (ed.) *The Handbook of Human Resource Management*, 2nd edn, Oxford: Blackwell.

Ravlin, E. C. (1995) Values. In N. Nicholson (ed.) *Blackwell Encyclopedic Dictionary of Organizational Behaviour*, Oxford: Blackwell.

Reeves, C. A. and Bednar, D. A. (1994) Defining quality: alternatives and implications. *The Academy of Management Review*, **19(3)**, pp. 419–45.

Robertson, I. T. (1994) Personality and personnel selection. In C. L. Cooper and D. M. Rousseau (eds) *Trends in Organizational Behaviour*, Chichester: Wiley.

Robertson, I. T. and Kinder, A. (1993) Personality and job competences: the criterion-related validity of some personality variables. *Journal of Occupational and Organizational Psychology*, **66**, pp. 225–44.

Robertson, I. T., Smith, M. and Cooper, D. (1992) *Motivation*, London: Institute of Personnel Management.

Rodgers, R. and Hunter, J. E. (1991) Impact of management by objectives on organizational productivity. *Journal of Applied Psychology Monograph Series*, **76(2)**, pp. 322–36.

Roe, R. A. (1989) Designing selection procedures. In P. Herriot (ed.) *Assessment and Selection in Organizations*, Chichester: Wiley.

Roethlisberger, F. G. and Dickson, W. J. (1939) *Management and the Worker*, Cambridge, MA: Harvard Business School Press.

Rogers, S. (1990) *Performance Management in Local Government*, Harlow, Essex: Longman.

Rosenfeld, P., Giacalone, R. A. and Riordan, C. A. (1995) *Impression Management in Organizations*, London: International Thomson Business Press.

Rummler, G. A. and Brache, A. P. (1995) *Improving Performance*, 2nd edn, San Francisco, CA: Jossey-Bass.

Sadri, G. and Robertson, I. T. (1993) Self-efficacy and work-related behaviour: a review and meta-analysis. *Applied Psychology: An International Review*, **42(2)**, pp. 139–52.

Schein, E. H. (1992) *Organizational Culture and Leadership*, 2nd edn, San Francisco, CA: Jossey-Bass.

Schmidt, F. L. (1993) Personnel psychology at the cutting edge. In N. Schmitt, W. C. Borman and Associates *Personnel Selection in Organizations*, San Francisco, CA: Jossey-Bass.

Schneider, B. (1987) The people make the place. *Personnel Psychology*, **40**, pp. 437–53.

Schneider, B. and Konz, A. M. (1989) Strategic job analysis. *Human Resource Management*, **28(1)**, pp. 51–85.

Schneider, B. and Schechter, D. (1991) Development of a personnel selection system for service jobs. In S. W. Brown, E. Gummesson, B. Edvardsson and B. Gustavsson (eds) *Service Quality*, Lexington, MA: Lexington Books.

Schneider, B., Smith, D. B. and Sipe, W. P. (2000) Personnel selection psychology: Multilevel considerations. In K. J. Klein and S. W. J. Kozlowski (eds) *Multilevel Theory, Research and Methods in Organizations: Foundations, Extensions and New Directions*, San Francisco: Jossey-Bass.

Schneider, R. J. and Hough, L. M. (1995) Personality and industrial/ organizational psychology. In C. L. Cooper and I. T. Robertson (eds) *International Review of Industrial and Organizational Psychology*, Chichester: Wiley.

Schneier, C. E., Beatty, R. W. and Baird, L. S. (1986) How to construct a successful performance appraisal system. *Training and Development Journal*, April.

Schneier, C. E., Beatty, R. W. and Baird, L. S. (eds) (1987) Introduction *The Performance Management Sourcebook*, Amherst, MA: Human Resource Development Press.

Schriesheim, C. A., Hinkin, T. R. and Tetrault, L. A. (1991) The discriminant validity of the Leader Reward and Punishment Questionnaire (LRPQ) and satisfaction with supervision. *Journal of Occupational Psychology*, **64**, pp. 159–66.

Schroder, H. M. (1989) *Managerial Competence: The Key to Excellence*, Iowa: Kendall Hunt.

Selznick, P. (1957) *Leadership in Administration*, New York: Harper & Row.

Shackleton, V. J. (1992) Using a competency approach in a business change setting. In R. Boam and P. Sparrow (eds) *Designing and Achieving Competency*, Maidenhead: McGraw-Hill.

Sheard, A. (1992) Learning to improve performance. *Personnel Management*, November, pp. 40–5.

Society of Telecom Executives (1992) *Stressing Performance*, London: Society of Telecom Executives.

Spangenberg, H. (1994) *Understanding and Implementing Performance Management*, Cape Town: Juda.

Sparrow, P. (1996) Too good to be true. *People Management*, December, pp. 22–7.

Sparrow, P. and Boam, R. (1992) Where do we go from here? In R. Boam and P. Sparrow (eds) *Designing and Achieving Competency*, Maidenhead: McGraw-Hill.

Sparrow, P. R. (1994) Organizational competencies: creating a strategic behavioural framework for selection and assessment. In N. Anderson and P. Herriot (eds) *Assessment and Selection in Organizations. First Update and Supplement*, Chichester: Wiley.

Sparrow, P. R. (1996) Too good to be true. *People Management*, December, 22–7.

Spencer, L. M. and Spencer, S. M. (1993) *Competence at Work*, New York: Wiley.

Steers, R. M. and Porter, L. W. (1991) Reward systems in organizations. In R. M. Steers and L. W. Porter (eds) *Motivation and Work Behaviour*, 5th edn, New York: McGraw-Hill.

Sternberg, R. J. (1990) *Metaphors of Mind: Conceptions of the Nature of Intelligence*, New York: Cambridge University Press.

Sternberg, R. J. (1994) Tacit knowledge and job success. In N. Anderson and P. Herriot (eds) *Assessment and Selection in Organizations. First Update and Supplement*, Chichester: Wiley.

Sternberg, R. J. and Wagner, R. K. (1986) *Practical Intelligence*, Cambridge: Cambridge University Press.

Sternberg, R. J., Forsythe, G. B., Hedlund, J., Horvath, J. A., Wagner, R. K., Williams, W. M., Snook, S. A. and Grigorenko, E. L. (2000) *Practical Intelligence in Everyday Life*, Cambridge: CUP.

Stewart, R. (1991) *Managing Today and Tomorrow*, Basingstoke: Macmillan.

Stiles, P., Gratton, L., Truss, C., Hope-Hailey, V. and McGovern, P. (1997) Performance management and the psychological contract. *Human Resource Management Journal*, 7(1), pp. 57–66.

Stinson, J. and Stokes, J. (1980) How to multi-appraise. *Management Today*, June, 43–53.

Stone, D. L. and Eddy, E. R. (1996) A model of individual and organizational factors affecting quality-related outcomes. *Journal of Quality Management*, 1(1), pp. 21–48.

Storey, J. and Sisson, K. (1993) *Managing Human Resources and Industrial Relations*, Buckingham: Open University Press.

Streufert, S. and Nogami, G. Y. (1989) Cognitive style and complexity. In C. L. Cooper and I. T. Robertson (eds) *International Review of Industrial and Organizational Psychology*, Chichester: Wiley.

Storey, J. and Sisson, K. (1993) *Managing Human Resources and Industrial Relations*, Buckingham: Open University Press.

Swanson, R. A. (1994) *Analyzing for Improving Performance*, San Francisco, CA: Berrett-Koehler.

Taylor, M. S., Fisher, C. D. and Ilgen, D. R. (1984) Individuals' reactions to performance feedback in organizations. *Research in Personnel and Human Resources Management*, 2, pp. 81–124.

Thatcher, M. (1996) Allowing everyone to have their say. *People Management*, March, pp. 28–30.

Thompson, J. L. (1990) *Strategic Management*, London: International Thomson Business Press.

Thompson, M. (1992) *Pay and performance: the employer experience*. Falmer, Sussex: Institute of Manpower Studies.

Thompson, M. (1993) *Pay and performance: the employee experience*. Falmer, Sussex: Institute of Manpower Studies.

Thornton, G. C. and Byham, W. C. (1982) *Assessment Centres and Managerial Performance*, New York: Academic Press.

Torrington, D. and Hall, L. (1995) *Personnel Management: HRM in Action*, 3rd edn, Hemel Hempstead: Prentice Hall.

Townley, B. (1994) Communicating with employees. In K. Sisson (ed.) *Personnel Management*, Oxford: Blackwell.

Tuxworth, E. (1989) Competence based education and training: background and origins. In J. W. Burke (ed.) *Competency Based Education and Training*, Lewes: Falmer Press.

Tziner, A., Latham, G. P., Price, B. S. and Haccoun, R. (1996) Development and validation of a questionnaire for measuring perceived political considerations in performance appraisal. *Journal of Organizational Behaviour*, 17, pp. 179–90.

Van Dyne, L., Cummings, L. L. and Parks, J. M. (1995) Extra-role behaviours. *Research in Organizational Behaviour*, 17, pp. 215–85.

Viswesvaran, C. and Ones, D. S. (2000) Perspectives on models of job performance. *International Journal of Selection and Assessment*, 8(4), pp. 216–26.

Wagner, J. A. (1994) Participation's effects on performance and satisfaction: A reconsideration of research evidence. *Academy of Management Review*, 19, pp. 312–30.

Waldman, D. A. (1994) The contributions of total quality management to a theory of work performance. *Academy of Management Review*, 19(3), 510–36.

Waldman, D. A., Atwater, L. E. and Antonioni, D. (1998) Has 360 degree feedback gone amok? *Academy of Management Executive*, 12(2), pp. 86–94.

Walker, A. and Smither, J. W. (1999) A five-year study of upward feedback: What managers do with their results matters. *Personnel Psychology*, 52, pp. 393–423.

Walters, M. (1995) Developing organizational measures. In M. Walters (ed.) *The Performance Management Handbook*, London: Institute of Personnel and Development.

Walters, M. (ed.) (1995) Introduction. *The Performance Management Handbook*. London: Institute of Personnel and Development.

Warr, P. (1996) Employee well-being. In P. Warr (ed.) *Psychology at Work*, 4th edn, Harmondsworth: Penguin.

Warr, P. and Conner, M. (1992) Job competence and cognition. *Research in Organizational Behaviour*, **14**, pp. 91–127.

Warr, P. B. (1987) Job characteristics and mental health. In P. B. Warr (ed.) *Psychology at Work*, 3rd edn, Harmondsworth: Penguin.

Warrick, D. D. and Zawacki, R. A. (1987) *High Performance Management*, Colorado Springs: Eagle Publishing Co.

Whetten, D., Cameron, K. and Woods, M. (1994) *Developing Management Skills for Europe*, London: HarperCollins.

Wild, R. (1995) *Production and Operations Management*, 5th edn, London: Casssell.

Wilkinson, A. and Willmott, H. (1995a) *Making Quality Critical*, London: International Thomson Business Press.

Wilkinson, A. and Willmott, H. (1995b) Introduction. *Making Quality Critical*, London: International Thomson Business Press.

Williams, A., Dobson, P. and Walters, M. (1993) *Changing Culture: New Organizational Approaches*, 2nd edn, London: Institute of Personnel Management.

Williams, R. S. (1989) Alternative raters and methods. In P. Herriot (ed.) *Assessment and Selection in Organizations*, Chichester: Wiley.

Williams, R. S. (1991) Communication in organizations. In M. Smith (ed.) *Analysing Organizational Behaviour*, Basingstoke: Macmillan.

Winstanley, D. and Stuart-Smith, K. (1996) Policing performance: the ethics of performance management. *Personnel Review*, **25(6)**, pp. 66–84.

Winterton, J. and Winterton, R. (1996) *The Business Benefits of Competence-based Management Development*, London: HMSO.

Wood, R. E. and Locke, E. A. (1990) Goal setting and strategy effects on complex tasks. *Research in Organizational Behaviour*, **12**, pp. 73–109.

Woodruffe, C. (1991) Competent by any other name. *Personnel Management*, September, pp. 30–3.

Woodruffe, C. (1992) What is meant by a competency? In R. Boam and P. Sparrow (eds) *Designing and Achieving Competency*, Maidenhead: McGraw-Hill.

Wright, P. (1996) *Managerial Leadership*, London: Routledge.

Yeates, J. D. (1990) *Performance Appraisal: A Guide for Design and Implementation*, Falmer, Sussex: Institute for Manpower Studies.

Yukl, G. (1994) *Leadership in Organizations*, 3rd edn, Englewood Cliffs, NJ: Prentice Hall.

Zairi, M. (1994) *Measuring Performance for Business Results*, London: Chapman & Hall.

Index